The Multilateral Dimension in Russian Foreign Policy

This book examines the place of multilateralism in Russia's foreign policy and Russia's engagement with multilateral institutions. Throughout the post-Soviet period, both Yeltsin and Putin consistently professed a deep attachment to the principles of multilateralism. However, multilateralism as a value, concept, strategy or general phenomenon in Russian foreign policy has seldom been assessed in its own right or from a comparative perspective. This book fills that gap, combining wider conceptual perspectives on the place of multilateralism in Russian foreign policy thought and action with detailed empirical case studies of Russian engagement at the global, transatlantic and European levels, and also in Russia's regional environment. It examines Russia's role and relationship with the UN, NATO, G8, EU, OSCE, Arctic Council, Eurasian Economic Community, Commonwealth of Independent States, Shanghai Co-operation Organization and Collective Security Treaty Organization, covering a wide range of issue areas including nuclear non-proliferation and trade. Throughout, it considers the political, economic and security interests that shape Russia's foreign relations, conception of multilateralism and activity in multilateral settings. Overall, this book is an important resource for anyone interested in Russian foreign policy and its role in international relations more generally.

Elana Wilson Rowe holds a PhD from the University of Cambridge and is a Senior Research Fellow at the Department for Russian and Eurasian Studies, Norwegian Institute of International Affairs (NUPI). Her research interests include regional co-operation in the circumpolar north and Russian foreign and energy policy.

Stina Torjesen holds a DPhil in International Relations from the University of Oxford and is a Senior Research Fellow at the Department for Russian and Eurasian studies, Norwegian Institute of International Affairs (NUPI). She has specialised on the international relations of Central Asia and works also on security and peacebuilding in Tajikistan and Afghanistan.

Routledge contemporary Russia and Eastern Europe series

The Multilateral Dimension in Russian Foreign Policy

Edited by
Elana Wilson Rowe
and Stina Torjesen

Routledge
Taylor & Francis Group

LONDON AND NEW YORK

First published 2009
by Routledge
2 Park Square, Milton Park, Abingdon, Oxon OX14 4RN

Simultaneously published in the USA and Canada
by Routledge
270 Madison Ave, New York, NY 10016

*Routledge is an imprint of the Taylor & Francis Group,
an informa business*

Typeset in Times New Roman by Keyword Group Ltd
Printed and bound in Great Britain by Biddles Digital, Kings Lynn

British Library Cataloguing-in-Publication Data
A catalogue record for this book is available
from the British Library

Library of Congress Cataloging in Publication Data
The multilateral dimension in Russian foreign policy/edited by Elana
Wilson Rowe and Stina Torjesen.
   p. cm.– (Routledge contemporary Russia and Eastern Europe
   series; 15)
   Includes bibliographical references and index.
   ISBN 978-0-415-47199-2 (hardback : alk. paper)
    – ISBN 978-0-203-89055-4 (ebook) 1. Russia (Federation)–Foreign
   relations. I. Wilson Rowe, Elana, 1980- II. Torjesen, Stina.
   JZ1616.M85 2008
   327.47–dc22   2008012960

ISBN10: 0-415-47199-0 (hbk)
ISBN10: 0-203-89055-8 (ebk)

ISBN13: 978-0-415-47199-2 (hbk)
ISBN13: 978-0-203-89055-4 (ebk)

Contents

List of tables

List of figures

List of contributors

Hannes Adomeit is Professor for Eastern Studies at the College of Europe in Natolin (Warsaw) and Senior Research Associate at the Stiftung Wissenschaft und Politik (SWP) in Berlin.

Pavel K. Baev is a Research Professor at the International Peace Research Institute, Oslo (PRIO); he is also affiliated with the Centre for the Study of Civil War at PRIO.

Julian Cooper is Professor of Russian Economic Studies at the Centre for Russian and East European Studies, European Research Institute, University of Birmingham.

Jakub M. Godzimirski is a Senior Research Fellow at the Department for Russian and Eurasian Studies, Norwegian Institute of International Affairs.

Robert Legvold is Marshall D. Shulman Professor in the Department of Political Science at Columbia University.

Margot Light is Emeritus Professor of International Relations at the London School of Economics and Political Science.

Alexander A. Pikayev is Director of the Department for Disarmament and Conflict Resolution at the Moscow-based Institute of World Economy and International Relations (IMEMO).

Stina Torjesen is a Senior Research Fellow at the Norwegian Institute of International Affairs.

Elana Wilson Rowe is a Senior Research Fellow at the Norwegian Institute of International Affairs, Department for Russian and Eurasian Studies.

Andrei Zagorski is Professor at the Center for War and Peace Studies, Moscow State Institute of International Relations (MGIMO-University).

Preface

The notion of examining and comparing Russia's participation across a spectrum of multilateral organizations first arose in brainstorming for themes for the Norwegian Institute of International Affairs (NUPI) Department for Russian and Eurasian Studies annual conference. In October 2006, this idea came to fruition with experts from Russia, the UK, the US, Germany and Norway convening in Oslo. Each scholar shed light upon Russian foreign policy thinking on the topic of multilateralism in and of itself as well as in-depth knowledge of Russian engagement in specific settings. Over the course of the conference, a number of key characteristics of Russian multilateral engagement – transcending the specific forum or issue area being analyzed by any one presentation – emerged. Partially overlapping and often intriguingly diverging sets of behaviour became evident in relationship to two geopolitical spaces – the former Soviet one and the world outside it. These characteristics and sets of behaviour are described in this volume. We are grateful to all of the contributing authors for shaping their presentations into chapters and for contributing their time, enthusiasm and insight. We also wish to extend our thanks to Tom Bates at Routledge, Domitilla Sagramoso at King's College London, Susan Høvik at NUPI and Dr Alex Pravda at the University of Oxford for their guidance in preparing this work. Professor S. Neil Macfarlane and Dr Christian Thorun, both from the University of Oxford, also gave useful advice in the preparation stages of the 2006 conference.

In writing about Russia, particularly on the eve of the second transition of presidential power since the end of the Soviet Union, one has the unsettling feeling of attempting to zero in on a shifting target. At the same time, some of the characteristics of Russian multilateral engagement described in the chapters to follow have endured several transitions. Certainly the time is ripe to investigate Russian foreign policy with an eye towards what remains consistent and what features may be more firmly institutionalized, even as this foreign policy continues to change. One could argue, as we do in the conclusion of Chapter 1, that a number of features of Russian multilateralism identified here are likely to persist beyond the election of a new president in March 2008.

Elana Wilson Rowe and Stina Torjesen
December 2007
Oslo, Norway

List of abbreviations

ACAP	Arctic Contaminants Action Programme
AMAP	Arctic Marine Assessment Programme
AMEC	Arctic Military Environmental Co-operation
ASEAN	Association of Southeast Asian Nations
CACO	Central Asian Co-operation Organization
CFE	Conventional Forces in Europe (CFE) Treaty
CFSP	Common Foreign and Security Policy (EU)
CIS	Commonwealth of Independent States
CSCE	Conference on Security and Co-operation in Europe
CST	Collective Security Treaty
CSTO	Collective Security Treaty Organization
EEC	The Eurasian Economic Community, *Evraziiskoe Ekonomicheskoe Soobshchestvo*
ENP	European Neighbourhood Policy
ESCAP	Economic and Social Commission for Asia and the Pacific (UN)
EU	European Union
GATT	General Agreement on Tariffs and Trade
GUAM	Georgia, Ukraine, Azerbaijan, Moldova
IAEA	International Atomic Energy Agency
IMF	International Monetary Fund
IPY	International Polar Year
ISAF	International Security Assistance Force (Afghanistan)
KFOR	International Security Assistance Force (Kosovo)
MERCOSUR	Southern Common Market
NATO	North Atlantic Treaty Organization
NRC	NATO–Russia Council
OECD	Organization for Economic Co-operation and Development
OPEC	Organization of Petroleum Exporting Countries
OSCE	Organization for Security and Co-operation in Europe
PAME	Protection of the Arctic Marine Environment (Arctic Council Working Group)

PCA	Partnership and Co-operation Agreement
PJC	Permanent Joint Council, NATO
RCA	revealed comparative advantage
RF	Russian Federation
SCO	Shanghai Co-operation Organization
SDWG	Sustainable Development Working Group
TACIS	Technical Assistance to the Commonwealth of Independent States (EU programme)
TAS	Central Asian Co-operation Organisation, *Tsentral'no-Aziatskoe Sotrudnichestvo*
UES	Unified Economic Space
UN	United Nations
UNSC	United Nations Security Council
WTO	World Trade Organisation

1 Key features of Russian multilateralism

Elana Wilson Rowe and Stina Torjesen

In the immediate post-Soviet years, multilateralism was seen an important instrument in Russian foreign policy to ameliorate some of the 'risks and pain of standing in the shadow of others'.[1] Both Boris Yeltsin and Vladimir Putin consistently professed a deep attachment to the principles of multilateralism. However, multilateralism as a concept, value and strategy in Russian foreign policy has seldom been assessed in its own right or from a comparative perspective. The contributions in this book examine Russia's engagement in multilateral institutions in both the former Soviet space and on a broader or global scale. The primary focus is on this engagement under the Putin presidency, although broader historical trends and key moments are also identified.

In this introductory chapter, some of the overarching tensions inherent to multilateralism itself are examined, followed by a brief review of the structure of this book and central aspects of Russian foreign policy under Putin. Key patterns of Russian engagement in multilateralism, internationally and in the former Soviet Union (FSU), are then identified and described.

By 'multilateralism' we refer to institutions and issue areas that involve multiple countries (three or more) working in concert in a sustained manner. Multilateralism must be distinguished from integration, which involves pooling certain aspects of state sovereignty and authority to a supra-national governmental body (such as the European Commission in the European Union).[2] While Russia often argues for intensive regional economic and political integration in the post-Soviet space through organizations like the Eurasian Economic Community (EEC), these proclaimed ambitions have rarely been accompanied by corresponding integrationist policies. It seems that Russia's leadership has, in practice, come to distinguish integration from multilateralism and favours (or is more capable of realizing) the latter over the former. Similarly, it is clear that Russia will not pursue any of the theoretically possible avenues for integration with the European Union (EU) (like membership or active involvement in the European Neighbourhood Policy), wanting, at most, a free trade zone with no more ambitious forms of co-operation. This unwillingness to alienate sovereignty via forms of political and economic integration[3] adds significance to multilateral co-operation as a tool for managing Russia's international relations.

Although these brief definitions may seem simple, the practice of multilateralism is complex. The changing international system, moving from the bipolarity of the Cold War and oscillating between unipolarity of the remaining superpower and signals of an emerging multipolar order, creates uncertainty around the significance and usages of multilateral forums. Multilateralism raises the question of the extent to which state interests can be pursued in tandem with other actors, and whether and how common overarching interests can be co-ordinated and institutionalized.

In this way, the study of Russian multilateralism speaks to key debates in International Relations (IR) theory, where multilateralism has been analysed in conjunction with studies of regimes.[4] While engaging with IR theory is not a key purpose of this book, it is worth noting that disagreements over the extent to which multilateral co-operation is expected to yield common goods and shape the way states maximize interests represent a central theoretical divide in IR.[5] Realists expect multilateralism to be limited to inter-state co-ordination and bargaining. Neo-liberal institutionalists, by contrast, see scope for mutually collaborative strategies between states that produce common goods beyond immediate interests of individual states. As will be highlighted in succeeding sections, both these visions surface in cases of Russia's multilateral engagement, although the more limited realist understanding of multilateralism as co-ordination seems, overall, to best capture the basic thrust of these multilateral strategies. Russia sees multilateralism as a value as well as a tool, and its multilateral engagement is shaped by political, economic and security interests specific to the particular issue areas and institutions in question.

A brief look at Russian and generalized 'European' responses to two critical issues further points up the diversity of approaches that states may take to multilateral co-operation, and the complexities involved in this. For example, examining international governance, one could say that European powers tend to favour a 'horizontal' multilateralism that affords a voice to both smaller and larger states. By contrast, Russia emphasizes 'great-power multilateralism', involving leading states that may or may not take into consideration the concerns and wishes of smaller states. Another tension centres around varying levels of willingness to limit state sovereignty and to allow international agreements and institutions to impinge on domestic affairs. Many European states have shown themselves willing to participate in multilateral agreements that involve real binding force and curtailment of state action, such as the International Criminal Court, where individuals can be prosecuted outside of their home country for genocide, crimes against humanity and war crimes. For Russia, by contrast, the primacy of state sovereignty in the international system and the sanctity of state borders have been key commitments. At the same time, as demonstrated in the chapters by Legvold, Adomeit and Godzimirski in their discussions of 'frozen conflicts' in the post-Soviet space, it must be noted that Russia has not been equally assiduous in respecting the sovereignty of other Commonwealth of Independent States (CIS) countries. Broadly put, Russia sees multilateralism, in its ideal form, as co-ordinated international action around key issue areas, rather than dense horizontal co-operation aimed at developing congruent policies that touch on or require change in domestic affairs.

Structure of the book

In this volume, we combine wider perspectives on the place of multilateralism in Russian foreign policy thinking and action in Section 1 (Chapters 1–3) and detailed case studies of Russian multilateral engagement with varying constellations of actors and issues at the global, trans-Atlantic and European levels (Section 2, Chapters 4–9) and in Russia's 'near abroad'[6] (Section 3, Chapters 10–12). The multilateral settings described and analysed in this volume entail a range of issues, opportunities and types of co-operation – economic, security and political. Consequently, they have tended to evoke varying kinds of political behaviour on the part of the Russian leadership.

To determine the extent to which these diverse institutions evoke common features of Russian multilateral engagement, the book and comparative analysis of this introduction are organized around the concept of multilateralism as operating in two geopolitical arenas: the post-Soviet space, and the world outside it. As Legvold points out in his contribution, Russia has tended to operate with a distinction between the areas it seeks to control ('near abroad') and areas it does not ('far abroad'). Indeed, trends specific to each sphere as well as important overlaps between the two levels can be identified. At the same time, these multilateral institutions and the behaviour of Russia's foreign-policy actors within them cannot be divorced from the various cross-cutting political, economic and security interests and influences that are explored in detail in subsequent chapters.

In Chapter 2, Robert Legvold examines key concepts and interests that shape Moscow's stake in contemporary multilateralism, such as the tension between mutual and collective security and the competing demands of global responsibility weighed against state sovereignty. The broad contours of how these concepts shape behaviour in a range of multilateral settings – NATO, the UN and the Collective Security Treaty Organization (CSTO) – are then traced. In Chapter 3, Andrei Zagorski takes up the overarching question of whether Russia is an 'instrumental' or 'principled' multilateralist, and examines its practical (particularly financial) commitment to multilateral initiatives.

Section 2 focuses on Russia's involvement in European, trans-Atlantic and global multilateral co-operation. Pavel Baev, in Chapter 4, examines Russia's involvement in the G8, including its recent (2006) chairmanship. In Chapter 5, Alexander Pikayev analyses Russia's role in nuclear non-proliferation regimes, focusing on how these issues are dealt with at the UN level. Margot Light, in Chapter 6, identifies key challenges facing the EU–Russia relationship, many of which speak to issues highlighted by Hannes Adomeit in his study of the NATO–Russia Council (Chapter 7). In Chapter 8, Jakub M. Godzimirski examines Russia's involvement in the Organization for Security and Co-operation in Europe (OSCE). Elana Wilson Rowe, in Chapter 9, analyses Russia's multilateral engagement in a non-post Soviet space regional co-operation, namely the Arctic Council.

Moving to the second geopolitical circle, the chapters in Section 2 look at multilateralism in the former Soviet space. Stina Torjesen, in Chapter 10, identifies key trends and dilemmas facing Russia's multilateral engagement in the near abroad and examines the extent to which it has managed to maintain the structures of and set agendas in the Commonwealth of Independent States (CIS) and the Eurasian Economic Community (EEC). In Chapter 11, Julian Cooper examines the bilateral and multilateral economic relations that connect the former Soviet space, and identifies the impact of plans for accession to the World Trade Organization (WTO) on this regional co-operation. Stina Torjesen, in the final chapter of this book, compares Russian security co-operation in the CSTO and the Shanghai Co-operation Organization (SCO).

Foreign policy under Putin

A review of key factors and central ideas shaping foreign policy under Putin is useful for contextualizing Russia's concepts of, stake in and approach to multilateralism.[7] In particular, we examine two enduring features of Putin's foreign policy – pragmatism and the pursuit of a multipolar world order – that have formed a basis for Moscow's international activity, including multilateralism. A more recent feature of Putin's presidency – an increasingly assertive foreign policy supported by the rising revenues from oil and gas – certainly also shapes Russia's engagement in multilateral institutions. Vigorous and recent efforts to counter NATO expansion in the former Soviet Union via alternative, competitive regional multilateral initiatives like the SCO and the CSTO, discussed below, can be understood as manifestations of both a commitment to the idea of multipolarity and this increasingly assertive trend. However, given the relative recentness of this development and the extent to which such assertiveness remains selectively and sometimes transiently applied, it is difficult to systematize and identify broad consequences for multilateralism of this new approach. Regardless, this and other chapters will flag when and how this more independent and aggressive foreign policy has played a role in shaping Russia's multilateral engagement.

While this section focuses on the Putin presidency as a key factor in shaping Russian foreign policy and, by extension, Russian multilateral engagement, it would be misleading to envision this foreign policy as micro-managed by the president himself or the presidential administration. As Lo puts it:

> Putin is the ultimate controller, he determines the country's strategic direction and involves himself selectively in the management of high-profile issues…but he delegates. What distinguishes him from Western leaders, however, is that he relies primarily on individuals instead of institutions, or rather he looks to individuals to ensure institutional compliance and efficiency and thereby implementation of policy.[8]

Consequently, it is reasonable to expect that other important institutions of foreign policy-making led by trusted individuals, such as the Ministry of Foreign Affairs, play a key and perhaps decisive role in lower-profile, stable and/or ongoing foreign policy issues.

Putin's presidency (2000–2008) has been marked by the pronounced marginalization of a debate that preoccupied the post-Soviet leadership under Boris Yeltsin – the question of whether Russia 'belongs' in the West, the East or somewhere in-between. Russia's foreign policy today cannot be understood as either pro-Western or anti-Western – in many ways, foreign policy has been de-ideologized in relationship to this formerly central question.[9] Prior to Putin's presidency, the question of identity and 'geographic' orientation had corresponded rather neatly with priority setting and the definition of national interests in Russian foreign policy. Yeltsin and Andrey Kozyrev (foreign minister, 1990–1996) attempted to cast the country's national interest as that of Western integration. Faced with many disappointments in this regard, Yeltsin and his subsequent foreign minister, Yevgeny Primakov (1996–1998), pursued a policy of counter-balancing the very same West, in part through an increased focus on maintaining hegemony in the post-Soviet space as a way of shoring up Russia's great-power status. In the words of Bobo Lo, this identity question 'was the conundrum facing Putin on his accession: how to transform the discussion of identity into a unifying force in society, while ensuring a plausible concordance between ambitious self-perceptions and uncomfortable realities'.[10] In many ways, this conundrum was resolved by Putin's clear orientation towards the United States – which became particularly prominent in the post-9/11 'global war on terror' – and Europe, early in his first presidential term. While Putin certainly shares the long-standing aim of restoring Russia's great-power status, his first term suggested that this pursuit was not to be at the expense of key relationships with the West.[11] His second term, however, has indicated a growing realization that Russia can afford to be more assertive and less clearly aligned at the international level without any immediate repercussions.

Another key element that distinguishes Putin's pursuit of great-power status from that of his predecessors is his acknowledgement that this status would have to be restored by deeds – not simply asserted through words, as in the Yeltsin era. Correspondingly, early in his first term, Putin placed considerable emphasis on economic modernization, repeatedly referring to the economic nature of power in the contemporary world and the political consequences of economic failure. Likewise, the first years of his second presidential term were marked by accelerated efforts to recentralize, to build a strong federal centre with the presidential administration at its core and to exercise Russia's economic soft power.[12] The sometimes rather harshly applied usages of this new economic soft power, particularly in relationship to energy (as discussed in Light's chapter on Russia–EU relationships and Cooper's chapter on CIS trading), show, however, that the focus on economic modernization cannot be taken to mean that Putin is a 'Western'-style liberal.

The emphasis on economic modernization and on the uses of economic soft power points to another important feature of Russia's foreign policy – pragmatism. The pragmatic approach adopted by Putin has been an attempt to find a way of maintaining Russia's great-power stance while creating a more realistic match between capacities and ambitions.[13] Trenin and Lo argue that the foundation of Putin's pragmatism lies in

> his readiness to absorb unpalatable realities and react positively by instigating major changes to domestic and foreign policy. This realist policy has been characterized by an opportunistic streak – with a twist. Putin has been quick to seize on openings afforded him by international circumstances...[14]

Although much of Russia's foreign-policy activity can still be usefully interpreted in light of the Kremlin's historical approach to foreign policy as a 'zero-sum game', Putin has actually tended to avoid making statements about zero-sum games, and notions of 'competing against the West' have been generally absent in his public rhetoric. Rather, Putin has attempted to re-set the agenda in positive terms, arguing about Russia's interests rather than casting its foreign-policy stances as efforts to diminish Western influence or thwart Western plans.[15] All the same, zero-sum or 'spheres of influence' thinking, where a gain for the West is a loss for Russia, continues to shape the Kremlin's foreign policy in many ways. This is shown particularly clearly in the studies of NATO and, to some extent, the EU in this volume.

At the same time, as Secrieru has argued, Moscow's emphasis on multipolarity means that Russia no longer sees *only* zero-sum outcomes and mutually exclusive solutions in international relations and, for example, that 'further integration in the CIS does not exclude closer co-operation with the EU or NATO'.[16] Whether or not the international system today is indeed a multipolar one, this concept is infinitely more palatable to the Russian foreign policy establishment than operating against the background of a unipolar world with the United States at the helm. The strategy of 'multipolarity', as first put forward by Primakov, called for the Russian foreign policy and defence establishments to see the international system as one in which the strategic unity of the West was breaking and in which several centres of power (e.g. the USA, Europe, Japan, China, Russia) were pursuing their own geopolitical agendas. Russia should react by capitalizing on and pursuing state interests in this fragmented system, playing these 'centres' against one another, building flexible alliances with some leading European states and emerging powers that might counter-balance US geopolitical dominance, and ensuring Russian dominance in the post-Soviet space. While the Yeltsin administration suffered some foreign policy losses through the uneven and disorganized pursuit of this multipolar policy, the idea has endured and remains a staple of Putin's foreign policy. In practice, this has entailed enhancing and deepening partnerships with China and India (see Chapter 2) and ensuring that Russia remains the dominant actor in political, economic and security affairs in the former Soviet space (see Section 3). In what it perceives to be a changing international system, Russia seems to seek to maintain as many positions of strength as feasible.[17] In this way, setbacks in one particular relationship or arena may not affect or may actually improve conditions in others.

On the other hand, Russia's preference for fluid relationships, rather than permanent alliances, with both great and emerging powers may have resulted in what Secrieru describes as a 'lack of long term priorities in relations with the main power centres and continued discrepancies between resources and ambitions'.[18] As Baev notes in Chapter 4, Russia may have realized some minor successes in its intensified foreign policy efforts in the Middle East in advance of the Russian G8 chairmanship. However, these small victories had fleeting results and were achieved by 'making friends' with leaders with whom other G8 members were unlikely to wish to be associated. Baev argues that such foreign policy endeavours linked to the logic of multipolarity do little to shore up Russia's great power stance.

On the other hand, multilateralism and building regional power in the CIS is an important feature of Russia's legitimacy as a global great power. Under Putin, relationships within the former Soviet Union have become more substantial and comprehensive than at any time since the end of the USSR. Particularly in his second term, Putin invested considerable political capital in building more empowered multilateral organizations encompassing the former Soviet space, such as the SCO and the EEC, and spoke publicly about his 'pleasant surprise' at seeing the SCO grow from a border-delineation and confidence-building endeavour into a broader economic and security community of sorts.[19] Interestingly, the rhetoric of Russia–CIS relations has, at the same time, continued to demonstrate a notable departure from more classic Soviet and post-Soviet thinking on 'spheres of influence'. As Lo notes,[20] even the notion of 'spheres of influence' has been expunged from official statements; the Kremlin seems to now understand that the term sends the wrong message of imperialism to former Soviet countries and international players alike. In response to a question from a reporter at a June 2007 press conference as to whether further economic integration in the post-Soviet area was meant to or could limit the involvement of former Soviet states in accession to the WTO or the EU, Putin emphasized both the importance and the relative innocuousness of these endeavours:

> Economic integration in the post-Soviet area is also immensely important in terms of ensuring the region's stability. The entire world has an interest in stable development in this part of Eurasia…[however] the integration projects we are pursuing in the post-Soviet area create no obstacles for anyone…and are not creating any barriers for countries' own development.[21]

Then again, even if Russia is increasingly engaging with the other former Soviet countries on the premises of reciprocal benefits and relationships between equals, playing a dominant role in the region has beneficial outcomes for Russia. The Russian leadership itself attributes international importance to the idea of Russia being 'one of the largest Eurasian powers... [which] predetermines Russia's responsibility for maintaining security in the world on both global and regional levels'.[22] In this way, Russia's role in the CIS as a guarantor of security has important political spin-offs that legitimize many of its aspirations to global significance. Here we can clearly recognize the interplay between the two concentric circles of geopolitics drawn upon as an organizing feature in this volume.

Importantly, the pursuit of great-power status, economic modernization, strategic interests and leadership in the post-Soviet space are seen as goals that can be achieved primarily through involvement in the international community and multilateral settings, rather than in isolation.[23] This makes Russia's behaviour in multilateral settings particularly interesting, as these should, in this light, be a key arena for achieving foreign policy objectives. A focus on potential gains to be had through multilateral institutions has been prominent throughout Putin's presidency – for example, a certain hopefulness about the possible benefits of economic integration in multilateral bodies like the WTO and the G8 (see chapter contributions by Cooper and Baev, respectively). More recently, however, in tandem with the more assertively independent foreign-policy style of Putin's second term,[24] there has been growing disenchantment with multilateral forums and what can be achieved within them, as well as more frequent reference to the notion that Russia is an 'energy superpower' and that a 'sovereign democracy' must assertively wield its economic soft power in order to achieve the desired geopolitical results. As discussed in further detail below, this shift may be connected with some of the enduring normative values associated with these multilateral settings.

Key features of Russia's multilateral engagement at the European/Transatlantic/International levels

Examination of Russia's multilateral engagement with the UN, G8, the NATO-Russia Council (NRC), the EU and the OSCE reveals several key features: (1) positive response to and a desire to belong to/be influential in 'great-power' clubs or forums that enable co-operation with other leading states; (2) expectations of acknowledgement and recompense for multilateral efforts; (3) preference for bilateralism when possible; (4) low ability to set the agenda within international forums; (5) negative response to normative expectations and/or critique of Russia's domestic politics; (6) tendency towards working primarily on 'low political' issues and (7) efforts to prevent non-Russian-controlled multilateralism from encroaching on the post-Soviet space.

Concert of great powers

Russia is particularly positive toward multilateralism when it relates to affirming great-power status and deals with issues of 'leading states'. Legvold's chapter demonstrates that a commitment to the concept of international governance occurring through a 'concert of great powers' is historically rooted in the Soviet period. Overall, Moscow prefers world affairs to be based on the leadership and multilateral interactions of the few great powers – as long as Russia is included among them.

Russia's rhetoric and behaviour in the UN exemplifies this commitment to great-power governance. Russian leaders, from Gorbachev to Putin, have consistently argued for the primacy of the UN, particularly when it comes to issues of peace and security. The UN Security Council with its five permanent members is a particularly important location where the vision of a concert of great powers is realized. As the findings in this volume show, Russia has been working actively to maintain the Security Council as the most respected and central international multilateral body. Both Pikayev and Zagorski highlight instances where Russia endeavoured to prevent divisive issues, like North Korea's nuclear programme, from reaching the UN Security Council, as subsequent debates and voting might reveal the Council as weak in responding to global challenges or insignificant in light of US unilateralism. This shows that Russia retains a powerful commitment to the arrangement on the discursive, if not financial levels (see Chapter 3).

The commitment to the leadership of great powers is also demonstrated in other forums and issue areas. Pikayev's chapter argues that, taking into consideration the heavy economic interests to be navigated, Russia can be seen to have a generally positive and basically committed stance towards multilateral co-ordination on nuclear non-proliferation issues, within both the UN and international regimes. This may be partly due to the fact that issues of nuclear non-proliferation attract the attention of and facilitate co-operation with leading states, most notably the USA. In his chapter on the Russian G8 chairmanship, Baev notes a certain exaggeration of the importance of the summit that is very much related to the high priority that Moscow assigns to this elite club.

Russia's commitment to multilateral co-operation with other great powers is also evident in its efforts to preserve the collective leadership of leading states. Gorbachev, Yeltsin and Putin, as Legvold documents, have all insisted on the special role of great powers and defended the place of the Security Council's five permanent members, arguing for efficiency over democratic representation and vociferously defending the veto. Similarly, Russia has opposed expansion of the G8 to include other countries (the 'G20' format with Brazil, South Africa, Saudi Arabia, etc.) – a reform seen to represent a belittling dilution of Russia's privileges. In organizations where it already clearly belongs to the right 'club', Russia is protective of the status quo and, in its vigorous campaigning, seems quite committed to those particular forums as they are. Fundamentally, Russia's vision of world affairs is linked to the vision of leading states, despite its occasional rhetoric about the democratization of international relations (e.g. the representation of all states, especially emerging powers) and the importance of a multipolar world.

More recalcitrant behaviour in other multilateral forums also demonstrates the fundamental belief that Russia must be a member of any globally significant multilateral organization. *Presence*, if not effectiveness or accomplishment of foreign policy objectives, is the primary aim. Adomeit, in his study of often-problematic Russia–NATO relations both within and outside of the NATO Russia Council, argues that much of Russia's involvement in NATO affairs is motivated by the desire to influence NATO decisions to the extent possible and to emphasize that Russia cannot be excluded from any important international organization On the other hand, participation in multilateral organizations outside of Russian control that do not acknowledge its 'great-power' status is firmly rejected. As Light outlines in her chapter, Russia's refusal to participate in the European Union Neighbourhood Policy (ENP) was based at least partly on a refusal to be put in the same category as Ukraine or Morocco. Instead, Moscow demanded direct EU–Russia relations, which eventually evolved into the 'four common spaces' policy programme. Although many of the objectives of the common programme remain to be realized and implemented, Russia's foreign-policy aim of parity in its relationship to the EU was achieved.

Acknowledgment and recompense of efforts at the international level

Pikayev's chapter on nuclear non-proliferation and Zagorski's study of key multilateral trends, particularly within the UN, demonstrate that the Russian foreign policy establishment expects its contributions to international joint efforts to be duly acknowledged by leading states with whom it co-operates and repaid in ways that increase economic or political capital. This may not be particularly surprising, and is certainly an aim that other states pursue at the international level whenever possible, particularly if co-operation on a particular issue is not seen to speak directly to state interests and security concerns. Pikayev highlights a vivid example of this expectation in relationship to the crisis over North Korea's nuclear programme. International clients had been central in maintaining the nuclear sector of the Russian economy during the transitional 1990s. At the time when the crisis over North Korea came to a head, Moscow had still been fulfilling previous agreements with Pyongyang, but, in accordance with international law, froze these activities. Subsequently, however, Russia found itself excluded from negotiations, which were led primarily by the USA, and was then excluded from plans/contracts to build the light-water reactor that had been offered to the North Korean leadership in exchange for freezing the country's nuclear programme. Such an experience may help to explain Russia's reluctance to sacrifice its own economic interests and immediately toe the line with the US and International Atomic Energy Agency (IAEA) stance on the Iranian nuclear programme.

On a related note, Zagorski and Adomeit both note that Russia has tended to maintain the independence of its own troops when it contributes to international peacekeeping operations. While this may not come as a surprise in connection with NATO-led operations, such as the Balkan peacekeeping operations of the 1990s, Russia also sent a small engineering unit into Lebanon in 2006 as part of a bilateral agreement with the Lebanese government. This was done in order to avoid taking part in a multilateral EU-led operation, even though the operation was under the aegis of the UN. Overall, Zagorski notes a limited commitment to spend money on international multilateral efforts, which becomes particularly clear when looking at the funds devoted within Russia to peacekeeping. At the same time, Russia, as Chapter 3 demonstrates, is often reluctant to participate in multilateral endeavours, even when it is prepared to contribute financially. Zagorski argues that by acting on the basis of bilateral arrangements, Moscow hopes to achieve a bigger and more obvious impact and to prevent its contributions from being rendered less noticeable as a consequence of a more multilateral approach.

Preference for bilateralism

The desire for efforts to be acknowledged and to result in specific return gains also speaks clearly to a rather obvious characteristic of Russian foreign policy – the overall preference for bilateral relationships. Light argues that this can be traced to the Soviet-era Warsaw Treaty Organization, which was, in fact, more of a web of bilateral agreements than a truly functional multilateral organization. The preference for bilateral relationships is evident in the Russia–EU relationship. A key Russian tool in working with European states, and often working around the EU, is the pursuit of bilateral relationships with leading European countries, like France and Germany, on key issue areas. The desire for bilateral relationships can certainly go both ways: many European countries, Light argues, have considered their relationships with Russia too important to be dealt with solely at the EU level. Russia managed to build a rather successful bilateral relationship with Germany around energy under Gerhard Schroeder's chancellorship, developing key deals on gas contracts and pipelines. However, the Ukrainian and Belarusian pipeline and transit disputes (see Chapter 6), led to a growing awareness within the EU of the need to present a united European front when dealing with Russia on energy issues. As Baev points out, an EU acting more cohesively around the energy issue torpedoed Putin's attempts to develop long-term gas contracts with the four European G8 countries (France, Germany, Italy and the United Kingdom). The clear tendency towards more 'straightforward' bilateral solutions and relationships may also indicate a lack of institutional capacity, compounded in some cases by a lack of political will, for navigating complex multilateral settings.

Limits to institutional power

Institutional power, in keeping with Michael Barnett and Raymond Duvall's definition of the term,[25] can be understood as the ability to shape the capacities of and outcomes for other actors indirectly, as 'when states design international institutions in ways that work to their long-term advantage and to the disadvantage of others'. Unsurprisingly, Russia's ability to set the agenda at the multilateral level varies according to the specific institution. While its involvement in the UN cannot be described as particularly pro-active in terms of introducing or following through on new forms of co-operation or key issue areas, Russia effectively wields its position and veto on the UN Security Council to realize its own foreign-policy aims (cf. Zagorski and Pikayev). By contrast, where it is a relative newcomer/outsider (as in the G8 or relations with the EU and NATO) and did not engage in the institution-building phase when 'long-term advantages' were being decided upon, Russia has often remained reactive, struggling to exert institutional power.

A telling example of Russia's lack of institutional power as a newcomer is its recent G8 chairmanship. As Baev describes in his chapter, Russia struggled to preside over typical G8 issues, like poverty, health and climate change. At the same time, in focusing on energy security – an effort to bring economic issues into the G8 when in reality these issues are currently handled by the finance ministers of the G7, where it is excluded – Russia was less successful, unable to handle important related issue areas like renewable energy and alternative fuel sources. That the Russian G8 chairmanship did not result in any concrete foreign policy achievements may have contributed, along with a growing general dissatisfaction with US foreign policy, to Putin's combative 'Munich speech'[26] in which he criticized the US and the 'unipolar' world. Here we can clearly see how encounters with the formidable institutional power of the USA and other 'Western' countries cause frustration for Russia.

The limitations to Russia's institutional power are not only linked to newcomer status in some institutions; structural incompatibilities and lack of capacity (or unwillingness to commit the funds that would help build such capacity) may also play a role. Structural incompatibilities, including the complexity of the bureaucracy in Brussels and a lack of qualified administrators in Russia for dealing with the EU, cause difficulties in EU–Russia interactions. Light argues that these structural and capacity problems result in Russia rarely proposing its own substantive proposals, reacting instead to EU proposals and then taking offence at the resulting impression that the EU is treating Russia as a 'junior partner'. The inability to exercise institutional power and to consistently shape long-term outcomes may make Russia's commitment to multilateralism selective rather than unconditional. As Zagorski notes, this may be in part because the Russian leadership may doubt its leverage within multilateral organizations and its ability to ensure desirable outcomes (or at the very least avoid undesirable ones). Interestingly, however, at the regional level, as evidenced in Wilson Rowe's chapter on the Arctic Council, Russia exerts a kind of 'automatic institutional power'. Capacity restraints, while certainly present, are to some extent mediated due to Russia's importance as a key Arctic state.

Norms dimension

Russia becomes negative towards multilateralism when this is linked with the assertion of values and norms – often a key feature of multilateral co-operation when European and North American states are involved. The problematic nature of the norms dimension is particularly clear when we look at the Russia–OSCE and Russia–EU relationships. The OSCE was long hailed by Russia as its favourite European structure. Russian then soured on the OSCE largely because of the criticism levelled at the human rights records of states in the post-Soviet space, including Russia. The EU's efforts to air concerns about the direction of Russia's domestic politics, particularly human rights issues relating to the second war in Chechnya, offended Russian counterparts and seriously complicated the relationship. As a result of other complicating issues – such the future status of Kosovo, energy security, treatment of the political opposition within Russia and particular bones of contention with the eastern EU member states of Poland and Estonia – the May 2007 EU–Russia summit concluded with only a few 'low politics' agreements on economic co-operation. Participation in the NATO Russia Council also carried with it 'normative baggage', in that NATO hoped that this co-operation would produce side-effects in the domestic realm within Russia, such as enhancing civilian control over defence, military reform and the resolution of 'frozen conflicts'. Even at the G8 – Russia's next-favourite in terms of multilateral co-operation – the spectre of normative criticism and expectations arose. As Baev argues, concerns over democratic values and domestic developments in Russia made it even more impossible for other G8 'great powers' to avoid normative statements. The Russia G8 summit was marked by lack of substantive/demonstrative gestures, and even the participation of G7 countries in all events did not conceal that no new Russia-US deal resulted from the summit.

Russian multilateralism remains more about co-ordinated action than fostering and adhering to common norms. Moreover, other leading states, when their critical interests align with Russia's, often are willing to de-emphasize the normative dimension of their co-operation. When interests diverge, however, the question of norms can become problematic.

'Low politics' by default

The studies on EU–Russia relations, NATO–Russia relations and Arctic multilateralism cite a similar characteristic of Russian participation in multilateral settings – a tendency to 1) have a clear definition between high and low politics and 2) end up working primarily on low political issues when co-operating multilaterally. Trenin and Lo argue that Russia, in keeping with the Soviet heritage, retains a strong distinction between 'high' and 'low' policy-making. In this dichotomy, 'high politics' involves questions of war and peace, foreign affairs, defence and domestic security; while 'low politics' concerns social and financial issues.[27] This distinction may be compounded by the now highly centralized political system and the primacy of the Russian presidential administration, as less powerful actors assigned to work multilaterally may not feel empowered to pursue co-operation that touches on what are seen as areas of high politics.

Thus it has been hoped that co-operation on the low political level, resulting in what Adomeit describes, in relation to the NRC, as a pleasant working atmosphere and symbolic rather than substantive results, would trickle up to and influence positively the high political level. In both the case of NATO and the EU, this desired spillover effect has yet to occur – indeed, perhaps the converse can be said to be true, with progress on low political issues often being hijacked by disagreements at the high politics level. To take an EU example, while the summit in Samara described above did result in certain concrete achievements in relationship to simplifying border controls and facilitating investment, little or no progress was made in terms of re-negotiating Moscow's strategic partnership with Brussels. Russia's engagement in the Arctic Council illustrates another key way in which the dichotomy between low and high politics can become problematic – namely when Russian actors seek to support fairly low level, technical co-operation with strategic documents/treaties in which other states are unwilling to invest time and resources to produce.

Defending spheres of influence

Although Putin assiduously avoids the 'spheres of influence' concept and imperialistic rhetoric when speaking about CIS space, Legvold notes that historically Russian leaders have become increasingly hostile toward multilateral endeavours initiated and controlled by others the closer such multilateralism comes to the borders of the post-Soviet space. EU expansion has caused new difficulties, although Putin has recently demonstrated a relatively pragmatic and non-combative stance relating to potential EU expansion. To take one example, in responding to a question about whether Russia would oppose Ukraine joining the EU, he voiced support for the EU – while also placing the possibility comfortably in the future, referring to Ukraine's economic and political problems and the EU's present limits to further expansion. He concluded: 'if the time comes when Ukraine is able to join the EU, we would not have anything against this idea.'[28] This positive tone may be related to the fact that EU–Russia relations now recognize that the countries sandwiched between the EU's expanded borders and Russia are a 'shared neighbourhood' requiring co-operation and co-ordination.

On the other hand, in the same interview, NATO expansion was viewed in a hostile light, due to the nature of the alliance as a 'political-military bloc'. Russia's engagement in the NRC has been primarily to limit the reach and significance of NATO in the post-Soviet space through direct involvement with it, as Adomeit argues, and Russia firmly rejects any role for NATO in resolving the Transnistrian separatist conflict in Moldova. As Chapter 8 documents, when the OSCE attempted to play a similar role in resolving the conflicts in the post-Soviet space, it came to be seen as a nuisance, and Russia has since actively worked to undermine the relevance of this multilateral organization.

Key features of Russia's multilateral engagement in Eurasia

Moving from the 'far abroad' to the 'near abroad', several distinct trends emerge when we examine Russia's multilateral engagement in the CIS, the CSTO, the Union State of Belarus and Russia, the Eurasian Economic Community (EEC), the Unified Economic Space (UES)[29] and the Shanghai Co-operation Organization (SCO). Key characteristics include: (1) the importance of Russian influence/dominance in the former Soviet area as a tool for enhancing great-power status globally; (2) an increasingly goal-oriented and pragmatic engagement in the 'near abroad'; (3) efforts to balance the introduction of market principles with the perceived imperative to entrench Russian leadership; (4) a reactive and competitive regional multilateralism, activated by encroaching 'Western' multilateral bodies; and (5) limits to Russian institutional power that result in multilateral efforts being supported by bilateralism and informal relationships between heads of state in the region.

Enhancing great-power status

Russia's efforts to defend its sphere of influence highlight the inter-linkages between the two concentric circles of global and regional geopolitics. Influence in the former Soviet counties not only serves immediate national interests (such as safeguarding Russian exports to neighbouring markets and enhancing national security by including neighbouring countries in Russian-dominated security structures), but also adds weight to Russia's claim to great-power status. In 2004, Deputy Prime Minister Victor Khristenko emphasized this dual importance of Russian-led multilateralism in the former Soviet space when he stated that 'our goal is creating a structure that is essential for the world; a structure in which the world would not be unable to function without Russia and the alliances involving it'.[30] The idea of Russia taking up a central position in a global multilateral concert of great powers by virtue of its regional leadership clearly emerges from Khristenko's statement. As Torjesen argues in chapters 10 and 12, Russia's vision for the EEC and the SCO offers further confirmation of this aim. A striking feature of Russia's activities within the SCO have been the initiatives to use this regional forum as a platform for generating joint statements that caution against US unilateralism globally as well as against US engagement in Eurasia.

Towards a more effective multilateral engagement

The importance of multilateral co-operation with the former Soviet states has been reiterated as a top foreign-policy concern since the early 1990s. In the Yeltsin years, official policy statements on the CIS gave an impression of policy coherence and prioritization of the CIS in Moscow's foreign policy.[31] According to Lo, however, the declared primacy of the CIS was an illusion – a 'foundation myth' perpetuated by the Yeltsin administration as a surrogate for policy action.[32]

Under Putin's presidency, just as the character of Russia's global foreign policy shifted from one of words to one of deeds, the character of its multilateral engagement in the former Soviet space became more substantial. Goals have been defined more narrowly, but strategies for achieving targets have become more effective. Russia has reduced its efforts to develop the CIS institutional framework into something more than a structure for facilitating dialogue and a 'civilized divorce' between the former Soviet states. Disillusionment with the CIS as a useful multilateral framework for deepening Russia's engagement in the region was made evident in 2004, when Putin noted that the CIS faced the prospect of 'withering away' and a corresponding 'reduction in interest in the CIS on the part of its member states'.[33]

Instead of working primarily through the CIS, Russia chose to further enhance several smaller multilateral groupings associated with the CIS, in particular the Union State of Belarus and Russia, the Unified Economic Space (UES) and the Eurasian Economic Community. Moscow's policies towards these multilateral arrangements has been one where issues of substance, like furthering free trade, are given priority over establishing elaborate formal structures for multilateral co-operation. This differed from the approach taken in relation to the CIS, which in the early and mid-1990s had been endowed with a formidable institutional structure, yet, as Cooper notes in his chapter, was left with 90 per cent of its agreements un-implemented. Moreover, Russia has advocated multi-speed and multi-level co-operation within the multilateral groups, particularly in the case of the Eurasian Economic Community. In their chapters in this volume, Cooper and Torjesen highlight how the countries most prepared for substantial multilateral co-operation – Belarus, Russia and Kazakhstan – were encouraged to spearhead the collaborative efforts, while those less prepared (like Uzbekistan) were pragmatically encouraged to remain in the group but engage in the multilateral initiatives at a slower pace. Rather than opting for a rhetorical or symbolic achievement through statements that the whole EEC bloc was intensifying its economic collaboration, Russia pushed for substantive co-operation with countries where the possibility of tangible and positive outcomes was greatest.

Balancing market principles and the pursuit of regional dominance

There have been significant incompatibilities in Russia's regional multilateral strategies, perhaps most prominently in relation to the tension between pursuing commercial and security/political interests at the same time. On the one hand, as Cooper shows in this volume, Russia under Putin has increasingly striven to bring market principles into its economic transactions with CIS member states and ensure that its own economic interests are met. On the other hand, Russia's wish to uphold substantial degrees of control over former Soviet states has often run counter to approaches based on cost-benefit analyses. While there has been a persistent policy of basing inter-state relations on economically sound exchanges, Torjesen argues in her chapter that economically beneficial interactions alone cannot fulfil the sizable project of safeguarding Russian political and security interests and influence in the former Soviet space. Torjesen also notes an increasing concern in the Russian leadership over the influence and presence of EU countries and the USA in the former Soviet space under the Putin presidency. This concern was significantly enhanced by the prolonged presence of US military bases in Central Asia following the terrorist attacks of 11 September 2001. The 'colour revolutions' in Georgia, Ukraine and Kyrgyzstan in 2004 and 2005 further aggravated Russian concerns about outside encroachment, since the new leadership in Ukraine and Georgian (less so in Kyrgyzstan) sought to strengthen ties with Europe and the USA at the expense of Russia. Both occurrences shaped Moscow's overall policies towards the states in the region and towards the outside countries engaging in the post-Soviet area. Most importantly in this context, these incidents led to an intensification of Russian-led multilateral institution building in Eurasia.

Reactive and competitive regional multilateralism[34]

Legvold and Adomeit show in their chapters that NATO expansion has been an important rationale for the development of the CSTO since its inception. Torjesen's final chapter highlights how Russia further intensified its efforts to turn CSTO and SCO into a viable multilateral security structures for Eurasia *after* the US deployed troops to former Soviet states in Central Asia. The string of 'colour revolutions' added further urgency to this task. Torjesen and Cooper note that the expansion of the EU and WTO membership negotiation by Russia and other CIS states provided an important backdrop to, and impetus for, Russia's invigorated attempts at establishing free trade arrangements in Eurasia through the UES and EEC initiatives.

The tendency to launch multilateral initiatives as *reaction* to policies and events pushed forward by European countries and the USA gives rise to the question of motivation. Are Russia's multilateral efforts primarily aimed at ensuring that there are the fewest possible 'inroads' available to outside powers seeking to entrench their engagement in the region? Or are these efforts best understood as directed towards developing institutionalized, inter-state co-operation in Eurasia? While it could be argued that both are at play – with the latter motivation manifested in some of the specific economic goals Russia pursues in its more market-oriented strategies and in the importance it assigns to a leading role in the region as part of the pursuit of great-power status – the timing of Russia's multilateral initiatives strongly points to the former. As Torjesen points out, reactivity and multilateralism aimed at keeping others out constitute a central feature of Russia's multilateral engagement.

Limits to institutional power

Russia is challenged by shortcomings in institutional power and this, in turn, imposes important limitations on its multilateral efforts in Eurasia. Clearly, Russia's institutional power is stronger in Eurasian than in global forums, where its structurally predominant position enables it to be the key initiator of multilateral endeavours. Nevertheless, it has not yet demonstrated in a Eurasian context that it is fully capable of exercising institutional power – what Barnett and Duvall have termed indirect and long-term control through the creation of international institutions.[35] As Light highlights in her chapter, the Kremlin's ministerial bureaucracies are not adept at dealing with the complex policy challenges associated with in-depth multilateral co-operation.

This explains why two other features so often accompany Moscow-led multilateralism in the former Soviet area: extensive bilateral arrangements and close informal ties with pro-Russian leaders in the former Soviet states. As Cooper argues in this volume, economic relations within the CIS have been most actively pursued by Russia via bilateral relations, rather than multilateral ones. Cooper suggests that instead of labelling Russia's policies 'multilateralism', a more appropriate term might be 'hegemonic bilateralism'. Irina Kobrinskaya has noted that Russia's strategies in Eurasia are increasingly characterized by efforts to ensure that political regimes in the near abroad are 'pro-Russian'. Bilateralism in combination with informal lobbying in domestic politics of the neighbouring states and tight informal networking with state leaders have at times substituted for developing formalized and institutionalized relations with the former Soviet states.[36] This is highlighted in Torjesen's chapter, where a discussion of Russian–Uzbekistani relations after 2005 offers a convincing illustration of the value placed by the Kremlin on 'pro-Russianness' over tangible contributions to Russian-led multilateral initiatives.

Concluding thoughts

The extent to which the foreign policy that underpins the characteristics of Russia's multilateral engagement identified above is a consolidated one remains a question. Even under the presidencies of Vladimir Putin, foreign policy and orientation towards multilateral organizations continued to evolve. More recently, in tandem with the more assertively independent foreign-policy style of Putin's second term, there has also been an increasing disenchantment with multilateral forums. For example, at a June 2007 economic forum in Russia, Putin called for a 'new architecture' in international economic relations, and argued that 'institutions created with a focus on a small number of active players sometimes look archaic, undemocratic and unwieldy. They are a far cry from recognizing the existing balance of power'.[37] While this shift in rhetoric is both strong and noteworthy, we should bear in mind that thus far it has remained just that – rhetoric and perhaps a jab to the players that have made Russia's path to WTO membership difficult. Tellingly, Russia continues its efforts to join the WTO, even though Putin cited the organization as a concrete example of 'archaic' tendencies. It is doubtful, as is discussed in this chapter and throughout the volume, that Russia has the political will and institutional capacity to create such a 'new architecture' for emerging centres of power.

Furthermore, many of the characteristics identified in the preceding sections point to aspects of Russia's engagement in multilateral regimes that have historical roots and that are also expressed consistently across a variety of forums. At the European/trans-Atlantic/global level, the commitment to great-power multilateralism, a desire for efforts made at the international level to be acknowledged and repaid, a tendency towards low political co-operation and a preference for bilateralism have a high likelihood of persisting, particularly given their long tradition and their expression across a range of forums. Unless significant efforts are made to increase capacity and come more closely in line with the long-term goals and fundamental values of 'Western'-dominated multilateral forums, Russia is unlikely to begin exercising increased institutional power. A closely related but more volatile question remains that of norms. While Russia currently shows no signs of acquiescing to norms imposed from outside or via co-operation in which it is not the dominant partner, this could change, if (1) internal politics and rhetoric should allow for adjustments that may bring Russia closer to Europe and North America in terms of values or (2) multilateral partners further allow the norms dimension of their co-operation with Russia to be eclipsed by practical interests. In the medium term, the latter seems more likely. For Moscow, the ideal form of multilateralism is one of co-operation around key issues in which the repercussions of such co-operation end at Russia's borders, or perhaps at the borders of the post-Soviet space.

Within the post-Soviet space, Russia has been involved in creating a form of multilateralism – flexible, regional and (importantly) free of normative baggage – that it wants multilateral organizations in the broader geopolitical arena to recognize. In his June 2007 speech cited above, Putin pointed to regional alliances and agreements that give 'the global market a new structure' as essential in augmenting existing global organizations like the WTO. The SCO is an example, albeit in primarily political and security co-operation, of such a flexible, relatively norm-free form of multilateral co-operation. The tendency to underpin such regional multilateralism with bilateral arrangements is likely to remain an enduring feature in the period ahead. It seems equally certain that Russia and the other former Soviet states will continue their resistance to yielding sovereignty to supra-national bodies, thereby firmly limiting inter-state arrangements in the region to multilateral co-operation rather than integration.

The longevity of the institutional arrangements forged in the Putin years in the post-Soviet space remains unclear. The pragmatic and goal-oriented efforts to further multilateralism under Putin could, in the medium term, be further strengthened and result in tangible and positive benefits for the states of Eurasia. However, the Kremlin's tendency to rely on informal networks and personal relationships with Eurasian heads of state raises doubts as to the robustness of regional institution-building. While the pursuit of foreign-policy dominance within the region will certainly remain an important legitimizing plank in Russia's status as a 'great power', the as-yet lightly institutionalized multilateralism of the post-Soviet space could change dramatically with new geopolitical circumstances. In particular, any changes in the constellation of conditions surrounding encroaching Western multilateralisms (such as NATO/EU), perceived negatively or positively by the Russian leadership, would be certain to result in changes to multilateralism regionally. After all, the investment in regional multilateralism was, in many ways, a reaction to precisely such external pressures.

As indicated in the opening of this chapter, although multilateralism may be simple by definition, it remains complex in practice. Russia's engagement in multilateralism encompasses many of the contradictions, problems, opportunities and key questions that shape the international system today. Russia can be seen as both an instrumental and a principled multilateralist – or, in other words, multilateralism in Russian foreign policy is *both* a tool and a value. And, as the subsequent chapters of this volume show in detail, this multilateralism is tempered by cross-cutting interests and intervening foreign policy objectives.

2 The role of multilateralism in Russian foreign policy

Robert Legvold

Russia's great-power dreams and frustrations get all the attention, but its leaders constantly insist that the bedrock of Russian foreign policy is their attachment to multilateralism. Not that the two are inconsistent. Multilateralism, as the Russians fancy it, complements their notion of how the international setting, if rightly organized, can aid Russia's return as a great power, and in the meantime minimize the risks and pain of standing in the shadow of others. Multilateralism, however, is not the framework within which analysts normally think about Russian foreign policy. Russia, of course, figures at every turn in multilateral institutions – sometimes playing a key role, such as one of the permanent five members in the UN Security Council; sometimes the role of a sceptic and even an opponent, as with NATO; sometimes the role of architect in various co-operative efforts in the post-Soviet space; sometimes as an object of concern, say, for the states that make up GUAM (Georgia, Ukraine, Azerbaijan and Moldova); sometimes as a member in name only, such as with the G8; sometimes as an aspirant, as with the WTO; sometimes as a free rider, as with OPEC; and sometimes as the co-manager, as with the Shanghai Co-operation Organization (SCO). Russia's relations with the European Union and NATO, its newer attempts to make something of the Unified Economic Space (UES) and the Collective Security Treaty Organization (CSTO), as well as its approach to the Non-Proliferation Treaty and the International Atomic Energy Agency (IAEA) are common themes, and the focus of much of this volume, but not much attention has been given to the place that multilateralism as a value, a concept, a strategy, or a general phenomenon occupies in Russian foreign policy. Multilateralism examined from this other, more basic perspective is the task of this chapter.

For some time now, the Russians have described multilateralism as both the foundation and the centrepiece of their foreign policy, and then embedded the claim in a set of basic linkages. Russia, they say, strives above all for the 'democratization of international relations based on the principle of multilateralism and respect for international law'. Multilateralism in turn is then hailed as the only legitimate basis for addressing problems of peace and security – including the use of force – and secondly as the best response to the challenges of globalization and global welfare. However, multilateralism has a further function. As noted in the joint declaration signed during Vladimir Putin's December 2004 visit to India, it also serves 'as an instrument to work toward the objective of a multipolar world'.[1] To finish the links in this chain, Russian commentators make the United Nations the institutional core of multilateralism, with the Security Council at its heart. And for the UN to better perform this role, they argue, it should be reformed and strengthened.

So, why is this interlocking set of propositions, fundamental as each is, not the first thing that comes to mind when analysing Russian foreign policy? The three easy answers are: first, Russian leaders do not mean it. For all the flowery language, it remains window-dressing, because the Russians neither put up the money or the men (when it comes to peace-keeping) essential to make multilateralism work, nor do they support multilateral efforts when these get in the way of particular Russian interests. Second – because of the Soviet Union's long antipathy to Western-dominated international institutions, its often obstreperous behaviour within the United Nations, and its passion for subordinating Soviet-led institutions to narrow self-interest – Russia, as the successor state, is not thought of as a deeply and long-committed proponent of multilateralism. And, third, multilateralism is not an easy envelope in which to insert any country's foreign policy – first, because much as a country may proclaim its devotion to the concept, too often it appears to act differently; and, second, the concept of multilateralism is itself slippery and shapeless.

Settling for easy answers, however, does not take us very far, nor does it force us to face the more complex questions raised by Russia's professed attachment to multilateralism. For the root of the analytical challenge resides in multilateralism's location at the intersection of a series of critical juxtapositions. First, as a concept, multilateralism overlaps both the notion of collective security (one for all, all against any peace-breaker) and mutual security (a self-selected set of states banded together against a named threat). Second, its prospects are buffeted by the prevailing polarity within an international system (torn between multipolarity and unipolarity today; by bipolarity yesterday). Third, multilateralism exists in two realms, one regional, the other global – and the dynamics, demands and effects are often quite different within the two. Fourth, at the level of norms, contemporary multilateralism is caught between the 'new norms of interventionism' ('humanitarian interventionism') and the old Westphalian norm of state sovereignty.[2]

Russia, like other countries that tout the virtues of multilateralism, cannot but struggle at the interstices where these contrasting and frequently conflicting impulses meet. Hence, any assessment of Russia's notion of, stake in, and approach to multilateralism will be oversimplified and abstract, if it ignores this confusing maze of cross-cutting influences. The meaning of multilateralism in Russian foreign policy cannot be reduced only to Russian behaviour at the United Nations or, alternatively, to its role in fledgling post-Soviet institutions. Rather, to measure the nature and significance of Moscow's stake in multilateralism, all aspects of contemporary multilateralism – the tension between collective and mutual security, the colliding effects of incipient multipolarity and fading unipolarity, the difference between global and regional multilateral enterprises and the competing demands of global responsibility weighed against state sovereignty – must be factored in. The Russian response to these conflicting pulls constitutes the grounds by which the place of multilateralism in Russian foreign policy should be judged.

Of course, it may be that Russia's stake in multilateralism is extrinsic not intrinsic; that the leadership supports the idea for instrumental, not principled reasons. Rallying around the slogan of multilateralism may simply be a stratagem for countering US unilateralism, not Moscow's preferred long-run design for managing international relations. If so, however, this too is best assessed by considering Russia's actions in the many different realms where the dilemmas of multilateralism unfold.

Collective versus mutual security and the challenge to multilateralism

Collective security, the notion of all for one, one for all, and all united against any state that would threaten the peace, is the twentieth-century invention that underpinned the League of Nations and still underpins the United Nations. In contrast, mutual security, by justifying the association of a limited number of states in defence against a particular threat or threats, is neither universal nor abstract. When institutionalized, it has as its embodiment NATO and similar agencies. One form need not exclude the other. Article 52 of the UN Charter allows for 'the existence of regional arrangements' to maintain 'international peace and security', provided that 'their activities are consistent' with UN 'purposes and principles', but the Charter requires that any 'enforcement action' taken by a regional organization be only 'with the authorization of the Security Council'. Hence, the framework of the United Nations, to the extent that it is honoured, subordinates mutual security to collective security, except in clear cases of self-defence as defined under Article 51. An institution like NATO is to be a tool of the United Nations, not the other way around.

The problem arises when the two concepts compete – or, somewhat more accurately, when the real world intrudes, for there never has been a period when the principle of mutual security bowed to collective security. Either collective security falls by the wayside because the great powers fail to act, as in the 1930s, or because some subset of states chooses to go off on its own, as often happened during the Cold War. Article 52 of the UN Charter has been honoured only in the breach, particularly when the interests of major powers have been involved. In our own times, the point was made when NATO went to war against Serbia in spring 1999 without Security Council sanction. Here too the issues at stake were deemed more important than guarding the principle of collective security. In this instance, however, Russia, along with China and India, rallied to the forsaken principle, but whether this was out of conviction or simply their objection to this particular instance of unilateral action was difficult to tell. The ambiguity underscores the mixed meanings that multilateralism has and the obstacles to making it the agreed-upon centrepiece of international politics.

Considerable history stands behind the standing that Putin's Russia gives to multilateralism, history that adds a useful vantage point from which to judge where today's approach fits in. For Russia the modern trajectory begins with Lenin and his Bolshevik colleagues, for whom, given their jaundiced revolutionary outlook, both the concept of collective security and its intended embodiment in the League of Nations were a sham facade behind which the Western powers continued to impose their sway over others. The legacy for the Soviet Union, even after it joined the League and later signed on to the United Nations, remained, as Alexander Dallin once wrote, 'the problem of a state with a "two-camp" world view trying to operate in a "one-world" organization'.[3] Along the way, if in the 1930s Stalin pursued collective security as one of the few means for blunting the Nazi German and Axis threat – and historians disagree on this score – no one would argue that it was for more than tactical reasons, not as a foundation for world order.[4] Even when the later phases of post-war de-colonization tilted the voting balance within the UN General Assembly more in Soviet favour, Stalin's successors continued to treat the United Nations and other multilateral institutions, like the IMF and World Bank, as, at best, arenas within which to pursue the struggle against the opposing camp, and, at worst, the inaccessible preserve of the imperialist powers. If this was multilateralism, it was multilateralism mobilized for battle, not a neutral concept intended to ensure international stability.

Real change came about only in the Soviet Union's final years under Mikhail Gorbachev. As his 'new political thinking' – the foreign policy slogan paralleling the home-front slogan of *perestroika* – coalesced into a corpus of conceptual innovations, freeing the Soviet Union from ideological encrustation, Gorbachev and those who joined him seemed to lift the weight of old bias from the notion of collective security, and to imagine it as a better way of running the international system. If, as he argued by autumn 1985, mutual security was to be made the prerequisite for national security, collective security became its logical institutional extension.

In short order, the Soviet Union radically altered its approach to the United Nations.[5] It agreed to pay approximately \$200 million in arrears, mostly back payments for peacekeeping operations (dismissed since the early-1960s Congo crisis as neo-imperialist smoke screens). After Chernobyl in spring 1986, it reversed its attitude toward the International Atomic Energy Agency (IAEA), and not only offered full co-operation in investigating the tragedy, but took the lead in supporting new conventions intended to cope with future nuclear accidents. It urged strengthening the role of the UN in dealing with environmental issues, human rights and terrorism. It championed expanded UN authority for coping with regional instability and a broader purview for the International Court of Justice. And it generally placed itself on the side of a stronger UN system, including more autonomy for the Secretary-General and even the invigoration of the moribund UN Military Staff Committee.

Most significantly, by 1988, Gorbachev and his like-minded political allies, in very un-Leninist fashion, had begun exhorting the international community to embrace the idea of 'comprehensive security'. By this they meant a fundamentally different tack on the part of the major powers – one that stressed early action to prevent crises rather than managing them after the fact; that merged economic with military well-being; and that privileged common interests over narrowly defined national interests.[6] It was a Wilsonian conception of international security more Wilsonian than Wilson's, with – as in his case too – fundamental implications for multilateralism *qua* collective security. For his Russian successors, it offered a sharp break from the Soviet legacy.

In one critical respect, however, Gorbachev preserved a *sine qua non* deeply rooted since Stalin's day. Collective security was to be of and by the great powers, albeit, at least in theory, for the greater good. Moreover, the institutional embodiment of great-power responsibility resided not merely in the United Nations, not merely within the UN Security Council, but within the permanent membership of the Security Council. For Stalin, the pre-eminence of the P-5 and the veto were the only things that made collective security safe. Gorbachev obviously was willing to place greater faith in the idea of collective security itself than Stalin, but he remained wedded to the primacy of the P-5 and the sanctity of the veto. His devotion to P-5 privilege may have been less inspired by disbelief in great-power goodwill and more by the urge to protect the Soviet Union's imperilled political standing, but this did not leave room for a more broad-based approach. In the end, Gorbachev's notion of collective security came closest to the nineteenth-century Concert of Europe model – an international system authored and managed by the great powers.

Gorbachev's successors with equal zeal have insisted on the special role of the great powers, and in the first instance of the Security Council's five permanent members. This raises the question of just how democratic Russia's pledged commitment to the 'democratization of international relations' really is. Even more than the other permanent five, the new Russia dragged its heels in the early 1990s when the pressures to reform the Security Council's membership mounted. Until 1993 the veto-wielding members had successfully waylaid efforts in the General Assembly to reconsider the basis of representation on the Security Council. During this period, Germany and Japan had also begun pressing their case for permanent seats on the Council. When in 1993 the United States, France and Great Britain gave up, acknowledged that the membership issue needed to be faced, and lent their noticeably unenthusiastic support to German and Japanese hopes, Russia stood exposed.

Its first response was to catalogue the reasons why neither country qualified for permanent membership, most of them having to do with their inability to contribute to UN peacekeeping operations. Eventually, as Berlin and Tokyo modified the domestic constraints on peacekeeping activity, and as the demands of General Assembly reformers swelled to include not only a vast enlargement of the Security Council and sharp limits on the veto or even its elimination, Moscow softened its opposition to additional permanent members, and retreated to a defence of its core interests – the veto, unmodified and in the hands of a few, along with sharp limits on an enlargement of Security Council membership. This allowed the Russians to rejoin the Americans, British and French who had embraced a two plus three formula for expanding the P-5 (Germany and Japan and, on a rotating basis, three developing countries) and who had sharply drawn the line against a Security Council with more than 20 members. Along with their other P-5 colleagues, Russian delegates argued that efficiency should take precedence over democratic representation. They reserved their real passion, however, for stifling any thought of tampering with the veto, or, as Sergei Lavrov, then Russia's UN ambassador, put it in 1998, 'the "in-built stabilizer" of the UN, a critically important and indispensable component of the mechanism of harmonizing positions and decision-making in the Council'.[7]

That the Russian commitment to multilateralism and collective security, with the UN Security Council as the command centre, has limits is scarcely surprising. Nor is it unexpected that Russia, in self-serving fashion, defines both in ways that promote its national interests – picking and choosing the moments when it wants the UN or other multilateral agencies to get involved. If there is a surprise it is in how large-minded, even idealistic, Gorbachev's embrace of multilateralism was. His radical shift in favour of collective security as an organizing principle for international politics and not merely a tactical recourse for Soviet policy, of course, could happen only because he did not have to confront either the agonizing imperatives created by the collapse of Soviet power or the rise of a preponderant, unilateralist United States. Had these story-changing events intervened, Gorbachev and those around him might well have done more or less what their successors have.

Because Russia's fall from grace converged with the United States' deepening venture into unilateralism, the dilemmas posed for Yeltsin and even more Putin intensified greatly. They revived the natural tension between collective and mutual security, thereby seriously clouding Russia's stake in multilateralism. To defend collective action among the great powers (assuming Russia's inclusion) as a general guideline was one thing when no mutual security enterprise was seen as threatening; it was quite another once Russia's attention had shifted to suddenly worrying trends within alliances. NATO enlargement and then the actions of an enlarged NATO, beginning with Kosovo in 1999, re-framed Russia's thinking about multilateralism. What from Moscow's vantage point was a negative form of multilateralism came to endanger – or perhaps more accurately, change the function of – multilateralism as collective security. After 1996, Russia's energies went into checking the former and, where possible, using the latter to this end.

In the Putin era, most of the country's energy has been spent on limning the idea of multilateralism with rather sour, defensive conditions. International institutions should not be used to interfere 'crudely in the domestic affairs of other countries, applying political pressure on them and imposing double standards when assessing election processes and the state of civil rights and freedoms'.[8] Multilateralism should not be a facade behind which some states or groups of states hide while attempting to push their way into the post-Soviet space, or to egg countries in this region to see their choices as starkly between East and West. Multilateral efforts in the struggle against terrorism should not be waged with 'double standards' or in a 'haughty, didactic tone', or 'used for various kinds of geopolitical games'.[9] Nor should key players assume that a UN vote in favour of Kosovo independence can be orchestrated without dire consequences in other separatist disputes. In particular, the resort to coercion should not be allowed to circumvent the UN Charter and the authority of the Security Council, nor should it be undertaken without supplying the Security Council with indisputable evidence to justify such use of force.

Beyond the edgy, guarded cast that the last decade's turn of events has given to Russia's view of multilateralism, even more have these events confused precisely what Moscow means by any of three central concepts – mutual security, collective security and the overarching notion of multilateralism. Russia insists that the United Nations should be the institutional foundation for multilateralism, but the principle at the very core of the UN is collective security, a principle that Russia accepts only so long as it remains under the control of the Security Council's privileged five, each possessing a veto that makes collective security impossible when the views of the five are not in harmony. In truth, therefore, Russia (as others among the five) prefers a great-power concert rather than a universal organization designed to make collective security work. Yet, as Pavel Baev highlights in his chapter, while Russia has sought to be included in the one organization closest to a great-power concert – the G8 – it is not eager to see the G8 displace the Security Council as the first among equals. Nor has its leadership been in a hurry to sponsor G8 membership for China or India.[10] Perhaps this reluctance stems from the G8's limited focus: from the start it has concentrated primarily on international economics, and only gradually and selectively on security issues. Or perhaps it is because of the G8's insistence that it is a club only for the *democratic* great powers. More likely, however, this has to do with the discomfort Moscow feels in a group where its right to be there is still questioned, its status is second-class on the economic matters central to the G8's identity, and its potential isolation on key political issues is unprotected by a veto.

For much of Russia's first decade and a half, the power holders did not think creatively or ambitiously about ways in which global governance could be re-institutionalized to enhance great-power responsibility, to increase the feasibility and effectiveness of multilateralism and to provide whatever new architecture could be created with broad legitimacy. Others had begun contemplating a G8 enlarged to include critical international players, then given the lead on both economic and security matters, and ultimately held accountable within a broader UN framework.[11] Robert Skidelsky, for example, was arguing that effective leadership of an inchoate international system requires greater collective responsibility on the part of the major powers – a greater willingness to address specific threats and the interlocking set of economic and political issues menacing long-term global stability and security. For this, he argued, there must be a forum enabling effective action, and one with broad-based legitimacy.[12] He has envisaged a G-10 or 11 that would include China, India and perhaps Brazil, a group with a far wider compass than the G8, and more effective machinery by which to carry on, while being embedded in the UN system and accountable to it. In this kind of dialogue, the Russian side had been simply missing.

Faint signs that this might be changing emerged in late 2007. 'What is needed', Lavrov was to say to the UN General Assembly in September 2007, 'is the collective leadership of major states that should represent the geographical and civilizational dimensions'.[13] The reference to geographical and cultural diversity seemed to imply a club that made room for China, India, Brazil and perhaps others. When, in the next sentence, he spoke of 'the basis for such an informal mechanism' as 'only... United Nations with its unique legitimacy', he seemed not too far from the Skidelsky idea. But Lavrov offered no details, and it remained to be seen whether the idea was the seed of a serious new direction in Russian foreign policy or merely another way of expressing Russia's discontent with, as he had said a moment earlier, an order based on 'diktat'. Throughout 2007 the Russian leadership, beginning with Putin, had grown more strident in excoriating both the underlying thrust of US foreign policy and what they termed an outmoded system of global governance still under the thumb of the major industrial countries of the West – in effect, the other seven members of the G8. Railing against a setup they disliked, however, was a far cry from developing a serious conceptualization of a different arrangement and then dedicating Russia to exercising strong positive leadership in order to bring it about.

Similarly, at another level – the regional level, where collective and mutual security also mix – the Russians have added to the muddle, twisting and turning among the misnomers and misconceptions by which each concept is represented. At times they have exhorted the fashioning of collective security at the regional level. Thus, for example, they originally hoped that the Organization of Security and Co-operation in Europe (OSCE: then the Conference on Security and Co-operation in Europe), could be made the backbone of a European security system, supplanting the mutual security pacts of the Cold-War era. The ill-fated attempt to bind together the defences of the post-Soviet states in 1992 was called a Collective Security Treaty, as with its more recent, much-truncated successor, the Collective Security Treaty Organization (2003). The OSCE, however, was much too weak and malformed to bear that responsibility, and the Russians never made more than a half-hearted case for it. Indeed, they eventually came to see the OSCE as a nuisance, particularly when others expected it to play a role in resolving conflicts in the post-Soviet space, an area that Moscow, with growing impatience, has regarded as its sphere of responsibility. More recently, Russian officials have begun to treat the OSCE as an obstacle to collective security or, at least, as an obstacle to a spirit conducive to collective security. The OSCE, Russia's foreign minister says, has been turned into a pillory where the EU, influenced by its newest members, is attempting to shame Russia for domestic policies to which it objects.[14]

The Collective Security Treaty and its successor, the CSTO, have come far closer to being a mutual security arrangement than a genuine collective security undertaking. The CSTO is neither inclusive nor intended to curb a rogue actor within its midst. It may be a collective action agency intended to deal with a thematic threat like terrorism, but as a military organization it points outward and is addressed to threats originating beyond the borders of its members. Not by accident, therefore, the entity that Russian leaders treat as a counterpart is NATO. And not surprisingly, in the muddy world of multilateralism, attempts to soften NATO's character as a mutual security pact and give it qualities of a collective security agency – the addition of the North Atlantic Co-operation Council (NACC) and now the Euro-Atlantic Partnership Council (EAPC) as well as the Partnership for Peace programme – have stirred no enthusiasm on the part of Russia.

Multilateralism and polarity

Even if the prospects of genuine collective security were better and the role of multilateralism clearer, nothing suggests that the Russians, rhetoric aside, actually would wish to make it the point of departure for their foreign policy. Rather than treat either as a feasible and adequate principle around which to build a new international system, they seem to view the first as beside the point and the second as a shield against other, more worrisome approaches to international security. This leads to the second juxtaposition: the way in which the tension between unipolarity and multipolarity affects Russia's stakes in multilateralism.

The tension, of course, replaces bipolarity's equally inauspicious impact on the concept. To go back to the start, Lenin rejected multilateralism (in the form of the League of Nations) in the name of bipolarity (between two political-economic systems), and, thus set in motion a dichotomy that would be at the heart of the Soviet Union's ever-changing, ever-unresolved relationship to the international system of the day. The Soviet Union of Lenin and then Stalin started from an insistence on two distinct sets of international law and two models of international behaviour: one for the orbit that it sought to control, the other for the outside world that it did not control. Only after Stalin's death did it begin to transcend this divide and look for a rationale by which it could accept a more unified standard. 'Peaceful co-existence' provided the answer. After 1956, prominent Soviet jurists like Grigory Tunkin used the idea to justify a set of principles (e.g. 'respect for sovereignty, non-aggression, non-interference in internal affairs and equality') offered as a common code.[15] Still, the reconciliation left 'class struggle' – for peaceful co-existence remained class struggle, with a nod to nuclear weapons – as the central dynamic in international politics and, by its very nature, the concept of class struggle ran contrary to the idea of multilateralism.

When Gorbachev began altering basic Soviet precepts, he soon demoted class struggle to an ancillary position – real, but inferior to the imperatives demanding international co-operation – thus at last freeing Soviet thought (and the prospects of multilateralism) from a deadening impediment. Yeltsin not only abandoned all traces of Marxism-Leninism, he assumed power in a world no longer bipolar, but the world that replaced it raised new challenges to multilateralism. Gradually, as the frustrations swirling around the post-Cold War reality of unipolarity gave rise to the aspirations of an unrealized multipolarity, Yeltsin's and then

Putin's Russia assigned to multilateralism a mission. Again, although for different reasons, polarity in international politics discouraged its leaders from embracing multilateralism as a principle – at least, in its most ambitious and basic sense – rather than as a stratagem.

To borrow from Bobo Lo, whenever the new Russia feared marginalization in a specific context – say, decision-making in the unfolding Balkan crises – or, more generally, whenever it sought a means of offsetting the United States' vast superiority in power, if left unfettered, it trumpeted the need for multilateralism and the primacy of the United Nations.[16] When, on the other hand, it played from a stronger hand – as in many of the conflicts near its own borders – multilateralism held less attraction. For Russian leaders, despite their general claim, multilateralism has been only a sometimes priority – a recourse, a foreign policy instrument, a way of levelling the playing field.

Compare that with a lesser power that has neither Russia's ambitions nor its frustrations. Like many smaller and middle powers, New Zealand places multilateralism at the centre of its foreign policy. 'From the perspective of a small nation', as its foreign minister noted in 2004, 'multilateralism and the associated rules-based international system is a critical and necessary alternative to a world in which the powerful can assert their will over the weaker'.[17] Russia, in contrast, would seem to favour multilateralism only where and when the most powerful can assert their will over the other powerful or would-be powerful.

Does that mean that Russia's praise of multipolarity and selective commitment to multilateralism is merely, as the French analyst François Heisberg once said of his own country's attachment to multipolarity, 'disguised anti-Americanism?' The answer is not easy. Actual motivations may be far more subtle. For example, Dominique de Villepin, as French foreign minister, defended France against this charge by insisting that his government's effort was not 'to develop an alliance of countries to contest US foreign policy, but a desire to develop autonomous aggregations of states able to act independently of US influence'.[18] The distinction is far from hair-splitting, whatever may have been the actual inspiration for France's actions. The former represents merely a blocking or check-mating enterprise. The latter imposes responsibilities on its protagonists.

Which is it for Russia? The answer is not clear, and the ambiguity is almost certainly because the country's leaders are not entirely sure themselves. Doubtless they would like to phrase their purpose in de Villepin's more neutral and constructive terms, and perhaps, at some level, the commitment is genuine. Yet, on too many occasions the lauding of multipolarity and the search for allies has come in response to US initiatives opposed by Moscow. Moreover, if Russia does want to see 'alternative aggregations of states' emerge, capable of assuming responsibility in crucial situations, it has done precious little to bring them about. With the exception of the Shanghai Co-operation Organization, it is difficult to identify any enterprise intended to compensate for the absence or failure of US global leadership to which Russia has contributed more than sideline commentary and encouragement.

The lack of clarity (or perhaps lack of deep thought) is also telltale in the way Moscow responds when Washington offers its own distinctly inadequate conception of multilateralism. The Bush administration speaks of 'effective multilateralism', by which it means multilateralism with teeth, manned by states with teeth and willing to use them. To this the Russian side has answered: 'No doubt multilateralism must be effective. But this can be done only through co-operative multilateralism, taking into account legitimate interests and the need for undiminished security for all states'.[19] Fair enough, but when they do not fill in the blanks, when they give no content to these broad imperatives, the words merely show discontent – discontent directed at the United States.

This neglect would be less noticeable, and therefore less the basis for suspecting that Russia's recent attachment to multilateralism has more to do with the polarity it resents than the real configuration of power it would prefer, were it not for the example set in the Gorbachev years. Then, when multilateralism seemed a new and serious commitment, the Soviet agenda had a sweep and depth missing now. Compare the goals pursued by the Soviets in the late 1980s, as ambitious as they were concrete, with the fencing that characterizes contemporary Russian policy. Gorbachev and his people urged efforts under UN auspices for easing debt in the weakest countries, for combating starvation where it was most acute, for enhancing 'ecological security', for liberalizing international economic relations, for weighing in more effectively on arms control issues and for addressing the threat of terrorism. Even more significantly, they then proposed specific ways of creating or strengthening the mechanisms essential to accomplish these tasks.

In contrast, Putin's Russia too speaks of the need to 'eradicate poverty and illiteracy', to 'bridge the gap between poor and rich states', to 'maintain environmental security', to 'avoid an arms race in space', and so on, but few specific ideas accompany these reminders, and fewer still are strenuously pursued by an active Russian diplomacy.[20] Lavrov, in his 2007 address before the UN General Assembly, underscored the need for 'steady socio-economic development in all the regions of the world' as an 'effective preventive to threats to peace and security', and promised that Russia would do its share as a donor.[21] But again, this came across as more of an afterthought or an offhanded display of good citizenship than as part of an ambitious programme to make multilateralism the backbone of an emerging international order.

Yevgeny Primakov, the Russian who served on Kofi Annan's 2004 'High-Level Panel on Threats, Challenges and Change', has argued that the UN should establish a structure capable of performing practical management functions in post-conflict conditions', but he has not offered suggestions for how this might be done.[22] His exhortation to give the UN a stronger 'military dimension' allowing it to be more effective in 'maintaining' or 'restoring' peace in 'hot spots' does contain specific recommendations ('permanent UN rapid deployment forces', UN 'agreements with certain regional organizations' to perform missions on its behalf, and 'within the UN a sort of expert pool' from states with advanced intelligence capabilities).[23] However, all of this is designed as 'an alternative to a unilateral decision on the use of force'. Yet, here too, Russian officials have put little energy into bringing any of this about.

Primakov is most specific about a function that has become central to Russia's stake in UN multilateralism: counter-terrorism. He supports the reorganization of the UN's Counter-Terrorism Committee, the strengthening of the Committee 1267 (the anti-terrorist sanctions committee), increased co-operation between the two, the elaboration of a 'Counter-Terrorism Charter', and the co-ordination of various regional sanctions committees.[24] Even his appeal to improve the efficiency with which the UN deals with more basic problems (of 'women, children, AIDS', etc.) is a prelude to zeroing in on the threat of terrorism. Primakov's emphasis parallels the general thrust of Russian policy at the UN. When, with some urgency, Russians advance specific ideas today, the inspiration usually appears to be the immediate threats most on their minds, not deep thinking about how the United Nations can be rendered effective for stabilizing the international setting.

Global versus regional multilateralism

Normally this is the level at which we think about Russia's behaviour in the world of multilateralism, but more rarely do we consider the tension between the two.[25] Russia's policy at the United Nations or within the IAEA or in pursuit of WTO membership is one thing. Its agitated but mixed relationship with NATO and its evolving struggle to come to terms with the EU are still another. How it thinks of and deals with other regional undertakings, such as the OSCE, ASEAN or the Black Sea Economic Co-operation organization, becomes yet a third topic. Separated even more sharply in much of the analysis is Russia's approach to regional organizations under its control or viewed as a tool of its foreign policy, such as the Eurasian Economic Community (EEC), the Collective Security Treaty Organization (CSTO), or the Shanghai Co-operation Organization (SCO).

In fact, however, all these entities form a borsch of more than letters: they blend powerful challenges and contradictory impulses into a single exceedingly variegated mix. For Russia they often have radically different valences, create radically different opportunities, serve radically different purposes and induce radically different behaviour. Not for Russia alone, of course, multilateralism designed to address over-arching global tasks often conflicts with the narrower, self-interested concerns motivating regional multilateral enterprises; and still more often the conflict may be between the stake of Russia (or that of any country) in one multilateral organization and its opposition to another.

One way to integrate these dimensions is to think geopolitically, locating multilateralism in concentric circles (the post-Soviet space, neighbouring strategic arenas and finally the larger world) and then assessing how developments in one circle interact with those in the next. One way to size up the divide between regional and global multilateralism is by judging each according to two criteria: how feasible or practical is the multilateralism of any enterprise in terms of the enterprise's own aims; and how reconcilable is any one form of multilateralism (regional) with the other (global), and, indeed, within a single form (inter-regional).

On the first score, thought of in terms of concentric circles, the contrasts between Russia's hopes, fears and frustrations among different multilateral forms stand out clearly. True, it not as though 'pro' and 'con' distinguishes one sphere from another. The mistrust Moscow has of the motives behind the collaboration of Georgia, Ukraine, Azerbaijan and Moldova in GUAM differs little from its wariness of NATO. In both cases, whatever the members claim to be the larger purposes of the organization and however much they disavow anti-Russian aims, Russians doubt the former and accent the latter. Multilateralism in these instances is at best undesirable and at worst dangerous.

However, there are differences that go beyond the comparative strengths of these two organizations – differences that reflect the geopolitics of multilateralism. If, in Russian eyes, both contribute to polarization, then, by setting one cluster of states against another, polarization has a more immediate and neuralgic effect inside the Soviet Union's former borders than in the wider world where Russians are accustomed to thinking in East–West terms. As a result, Russian policy-makers feel no urge to introduce nuances into their view of GUAM or to contemplate ways of co-operating with it. NATO, on the other hand, because it operates outside the area that Russia regards as its natural writ and because it has multiple missions, some of which Moscow approves, requires a more considered and many-sided approach. Russia, particularly its military, objects to NATO bringing troops and arms to its borders, especially in new forms like theatre missile defence, and it resents NATO efforts to work with and transform the militaries of other post-Soviet states, but it also wants to be involved with NATO, to develop areas of co-operation (outside the post-Soviet space) and to create mechanisms by which it can be given in a voice in NATO activities, such as the NATO–Russia Council created in 2002. Russia violently opposed NATO's 1999 war in Kosovo, fearing that NATO might be emboldened try the same in Russia's backyard, but its troops served alongside those of NATO in policing the Bosnian peace, and it has welcomed the role NATO plays in trying to pacify post-war Afghanistan.

Russia's two-sided view of NATO forces it to face the challenge of reconciling regional with global multilateralism. Its answer is a division of labour. As Yuri Fedotov said to a 2004 conference in New Delhi: The UN's success in dealing with crises from Afghanistan to the Balkans, from East Timor to Africa, owed 'to the unique capability of the UN to combine political, security and reconstruction activities while sharing responsibility with sub-regional organizations, arrangements and coalitions of the willing in accordance with Chapter VIII of the UN Charter'.[26]

Primakov, in speaking of strengthening the 'military dimension' of the United Nations, has raised the possibility of the UN signing 'special agreements with a number of regional organizations and individual states that, should the Security Council take an appropriate decision, they will send their rapid deployment units to conduct operations either under the UN flag or jointly with the UN'.[27] The critical conditionality, of course, is that this be done at the behest of and under the authority of the United Nations, but NATO clearly qualifies, because a sentence or two earlier Primakov included Afghanistan on his list of 'positive examples'.

On the other hand, the black side of Russia's view of NATO (and GUAM) prompts it to set against them competing forms of multilateralism. Whatever intrinsic security objectives Russia assigns to the CSTO, a further – perhaps the central – purpose is to fill space or meet needs that NATO and other organizations might otherwise exploit. Indeed, Article 1 of the CSTO's institutional forerunner, the Collective Security Treaty, proscribes members from joining any military alliance or grouping directed against other members.[28] As Stina Torjesen discusses in detail elsewhere in this book, after years of inaction, the sudden surge of activity following the formal creation of the CSTO in autumn 2002 was almost surely stimulated by the post-September 11 arrival of US and NATO forces on post-Soviet soil. Talk and wheel-spinning no longer sufficed. If Russia and those states ready to work with it wanted to take security matters into their own hands, they would have to create real machinery – working command structures, an integrated air defence and a staffed, trained collective rapid deployment force. Endowed with these components, given real rather than virtual headquarters at the Kant airbase in Kyrgyzstan, under a Russian secretary general and divided into regional military groupings covering Central Asia, the Caucasus and 'Eastern Europe', the CSTO represents Russia's determination to ensure that multilateral security institutions in the post-Soviet space remain under its control.

If Russia urges co-operation between the CSTO and NATO and welcomes the 2004 joint agreement to co-ordinate counter-terrorism efforts, there is not much doubt that it expects the CSTO to be, and be seen as, the dominant security institution in the post-Soviet space. In this division of labour, NATO's contribution is to be made beyond former Soviet borders. Thus, when NATO activity challenges this schema – whether by nurturing a NATO option for Georgia and Ukraine, or implying that it might be interested in facilities in the region – a sense of rivalry not a spirit of co-operation dominants Russia's reaction. Whether in this division of labour, when it comes to acting, Russia would subordinate the CSTO to UN Security Council authority, as it demands of NATO, remains to be tested. Moreover, if Russia expects, as it did in 1993–1994, to be simply 'deputized' by the UN as the 'security manager' for the post-Soviet space, and if the CSTO is merely a new guise for an old aspiration, then Moscow is not going to have its way and its pursuit will sharpen the clash between regional and global multilateralism.

It would be a mistake, however, to render too crudely Moscow's stake in the CSTO. Good, practical, even urgent interests parallel the instinctive desire to keep outsiders, beginning with the United States (and NATO), at bay. By 2007, Russian officials had began stressing a far more expansive agenda for the organization, one inspired by the pressing challenges plaguing all members of the CSTO. For all face the burgeoning problems of illegal immigration, drug and human trafficking, transnational crime and unsanctioned arms trade. These issues, alongside the struggle against terrorism, have been increasingly featured in the six working bodies of the organization, culminating in the decision of the September 2007 Bishkek meeting of the CSTO Committee of Secretaries of National Security to create a joint committee uniting officials from the special services, law-enforcement agencies, units dealing with illegal immigration and those charged with dealing with emergency situations.[29] It is not necessary to search for ulterior motives to understand why Russia wanted to co-ordinate bureaucracies and concentrate resources in this case.

In one instance, Russia has surmounted the natural geopolitical tensions surrounding multilateralism. The Shanghai Co-operation Organization dulls the normal anxiety Russians feel when major powers from outside the region play a significant and growing role within it. Indeed, in this case, in addition to devising an agenda addressed to the economic and increasingly intrusive security issues that link Russia, China and the Central Asian states, Moscow and Beijing share a common interest in keeping US and NATO influence to a minimum. Here multilateralism reaches into the next concentric circle harmoniously, not least because it counters multilateralism that does not. Moreover, the SCO has succeeded in transcending regional and global divides, attracting the support of other multilateral institutions at both levels. With an organization like ASEAN, it has done so by being Asia's major voice (represented by China and Russia) on two key issues: North Korean nuclear weapons and the Iraq imbroglio. With the UN, as testified to by Kofi Annan's praise for SCO in June 2006, the bridge is built around the SCO's energetic efforts to work with the UN's Economic and Social Commission for Asia and the Pacific (ESCAP), the UNDP and other UN agencies, as well as the respect it has shown for the high-level meetings organized by the UN with regional and other inter-governmental organizations.[30]

For Russia, the geopolitical and the practical tensions inherent in multilateralism are as pronounced in the economic as in the security sphere. Both plague its most recent effort to promote economic integration within the post-Soviet space. From a geopolitical perspective, the attempt to forge from Russia, Ukraine, Belarus and Kazakhstan a Unified Economic Space, the name given to this 2003 initiative, soon conflicts with the influences emanating from the next concentric circle – from the European Union. The UES has been conceived of as a three-stage process, beginning with the creation of a free-trade zone, then advancing to a customs union and finally emerging as a fully integrated single economic space operating with a common currency and free-flowing services, capital, goods and labour. Without Ukraine, however, the UES has little meaning and fewer prospects: and Ukraine refuses to go to the second stage, because membership in a customs union would preclude membership in the EU, or perhaps even a free-trade agreement with it – the lesser goal a stymied Ukraine has set.

Even were that to change (presumably only if the door to the EU remains closed for Ukraine), Russia's hopes for the UES would then confront the practical problems inherent in the enterprise itself. The UES is not the first undertaking in the post-Soviet space to envisage a three-stage process of integration. The agreement on the 'Creation of the Economic Union' early in the history of the CIS also anticipated a staged-process beginning with the freer movement of trade, and from there to co-ordinated monetary and fiscal policy, and ultimately a fully integrated EU-like structure. It never got off the ground.

The failure resulted not only from the desire of its most fervent advocates to preserve in a new form the old features of a state trading system; not only from the disorienting effects of disintegrating institutions; not only from the natural inclination of weak and impoverished states to free-ride; and, in particular, not only from the unwillingness of Russia, as the only state capable of underwriting the enterprise, to play the role that, say, West Germany played in facilitating economic integration in Europe. Even more important was a fundamental obstacle that goes to the heart of the issue and remains there today: Namely, the unwillingness of any of these states to cede sovereignty. This, of course, is what makes 'integration' different from 'multilateralism'. So long as the members of an undertaking refuse to cross this threshold, multilateral co-operation will remain the only option.

For the geopolitical reason, the Russian emphasis is likely to turn away from the UES and toward the Eurasian Economic Community (EEC), an organization of contiguous states (but without Ukraine) to which the remaining UES members belong. For the practical reason, the EEC, even as a multilateral undertaking, is unlikely to proceed much beyond the lower levels of economic co-ordination, at best something in the nature of a free-trade zone. Putin's Russia still speaks of integrating the post-Soviet space as among the highest priorities of its foreign policy; but, if this is conceived as achieving what Europe has, or even an entity like Latin America's MERCOSUR, it is too high a goal.

Signs are, however, that Russia's leadership over the last decade has come to understand the realities distinguishing integration from multilateralism in its part of the world. At the most basic level, no longer do Russian leaders imagine an integration *of* the post-Soviet space – they rather aspire to integration *in* it. Beginning with the Eurasian Economic Agreement in 1996, the focus has shifted to groupings drawing together limited numbers of like-minded states, in this case initially Belarus, Kazakhstan, Kyrgyzstan and Russia. As Evgeny Vinokurov has noted, the approach has become increasingly pragmatic and flexible, concentrating 'less on institution building and more on preparing a legal base for trade liberalization and economic expansion', while accepting 'a union with fewer participants and with the built-in concept of multi-speed and multi-level integration'.[31] These days Russia confines its hopes to undertakings like the UES, CSTO, EEC and various functional offspring of the CIS. As for the CIS itself, it lingers on, but largely as a forum, not a multilateral IGO. In instances such as the CIS collective security arrangement, it has given way to these new, more modest institutional forms (here the CSTO).

By 2007 the glimmering of another advance in Russian thinking appeared. It seemed to have two related parts. The first and more direct aspect centred on weaving together relevant multilateral institutions within the post-Soviet space, the CSTO and the EEC in particular. A year earlier they had begun holding joint summits at the heads-of-state level, and planning for joint co-ordination at the working-group level. In 2007 they pushed the idea along, emphasizing the synergies expected to develop where the agendas of the two organizations intersected – in combating terrorism, undocumented immigration, crime and trafficking in drugs, humans and arms.

While much of this remained hortatory rather than reality, the intent appeared serious, and suggested a second, more fundamental but unarticulated aspect of evolving thought. The Russian leadership, it seemed, was increasingly inclined to make regional multilateralism the primary focus of its commitment to multilateralism. Much less emphasis was placed on enhancing multilateralism at the global level, and far more on stressing its central role regionally. Not only did Putin and those around him invest a good deal more in making something of the CSTO and EEC, they also put far greater stress on securing official recognition from the UN for the role these institutions were to play in advancing the UN's own agenda.

The shift toward greater pragmatism has another advantage: realism in approaching multilateral (economic) co-operation in the post-Soviet space eases the task of advancing Russia's relationship with institutions like as the European Union, institutions dominant in the next concentric circle, institutions embodying integration – an integration whose radiating influence Russia can ill afford to ignore, let alone contest.[32] The mechanism or framework within which this takes place between Russia and the EU is the second of the so-called 'four common spaces', the common economic space. Not accidentally, as the Russians like to say, the idea came into being in 2003, under the converging effects of EU enlargement, which brought the EU to Russian borders, and Russia's readiness to tackle the large array of very specific and very practical issues affecting the economic relationship with its largest set of trading partners.

How the Russians have gone about this displays both the shifting tenor of Russian policy and the unresolved tensions between the regional and extra-regional dimensions of multilateralism. For example, between 2003 and 2005, as the two sides attempted to work out the 'road maps' by which the four common spaces would be advanced, the EU sought to stress the linkages across the four; the Russians, fearing that the common space dealing with 'justice, security and freedom', if linked to the second space, would be used to apply economic pressure on Russian actions, say, in the Chechen war, successfully resisted. Indeed, in general, in negotiating the four common spaces, the Russian side has generally preferred to concentrate on narrow, practical details and avoid larger, fundamental issues, such as, in particular, shared political values. Partially this stems from the monopoly that bureaucrats have over policy formation, but the deeper reason brings us back to the challenge that multilateralism beyond post-Soviet borders poses for Russia: how to accommodate and benefit from it, without yielding excessive leverage over Russian choices.[33]

The other example joins the regional and the extra-regional even more directly. At key stages in developing the common economic space, Moscow has concentrated on easing trade for particular sectors of the Russian economy, rather than featuring broad, basic steps designed to promote the free movement of goods and services, capital, labour and persons. With Europe Russia wants what

Ukraine wants vis-à-vis the post-Soviet space: a free-trade zone without more ambitious forms of economic integration. This it wants in no small part so as to preserve its economic options within the post-Soviet space. Thus, the unresolved dilemma for Russian policymakers is how to forge multilateral institutions that increase Russia's influence over economic trends within the post-Soviet space, without weakening their hand when dealing with multilateral institutions on the outside.

The complexities of the linkages across the different geopolitical dimensions of multilateralism do not end here. The regional, inter-regional and global are interconnected. Russia's pursuit of membership in the WTO, for example, has ensured as much. At the inter-regional level, its chances of entering the WTO required an arduous and lengthy negotiation within the EU–Russia bilateral working group. Then, in reverse, the delay in Russia's entry into the WTO remained a chief stumbling block to advancing the second (economic) space. At the regional level, one of Russia's key objectives in the UES and EEC has been to persuade other WTO aspirants to form a common front with Russia as each negotiates its way toward membership. This has been, at best, a mottled success, and the reasons one or another state resists underscore the obstacles facing higher degrees of integration within post-Soviet institutions. Even at the one level where the reconciliation of the regional with the inter-regional appears easiest – the co-ordination of the swelling parallel security agendas of the CSTO and SCO, leading in autumn 2007 to a formal agreement between the two organizations – the process has been slow and impeded. As Nikolai Bordyuzha, the secretary general of CSTO confessed, for all his efforts to persuade the SCO leadership to join hands, particularly in countering the narcotics traffic emanating from Afghanistan, 'the co-operation with the SCO to this point is not as intensive as one would like'.[34]

Norms and multilateralism

Fourth and finally, the tensions swirling about new and old core international norms further complicate Russia's stake in and approach to multilateralism. Since the end of the Cold War, and not least because of the human suffering generated in the ensuing disorder in places like Rwanda, Bosnia and East Timor, new norms of intervention have risen to challenge the venerable sanctity of state sovereignty, the reigning norm post-1648. Count the Russians, along with the Chinese and the Indians, among those least ready to see it supplanted.

In the case of Russia, this attachment has a long, tortuous, and by no means dead history. When Putin's Bolshevik ancestors came to power, they assumed that the very idea of sovereignty would soon be extinct, buried in the revolutionary onslaught. A harsher reality, however, in short order persuaded them – Lenin soonest among them – that Soviet power was best not sacrificed on the altar of revolution. The choice turned them into instant and tenacious defenders of sovereignty. Sovereignty for them was a shield. They embraced it to discredit what they assumed was imperialism's permanent nefarious plan to intervene again, as in Russia's 1918–1922 civil war. Eventually, under Stalin and his successors, the fear mutated, from one of crude, direct military intervention, into a general wariness of the West's determination to question, harass and where possible subvert the Soviet Union's freedom of action at home and in its new extended empire. Sovereignty remained the bulwark behind which the Soviets guarded against this interference – in particular, against the use of international institutions for these ends. It later also became the basis for attacking US and Western policies in those parts of the Third World favoured by Moscow, especially what were seen as progressive regimes like those of Castro, Nasser, Ben Bella, and Nkrumah.

The Soviet conception of sovereignty, however, retained an odd feature: The free hand it shielded permitted Moscow to disregard the sovereignty of states within its sphere of influence. Hence the derogated sovereignty implicit in the creation of the East European satellite regimes after 1948. Hence the interventions in 1953, 1956, 1968 and by proxy in 1981. And hence the pretext for war in Afghanistan in 1979.

Today's Russia clings to the principle of sovereignty for roughly analogous reasons. Not only does the notion of intervention – humanitarian or otherwise – evoke historical memory. (As one acute observer has noted, the word itself has a negative connotation in Russian.)[35] It carries the taint of values, ideas and preferences imposed by outsiders on countries whose ways differ or displease. The more defensive or simply impatient that Putin and his colleagues have become over US or EU efforts to influence their domestic policies or actions in Chechnya, the more have they raised the banner of sovereignty. Like their Soviet predecessors, Russia's leaders rally to the idea less as an ordering principle in international politics than as a defence mechanism. In this they are joined by the Chinese, and largely for the same reasons. Sovereignty is a rampart behind which Beijing strives to fend off interference in its internal affairs, which by its definition includes the issue of Taiwan. So, when leaders from the two countries gather, they formally condemn 'attempts at subversion of the fundamental norms of international law by means of such concepts as humanitarian intervention and limited sovereignty'.[36]

Yet, at the same time, the Russians have been less zealous protagonists of full-blooded sovereignty when it comes to the unimpeded independence of nearby states. They may profess their commitment to the sovereignty and territorial integrity of these new neighbours, but it is difficult to argue that Russian leaders have done all they could – or avoided all they should – in order to facilitate reconciliation between Georgia and the breakaway territories within it, or between Moldova and that within it, or Azerbaijan and the separatists in Nagorno-Karabakh. Nor has Moscow been hesitant to make demands reflecting less than full respect for the sovereignty of these states – whether in the form of pressure to create dual citizenship, reluctance to vacate Soviet-era military facilities, disregard of borders when weak or uncontrolled, and heavy-handed moves to acquire control over their resources, infrastructure or installations.

Multilateralism figures in this picture, because the Russians lean on the UN, albeit selectively, to buttress their conception of sovereignty. NATO's 1999 Kosovo war brought this association into sharp relief. When, in the name of humanitarian intervention, NATO bypassed the UN Security Council, and used military force to bring Slobodan Milošević's Serbia to heel, everything Moscow objected to in a putative new international norm and its potential abuse by a unilateralist USA came to a head. Yeltsin's Russia not only rejected NATO's approach: it feared a precedent that could be duplicated in other places where Russian interests and perhaps Russia itself were directly implicated.[37] So Moscow worked hard to de-legitimize the Kosovo model – and with it the idea of circumscribing sovereignty to make room for international actions justified on the grounds of ending egregious human rights abuses.

What happened in Rwanda, Bosnia and Kosovo, however, could not be ignored, not when new humanitarian tragedies in Indonesia and other ethnically explosive settings loomed. Thus, the story does not end here; it simply grows more complex. Russia and other countries that share its view, such as China and India, have been forced to consider what role the international community must assume in the face of these crises. Indeed, even amidst the fury over NATO's Kosovo war, Russian leaders began grappling with the issue of when and how the use of force might be necessary and legitimate. Days after the conclusion of the NATO bombing campaign against Yugoslavia, Yeltsin arrived in Cologne for the G8 summit ready to reconsider legal standards for the use of force in a changing international setting. Similarly, while the *Foreign Policy Concept* (2000), issued early in Putin's tenure, condemned humanitarian intervention as a way of skirting state sovereignty, it also acknowledged the need to fashion 'concrete forms' by which the international community can react 'in different acute situations, including humanitarian crises'.[38] And it repeated the call 'for a constructive dialogue on upgrading the legal aspects of employing force in international relations in conditions of globalization'.

Lavrov, in his address to the 2004 conference on global governance, recognized that 'the numerous disputes over the theme of "humanitarian interventions" raise the question of the correlation between state sovereignty and the need to respond to crises in one or another country'.[39] By then the Russians were struggling with a way to square the circle. Initially the result was the jejune proposition that external intervention would be all right if invited by the state in which it was to take place; but there were others, whom Vladimir Baranovsky quotes, who were ready to argue that 'In exceptional cases … the UN should get the right to intervene in a domestic conflict, notwithstanding the position of the state where this conflict takes place' – such, for example, in the case of 'massive crimes against humanity, genocide, brutal repression against the civil population, combatants, and POWs'.[40] Later Primakov went further. Not only in the face of 'an acute humanitarian crisis, such as mass murder of civilians, gross violations of international humanitarian law, rights to life and property, and the mass exodus of refugees', but also when the central government is unable 'to take control over non-state entities' operating on its soil and posing 'a threat to international security', or when the Nuclear Non-Proliferation Treaty is in danger of violation, particular with the risk of 'nuclear arms being transferred to a terrorist organization', then 'coercive action' by the UN Security Council is not only permitted but required.[41] This does not mean 'a rejection of the principle of the sovereignty of states per se', he maintained, but then displayed how far Russian thinking had evolved by adding: 'the ban on interference in a state's internal affairs is firm only when the development of events within this state do not present a threat to either part or all of the global community'.

What had impelled this re-thinking was more powerful than merely the discomfort of standing aside while brutal regimes or lethal chaos destroyed large numbers of people. It was the sudden swollen threat of global terrorism. Safe havens and help for terrorists from sympathetic regimes considerably diluted Russia's unalloyed belief in the sanctity of state sovereignty – at least for those states. The Russians were coming to terms with the imperative of mobilizing outsiders to deal with humanitarian crises, provided – and here norms and multilateralism re-converged – the actions were sanctioned by the UN Security Council.[42] Hence, notwithstanding the general lack of enthusiasm among the Russian public and political elite for involvement in such messy situations, Russia, like China, did sign on to the UN-sponsored military intervention in East Timor in September 1999.

What changed the Russian mind was a new overriding concern with terrorism. In the words of Minister of Defence Sergei Ivanov, 'if, fighting with such a terrible evil as international terrorism, we strictly observe the rules, then we'll be losing all the time'.[43] Not only did Putin in autumn 2002 seize on the Bush administration's distinctly sovereignty-insensitive doctrine of pre-emption to justify a comparable right for his country. Russian defence officials have on various occasions indicated that deciding when and how Russia and its CIS partners would respond to terrorist threats emanating from other countries would be done by them, presumably without the niceties of UN consultations. On other occasions, Russian officials have continued to insist that the 'preventive use of force' must follow a UN Security Council lead, be sanctioned by it and be accountable to it; but it is clear that neither Russia's leaders nor outside observers can be sure which impulse will prevail in a crunch. It is also clear that the challenge posed by global terrorism has further complicated the tensions between competing international norms and Russia's far-from-straightforward stake in multilateralism.

Trilateralism as multilateralism

There is one other new and potentially radically dramatic factor capable of altering the place of multilateralism in Russian foreign policy: the evolving relations among Russia, China and India. The significance of this three-way relationship far transcends its implications for formal multilateral institutions. If the three move beyond what divides them, if they begin to make common cause on a wide range of fundamental international issues, then this will be a particularly important incarnation of multilateralism understood in its broadest sense.

Not to be misunderstood: the three have not achieved – and may not wish to achieve – a level of convergence that would bring into being a new and influential 'trilateralism'. Each of the three – India and China in particular –

has other relationships, including with the United States, that remain priorities. Moreover, India and China still have matters (from relations with Pakistan, to sanctuary for the Dalai Lama), that set them apart, and China's rising power is likely to be of growing concern to the other two. But something new and arresting is underfoot. At the close of the St. Petersburg G8 summit in summer 2006, Hu Jintao, Manmohan Singh and Vladimir Putin met separately during the summit's 'outreach' portion. Hu praised the idea of the three acting together to enhance 'communication and co-ordination on major international and regional disputes', to help resolve 'disputes through negotiation and dialogue', and, above all to uphold 'multilateralism'.[44] A year earlier, Lavrov had joined his counterparts, Li Zhaoxing and Natwar Singh, in Vladivostok for the first stand-alone foreign minister meeting of the three, following three prior encounters on the sidelines of the UN or ASEAN. They spoke of trilateral co-operation in practical areas such as transport, agriculture, energy and high technology, but they also stressed their parallel approach to new security threats and the struggle against terrorism. Then, in a telling twist on the latter, their joint statement warned against 'double standards in fighting terrorism', a complaint Russians have often levelled against the United States and Europe in the wake of September 11.

The three countries are scarcely on the verge of forming the 'strategic triangle', that Primakov had called for in December 1998, only to be openly rebuffed by both Beijing and New Delhi; but so are they a long way from the point in May 1998, when India's defence minister, George Fernandes, referred to China as 'enemy number one'. Witness Chinese Prime Minister Wen Jiabao in India in April 2005 saying that co-operation between China, India and Russia would help to democratize international relations and safeguard world peace, security and stability, and then going on to underscore the three countries' 'identical and similar' views on many issues.[45] Or after meeting with his colleagues from what he called the 'Moscow–Beijing–New Delhi triangle' during the 2003 ASEAN session, Igor Ivanov's praise for the interaction as crucial to 'international stability in general', not least because the three share a common commitment to a 'multipolar and just world'.[46] Indeed, by autumn 2007, Lavrov, in a speech before students at the Moscow State Institute for International Relations, was referring to the relationship as a 'troika', and celebrating the 'successful development of co-operation' within it.[47]

Rhetoric, of course, may be only that, but in this case not only are the three countries pushing forward their bilateral relationships in a variety of increasingly ambitious forms (admittedly in some cases from a low point, like Indian–Russian trade or Russo–Chinese energy collaboration), they appear genuinely earnest in promoting three-way co-operation. The Russian side has celebrated measures to improve Indian–Chinese relations, urging (as Putin did in 2000 on the eve of his first visit to India) that China and India join hands to defend Asia's common interests based on 'openness and transparency', and strongly approving Prime Minister Atal Bihari Vajpayee's June 2003 trip to China as key to global stability.[48]

The Indian side likes to think of the relationship as a 'trialogue', and indeed, all three sides stress what are called the three 'no's: no alliance, no confrontation and no third country targeted.[49] Each of the three has a different stake in the trilateralism, and these locutions serve as an overarching umbrella covering the differences. For India, whose central foreign-policy objective is a prominent but independent role in international affairs, ties with China and Russia complement its refurbished relationship with the United States. For China, closer working relations with India and Russia secure its geostrategic rear while it struggles to find a way of making its rising power acceptable to the United States and Japan. And, for Russia, fraternity with the other two, on the one hand, suggests that Russia has alternatives to alignment with the West, and, on the other hand, helps to dampen competition with a surging China.

However, these are not differences that set the three countries at cross purposes. Increasingly they focus on the common ground uniting them, which is by no means trivial or hollow. All three speak favourably and invidiously of a multipolar world, because all three are less than enamoured of US behaviour during the 'moment of unipolarity'. All three stress the need to establish 'a just and fair new international order', in which states other than the industrialized countries of the West have a say. All three see eye-to-eye on issues like terrorism, the weaponization of space, Taiwan, and, when it comes to international norms, the priority of sovereignty over any competing norm; and, of particular significance to this discussion, all three put special emphasis on the role of the United Nations, particularly the Security Council – in India's case, if and when it becomes a permanent member; they also speak of co-ordinating their positions within the WTO – in this case, if and when Russia becomes a member.

This is not the place to explore the character and extent of the three-way relationship, other than to note that the most crucial dimension is Russia's unfolding ties with China. In the trilateral relationship, China–India tensions are a crucial obstacle to be overcome, whereas Russia–India relations remain to be developed, but it is the future of Russia–China relations in all their complexity that will determine whether a foundation can be created on which to build a wider collaboration among the three. If this advances beyond the incipient dialogue of our day; if the three great Eurasian powers do synchronize their foreign policies; and particularly if the synchronization rests on a similar approach to underlying international issues, including the role of international institutions, then the meaning of multilateralism in Russian foreign policy will change dramatically.

Conclusion

It would be unfair and inaccurate to ignore or dismiss Russia's stake in multilateralism. Weighed, as it should be, in the many contexts in which it unfolds, the Russian stake is not a simple matter, nor is it insignificant. True, this stake almost surely is more instrumental and less principled than the Russians claim. The high-minded syllogism that they insist guides them – a 'democratized' international system, with multilateralism and a respect for international law as the basis for determining the use of force, and the UN as multilateralism's institutional core – in all likelihood serve narrower and less noble aims. As many have assumed, including several Russian commentators, its first inspiration may be heavily tied to time and space – designed to constrain what for the moment Russia cannot constrain by its own resources, and, during this interlude, to offer a recourse that can offset Russia's relatively weakened international position.

This matters, because, if Russia's stake is only as an expedient dictated by particular circumstances, then presumably it will weaken or disappear when these circumstances change. Solve Russia's momentary frustrations, alter its disadvantages, and the commitment to multilateralism might well vanish. That is a fair point, but also only half the point. Even if the impulse behind Russia's devotion to multilateralism over unilateralism is highly self-regarding, for nearly a decade, through the Yeltsin and Putin eras, its leaders have stood by this position. Over this time, when addressing the core international challenges of the day – whether regional conflict, dealing with so-called 'rogue states', preventing the proliferation of nuclear and other weapons of mass destruction, or addressing humanitarian crises – they have been relatively consistent in demanding that the UN Charter be honoured and that the UN Security Council be made the first and ultimate arbiter. Granted, most of the time, as Andrei Zagorski makes plain in his chapter, Moscow has pursued this course on the cheap, but the guideline has remained in place throughout; and, to the extent that Russia has sought to coalesce with others, this has been with states that think and act similarly.

Thus, rather than emphasize the fragile or self-serving aspect of Russia's stake in multilateralism, it would be more sensible for policy-makers in Europe and North America to focus on ways of converting Russia's motivation into something more basic, general and permanent. However, almost certainly, this will not – indeed, cannot – happen so long as any major power whose foreign policy is of concern to Russia, let alone the world's dominant power, refuses to make the same commitment. In the end, Russia's investment in multilateralism as the core *modus operandi* in international politics will be a function of the behaviour of others, not simply or even primarily the product of its own preconceptions or internal impulses. No more than any other major power, can Russia be expected to sacrifice its freedom of action to multilateral co-operation, if other key players choose another path. This is not to say, even were, for example, the United States to recommit itself to multilateralism or seek a balance between multilateralism and unilateralism acceptable to others, that Putin and his successor could or would easily move beyond the narrowly self-serving aspects of their own commitment, or soon be willing to make the needed sacrifices to render multilateralism, particularly at the level of the United Nations, central to international politics.

Nor is this to suggest that the awkward tensions that exist in Russia's attitude toward multilateralism can be easily overcome. The closer multilateralism comes to the post-Soviet space, particularly those forms not of Moscow's making or under its control, the more ambivalent and often hostile Russian leaders become. In this case, they tend to see multilateralism as a competitive business – 'ours' and 'theirs' – expending considerable energy on buttressing 'ours'; with mixed emotions, exploring areas of potential co-operation with 'theirs', and ever-ready to see and parry a threat.

Here the problem is less with the world outside, and more with Russia's edgy insecurities at home and nearby. For the European and North American policy-maker the hope would be a gradual Russian evolution toward a stake in multilateralism that is mutually reinforcing at all levels, not a fragmented and compartmentalized version pulling in different directions. This does not free NATO or the EU from considering carefully how they might go about their business in ways inducing the Russians to place greater faith in the positive synergies among multilateral enterprises and to design those it controls with this aim in mind.[50] Ultimately it will be the Russians who make this happen – either because the things they fear ease, or because they decide this offers a better path to their own welfare and security.

3 Multilateralism in Russian foreign policy approaches

Andrei Zagorski

This chapter builds on the Introduction to this volume and Robert Legvold's contributions by exploring in greater detail some of the key themes signalled in the two preceding chapters. The centrality of a 'great-power concert' in multilateralism as practised by Russia is discussed further, and the tensions between instrumental versus principled multilateralism highlighted. This includes underlining the dualism in Russia's approaches to multilateralism through examination of regional (CSTO, SCO, CIS) and global (UN) multilateral initiatives. The chapter also assesses its tangible contributions to multilateral initiatives, as in international peacekeeping, and notes general trends, such as Russian concerns about proper acknowledgement and recompense for its efforts at the international level.

In global politics, there is an implicit tension between what Robert Kagan has called 'principled' and 'instrumental' multilateralism.[1] There is a divide between those nations – particularly the USA – which would be prepared to take coercive action unilaterally and pursue a policy which they hold to be right even if it does not receive support in the United Nations, and those – particularly many European states – which would emphasize that especially a military intervention must be subject to authorization by the United Nations Security Council (UNSC).

This chapter asks where Russia finds itself in connection with this divide, and suggests that it is difficult to place Russia's multilateralism on either side. A better approach is to emphasize the dualism of Moscow's policies. As a medium-sized power in world politics that seeks to maintain the *status quo,* Russia tends to perform rhetorically as a proponent of the kind of multilateralism embodied in the United Nations. Indeed, Moscow's language on the central role of the UN is exactly that of a 'principled multilateralist'. However, Russia remains a rather conditional supporter of multilateralist approach in international relations: it mainly seeks to use existing institutions to restrain US policy, and it does not show strong support to international organizations, instead hesitating to call on them, or failing to contribute substantially to their practical activities.

On the other hand, Russia has revealed stronger ambitions to assert itself as a regional power in its immediate neighbourhood. Here it tends to act either unilaterally or as an 'instrumental multilateralist', predominantly making use of regional institutions or *ad hoc* agreements in order to legitimize its actions.

The first section of this chapter characterizes the concept of multilateralism as applied in the Kremlin's official foreign Policy doctrine, particularly in the recent *Foreign Policy Review of the Russian Federation,* which was completed late in 2006 and made public in March 2007.[2] It also reveals differing interpretations of this principle, reflecting the dual approach taken by Moscow. The second section highlights the practical/financial limitations to multilateralism as practised by Russian policy-makers and brings out the underlying dualism and tensions involved in the apparent commitment to 'principled multilateralism' at the global level, primarily through a study of UN involvement. The third and final section addresses the predominantly unilateralist or 'instrumental multilateralist' policy of Russia as a regional power.

The Russian concept of multilateralism

Any review of Moscow's attitude towards the concept of multilateralism must begin by establishing that this concept has not yet taken firm root in the official political lexicon, even though 'effective multilateralism' is mentioned in several joint declarations issued by Russia and the European Union. The next equivalent concept used in official documents to describe the concept of 'multiple nations acting in concert' is *multilateral diplomacy.* In his Munich speech of 10 February 2007, President Vladimir Putin explicitly used this concept as the only reasonable alternative to the concept of a unipolar world;[3] the 2006 Russian foreign policy review does likewise.[4]

Multilateral diplomacy, as understood by Moscow, is much closer to an interest-based concert of powers, than to the evolving EU understanding of effective multilateralism as a means to greater value-based convergence of policies of the countries concerned. The Russian concept is characterized by three important features.

First, it implies the concept of a 'collective leadership of leading states' which objectively assume special responsibility for the state of world affairs' (as stated in the introduction to the *Foreign Policy Review*) as opposed to the leadership ambition of a single superpower.

Second, the very notion of multilateral diplomacy implies that the concerted multilateral policy is to be negotiated among the relevant nations, including the Russian Federation. This means that Russia would not accept the legitimacy of the outcome of negotiations in any forum where it had not been part of the decision-making and which it had not endorsed. Nor does it see legitimacy as flowing from any multilateral decisions taken in regional organizations, such as NATO or the European Union, where Russia is not included. In his Munich speech in February 2007, Putin particularly attacked and dismissed any proposition that decisions by either of these organizations entailing the use of force against third countries could at any time substitute the legitimacy that can be given only by the United Nations.

Third, such multilateral diplomacy is intended to become the foundation and reflect the distribution of power in the emerging multi-polar world. This implies, for example, that it must embrace the rising China, India and Brazil – the three fast-growing powers to which Moscow pays special attention.

Within this perspective, it is not surprising that Moscow focuses on the United Nations as the single most important international organization to institutionalize and practise the concept of multilateralism:

> The UN remains the universal forum that has been given unique legitimacy, […] and the main element of contemporary multilateral diplomacy. Our principle choice in favour of collective action by the world community implies strengthening of the central role of the World organization in all areas of international life.[5]

The UN fits these criteria for multilateralism almost perfectly. The group of five permanent members of its Security Council might be regarded as an embryonic collective leadership – although its composition does not exhaust the list of nations which, from the Russian perspective, would qualify for membership in the group of nations that would assume responsibility for managing world affairs. In theory, the veto power of the permanent members is meant to force them to seek negotiated solutions, so that collective action shall include the perspectives and respond to the concerns of all members of the group. However, Moscow still complains that the composition of this group does not fully reflect the power distribution among the main actors of the forthcoming 'multipolar world', and that the Council is often too strongly influenced by US policies and positions.

Proceeding on this basis, Moscow has been pursuing a cautious policy regarding potential reform of the UN Security Council. It gives clear preference to keeping the UNSC a compact body, while at the same time it admits the need to increase the representation of 'influential developing countries'. The bottom line of the Russian policy is to exclude any possible damage to its status as one of the few veto powers on the Council.[6]

As Pavel Baev notes, Russia regards the G8, which it has gradually joined only recently, as the second-most important avenue for the pursuit of its multilateral policy. The *Foreign Policy Review* explicitly attributes to this group the capacity of an evolving informal global 'mechanism of exercising collective and constructive leadership by the leading states which ought to be representative in geographic and civilizational terms'.

These two institutions top the list of international bodies seen as capable of institutionalizing the Russian concept of multilateralism. However, as discussed below, the principle of multilateral diplomacy is also meant to apply at the regional level.

In fact, Russian policy remains ambiguous. The increasing emphasis on the principle of sovereignty and on the need to retain a free hand in connection with world politics, and repeated reluctance to hand over key international security issues to the UNSC all suggest that, while rhetorically emphasizing the principle of multilateralism, Moscow's foreign and security policy remains oriented mainly towards unilateral action and *ad hoc* coalitions. It is thus neither purely multilateral

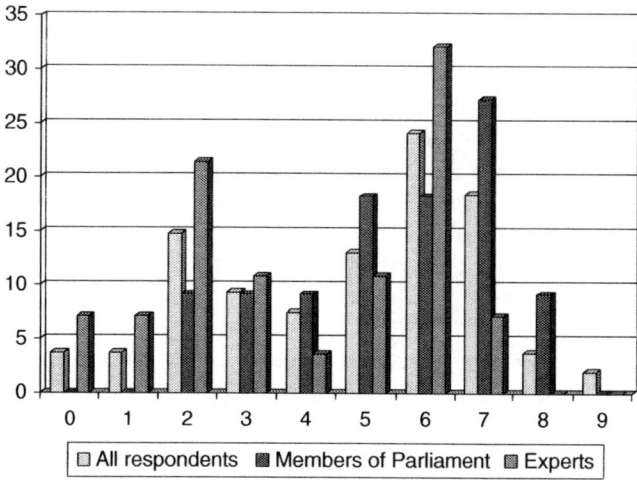

Figure 3.1 Unilateral versus multilateral security policy (%).

nor purely unilateral, but a highly complex mix of both. This conclusion is largely supported by the findings of a survey conducted in 2006 among Russian MPs and experts.[7] The survey showed wide differences in the responses of both groups, as well as that a comparatively high number of those polled agreed that Russian security policy tends to be more unilateral than multilateral.

Figure 3.1 reflects this split. Survey participants were asked to select the most appropriate description of Russian policy, on a scale where zero would mean a purely unilateral approach, nine a purely multilateral one, and five a balanced mix of both. Although responses were distributed unevenly along that scale, both the zero and the nine margins were much more poorly represented, with the relative majority of responses situated in-between the balanced five and the slightly more multilateral seven.

This confusion reflects the dualism which reveals multiple patterns of policy towards various international organizations. Although the leaders may profess their commitment to multilateralism as a principled and fundamental stance, Russia's multilateral engagement is, unsurprisingly, tempered by the existence of important cross-cutting interests to be pursued at the international level. As a country that explicitly identifies itself as a great power and sees this status confirmed by being one of the five permanent members of the UN Security Council as well as a member of the G8 – the two global exclusive clubs it is proud to be part of – Russia often acts as an 'instrumental multilateralist' seeking to work through international organizations whenever it thinks this would help in achieving its goals and/or would provide additional legitimacy to its actions. By the same token, Russia tends to act unilaterally or on the basis of bilateralism if this is seen as better serving its interests.

More often, however, acting as a medium-sized power, Moscow tries to restrict the freedom of unilateral action of the single remaining superpower – the USA – by seeking to bind it into the consensus available within the United Nations. Whenever it fears, however, that attempts to restrict the USA's freedom of action could fail and, instead, might result in the UN legitimizing the latter's action, Moscow avoids calling on the United Nations, in order to avoid the unpleasant policy choice of either vetoing a US-sponsored Security Council resolution or endorsing it at least tacitly by abstaining. In either case, Moscow would feel uneasy at either taking part of the responsibility for the US action, or running the risk of undermining the role of the Security Council (and its own, as a permanent member) should Washington decide to act outside the UN framework, as indeed it has done several times in the past ten years.

Finally, acting as a regional power, Moscow seeks to avoid a situation where its own freedom of action is restricted by neighbouring states. This is achieved both through post-Soviet regional organizations that have been created after the collapse of the Soviet Union and by seeking to benefit from existing global multinational arrangements in order to obtain additional legitimacy for its regional posture. The latter is exemplified by Moscow's demand that the European Union, while pursuing its neighbourhood policy, should respect the existing Russia-led integration initiatives, or by legitimizing the presence of Russian peacekeepers in Abkhazia (Georgia) through decisions taken within the framework of the CIS. Notably, Moscow has been seeking an agreement with NATO on mutual recognition of the respective 'areas of responsibility' of the Alliance and of the Russia-led Collective Security Treaty Organization.

Selective multilateralism

The list of different patterns of Russian policy within and with regard to the United Nations as well as other international organizations clearly indicates that its support to multilateral institutions can hardly be expected to be unlimited and unconditional. As the data presented below reveal, Russia's contribution to multilateral activities under the aegis of either the UN or other multilateral frameworks is also well below the level to be expected of a member of the exclusive group of 'most relevant' nations.

Ever since the 1990s, with few exceptions, Moscow has sought to minimize its financial contributions to international organizations. However, it still maintains the principle that the level of fees payable by individual member states shall be determined on the basis on their solvency[8] – even though Russia has significantly improved its financial situation in recent years.

One of the rare exceptions to this rule is the G8. Seeking full integration into the group, Russia has pledged to be the biggest sponsor of the global partnership against the proliferation of weapons of mass destruction (although all funds pledged for this partnership are to be spent exclusively on Russian programmes of chemical weapons destruction and on the disposal of decommissioned nuclear-powered submarines), as well as the biggest contributor to the programme for writing off the external debt of the poorest nations. Moscow is symbolically co-funding several other G8-sponsored programmes in order to demonstrate its equal status within the group.

Nevertheless, Moscow clearly limits its participation or recourse to the United Nations, which it praises as the centrepiece of multilateral diplomacy, particularly when international security is concerned. This policy can be seen in the minimal contribution that Russia renders to UN peacekeeping, as well as in its reluctance to address significant issues of international security in the UN Security Council, or to join in multilateral action once this has been sanctioned by either the UN or other multilateral bodies.

Moscow puts on the record that Russian personnel have participated in 13 out of the 19 current UN peace-keeping operations. However, the Foreign Ministry openly admits that neither numerically (only the fortieth biggest personnel contributor to those operations), nor financially (only 1.4 per cent of the total peace-keeping budget of the UN and being one of the 20 biggest donors of these activities) is its contribution commensurate with the responsibilities expected of a permanent member of the Security Council.[9] To judge from budgetary appropriations policy of the Ministry of Defence, this low-key policy is quite unlikely to change soon. Figure 3.2 shows the decline in spending for peacekeeping purposes. Together with Table 3.1, which shows the share of defence and peacekeeping appropriations in the total state budget, it clearly indicates that the Ministry of Defence pursues other priorities and reveals little intention to spend more on (and thus participate in) international peace-keeping. Despite the constant growth in defence appropriations, the ministry has chosen to concentrate available resources on the technical modernization of armed forces, while seeking to save on budgetary items that appear less relevant for that purpose – peace-keeping and mobilization capabilities in particular.

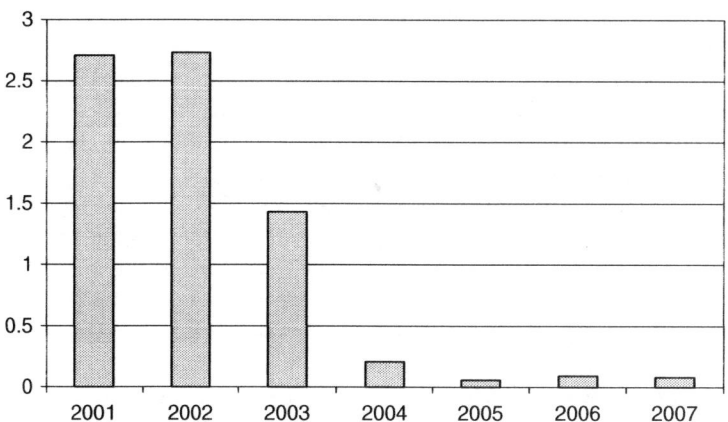

Figure 3.2 Peace-keeping budget of the Russian Federation 2001–2007 (in billion roubles).

Source: State budget data available from the Russian Ministry of Finance (www.minfin.ru).

Table 3.1 Appropriations for defence and peace-keeping, Russian Federation state budget
2001–2007 (%)

	2001	*2002*	*2003*	*2004*	*2005*	*2006*	*2007*
Defence in general	18.0	14.6	14.7	15.5	17.4	15.6	16.0
Peace-keeping	0.23	0.14	0.06	0.01	0.002	0.002	0.0001

Source: Calculated on the basis of state budget data available from the Russian Ministry of Finance
(www.minfin.ru).

Probably an even more telling example of the limited and selective support
Russia gives to the UN and other multilateral institutions is found in its
occasional reluctance to act as part of the multinational effort, deliberately choosing
instead to contribute to achieving the mutually-agreed goals on the basis of
bilateral arrangements with the countries concerned. Such a choice was clearly
demonstrated in 2006 in Lebanon when Moscow, after some hesitation, decided
to contribute a military engineering unit to assist with the reconstruction of bridges;
but it did so explicitly on the basis of a bilateral arrangement with the Lebanese
government, and not as part of the multilateral effort of the EU-led operation under
the aegis of the United Nations.

Also other examples confirm that, when confronted with the choice of either
joining in multinational efforts, or acting bilaterally or unilaterally, Moscow
often goes for the latter option. Although it was one of the original founders
of the Stability Pact for South Eastern Europe in 1999, Russia never joined
the donors' conferences with the objective of financially supporting any of
the projects selected by the various Stability Pact 'tables' to address the
problems of developing democratic institutions, supporting economic reconstruction or improving security in the region. Instead, Moscow preferred to
participate in the economic reconstruction of Serbia on the basis of bilateral
arrangements.

The same policy pattern occurred after the war in Iraq had ended. After 2003,
Moscow participated in the reconstruction of the country's energy sector on the
basis of bilateral arrangements, as long as the security situation permitted the
employment of Russian national construction personnel.

These instances reveal that Moscow is not only unwilling to devote more funding
to multilateral institutions, but often is reluctant to join in multinational efforts –
even if it is prepared to spend some money in order to obtain multilaterally-
agreed objectives. The reason for both is probably that Moscow expects a greater
effect in terms of achieving national objectives by acting on the basis of bilateral
arrangements, while it may fear that its contribution and impact on decision-
making would be less noticeable if diluted through multilateral procedures and
projects.

The limits of Russian engagement of and within the UN are also revealed
by Moscow's reluctance to involve the Security Council in cases relevant to
international peace and security. This pattern occurred repeatedly after Moscow

failed, in 1998 and 1999, to prevent air strikes in Iraq and the NATO intervention in Kosovo, by threatening to veto resolutions of the Council. In both cases the USA and the UK, and later NATO, simply circumvented the UN and acted without authorization from the UNSC. These developments signalled to Moscow that failure to reach agreement within the Security Council could easily lead to a decline in the prestige of the latter, as well as in the privileges Russia enjoys as a permanent member.

Largely for that reason, Moscow has changed its policy since earlier in this decade, and has sought to avoid bringing to the Security Council any controversial issues that might push Russia into the dilemma of either endorsing the US action at least tacitly (through an abstention vote), or by vetoing it – which could put the Security Council at risk of failing to act, and, in consequence, further diminishing its importance.

Acting in line with this logic, Moscow vehemently opposed bringing the North Korean nuclear dossier to the Security Council, preferring instead to set up an *ad hoc* format for negotiations to address the issue. Until spring 2003, when North Korea accepted the formula of six-party talks, Moscow was prepared to pursue this policy line even at the price of not being included in the circle of those participating in negotiations. Then, after North Korea had conducted its nuclear test, Moscow was no longer able to prevent the Security Council from discussing the issue. However, this case can be so far regarded as a relative success for Russia's tactics, since the six-party talks were (again) resumed, even producing a new agreement between the parties early in 2007, and thus effectively keeping the case outside the UN framework.

This policy worked out differently in the case of Iraq, however. Initially, after the UNSCOM mission had been expelled from Iraq in 1998, Moscow successfully resisted attempts by the United States to bring the case before the Security Council, including early in 2002. However, by autumn that year, Moscow found this tack no longer possible, in view of the risk that Washington might again decide to bypass the UNSC. Having accepted this, Moscow was no longer able to prevent the escalation of the discussion on measures to be taken by the Security Council, and found itself, in February 2003, confronted with precisely the choice it had sought to avoid – vetoing the US co-sponsored resolution implying the possibility of coercive action, or endorsing it by abstention. In fact, this never came to the vote in the UNSC: the UN mechanism was again bypassed when the USA proceed to invade Iraq without explicit authorization from the Security Council.

As Pikayev explores in more detail in this volume, discussions of the Iranian nuclear dossier went through a relatively similar process. From 2002 through 2006, Moscow resisted the idea of turning the case over to the UN Security Council, and welcomed the efforts of the three EU nations (France, Germany and UK) that sought to reach a political deal with Tehran. After the EU countries failed in 2005 and began to drift towards calling on the Security Council, Moscow made an enormous effort to get Iran to suspend its controversial nuclear activities, and to co-operate fully with the IAEA. However, Moscow was unable to sway Tehran, and thus failed to prevent the case from going to the UN Security Council – which later also meant a failure to get the issue returned to the IAEA. The issue is still predominantly handled within the group of six countries – the five permanent members of the UNSC plus Germany. However, the potential for further escalation of the conflict remains high. Moscow has not excluded an escalation of the controversy over the Iranian nuclear dossier in a similar way it did in the Iraqi case. Thus Russia might again find itself confronted with the dilemma of either endorsing US action, or vetoing it and thereby risking that the Security Council could again be bypassed – incurring further damage to its prestige.

Those three cases reveal the dilemmas facing Moscow, and its hesitations whenever confronted with the choice of whether or not to involve the Security Council. During this decade, it has obviously preferred the second option, but not always with success. These cases highlight both the emphasis that Russia places on the UN as a key venue for its principled multilateral engagement, and the limitations that it encounters when attempting to be an effective 'instrumental multilateralist' within this forum. Russia cannot, as these examples reveal, exercise sufficient leverage within the world organization to forestall undesired outcomes or to realize the desired ones, particularly when it comes to preventing tricky cases from being turned over to the UN Security Council.

Russia as a regional power

Revealing an increasing ambition to act as a regional power in the post-Soviet space, or in its immediate neighbourhood, Russia was from the early 1990s engaged in constructing multiple multilateral frameworks intended to help it to resist the challenges to the status quo that arose with the collapse of the Soviet Union, and to retain a dominant position in the region. This chapter argues that, in such regional initiatives, Moscow's instrumental use of multilateralism becomes particularly clear.

As the chapters in Section 3 of this volume highlight, many of these Russian initiatives failed as its situation continued to erode. The effectiveness of the remaining multilateral institutions and of their regulatory capacity remains low. Still, Moscow pays attention to the maintenance and external recognition of those few that help it to maintain its vision of the post-Soviet space as a geopolitical entity. Prominent among these are the Commonwealth of Independent States (CIS), which includes 12 newly independent states of the former Soviet Union, the Eurasian Economic Community (EEC) and the Collective Security Treaty Organization (CSTO). The latter two organizations effectively institutionalize an economic and security alliance of Russia with Central Asian states (with the exception of Turkmenistan). They are joined by Armenia as member of the CSTO, and Belarus as member of both frameworks. Special attention is paid in Moscow to the role to be performed by the Shanghai Co-operation Organization (SCO) in bringing together Russia, China and most of the Central Asian states.

While the first three – the CIS, EEC and CSTO – are multilateral institutions that largely serve to legitimize Russia's leadership ambitions in the region, the SCO is intended more as an instrument for monitoring and mitigating any expansion of Chinese influence in Central Asia. Thus all these organizations are widely seen in Moscow in terms of 'instrumental multilateralism', as they are meant to serve the objectives of the Russian policy as best they can. As for the development of true multilateralism in the region, it is confronted with a number of challenges.

Bringing together politically, economically and culturally heterogeneous countries, all post-Soviet multilateral institutions have fallen short of meeting the criteria of 'multiple nations acting in concert', as they have generally failed to produce and anchor any culture of common action. Many of the former Soviet states have seen the CIS and other forms of regional multilateralism largely as an interim, second-best affiliation on their way to mature independence. Many of them have recognized the rationale of belonging to a Russia-led group, maximizing the economic and/or political benefits Moscow might be prepared to grant (particularly to members of the EEC and the CSTO), while minimizing their own political commitments. However, many of them have also feared that Moscow's dominance could make them hostage to Russian geopolitics, and have sought to escape it as far as possible.

This is one (but not the only) reason why all post-Soviet multilateral institutions have largely failed to bring about free trade, or a real regional peacekeeping capacity, or a genuine commitment to granting each other mutual security assistance. As Cooper's chapter shows, the most sensitive trade issues have been dealt with through bilateral treatment. In the security field, the CSTO has remained mainly a multilateral umbrella for bilateral arrangements of individual member states with Russia. The single CIS-endorsed peacekeeping operation in Abkhazia (Georgia), despite Moscow's initial efforts to make it at least symbolically multinational, remained purely Russian in political supervision, military command and reporting, as well as in personnel.

Repeated attempts to improve the decision-making procedures within those institutions in order to make the process more efficient have collapsed, because the individual member states have feared to give up their sovereignty for the benefit of Russia, and because of Moscow's reluctance to admit the slightest possibility of being outvoted. Indeed, throughout most of the post-Soviet period, the Russian authorities have relied more on striking bilateral deals with neighbouring countries, instead of basing their policy on otherwise more expensive, inefficient and generally symbolic regional institutions. In this we can see the justification for Cooper's suggestion that 'hegemonic bilateralism' has dominated the regional multilateralism of Russia.

Nevertheless, 'regional multilateralism', symbolic as it may be, has served and continues to serve the purposes of Russian politics. It strengthens Moscow's pretensions of having a special role to play in the post-Soviet space. It helps to legitimize Russia's political and military role, especially in dealing with frozen conflicts whenever this role is challenged by criticism – whether from outside or from within the region itself, particularly from countries like Georgia and Moldova that seek to replace Russian peacekeepers and negotiations mediators with representatives from the UN, the OSCE, NATO or the European Union. Finally, it serves as an argument in opposing the growing attraction of the European Union to several states in the CIS, by demanding that the EU should respect both the existing formats of negotiations on frozen conflicts, and existing integration initiatives within the Commonwealth of Independent States.

As a result, while presenting itself as a champion of multilateralism and even widest possible integration in its immediate neighbourhood, Russia largely acts as an 'instrumental multilateralist', seeking to pursue its objectives and legitimize its role and activities within the region through existing organizations.

Conclusions

The Russian concept of multilateralism – or, rather, that of 'multilateral diplomacy', to use official Russian terminology – combines three important elements. It is largely understood as an institutionalized 'collective leadership' (or a concert of major powers) including Russia itself, that must duly respect and reflect the emergence of a multipolar world. This concept seeks to serve the purpose of managing the challenges of globalization on the basis of strategies to be negotiated by these major powers.

There are two approaches that are perceived in Moscow as most appropriate for institutionalizing and practising such a 'collective leadership'. The one involves the UN, which, by granting special rights to the five permanent members of its Security Council, almost perfectly fits the criteria of the Russian concept of multilateralism. The second is the G8. By working through both avenues, Moscow aims to achieve the important goal of restricting the unilateralism of US policies.

However, by invoking a principled commitment to multilateral diplomacy, Russian policy emerges as ambiguous. It remains neither purely multilateral, nor purely unilateral, but a highly complex mix of both. In this it reflects the dualism of Russian policy, which reveals multiple and sometimes diverging patterns of policy towards international organizations. Moscow often acts as an 'instrumental multilateralist', seeking to work through international organizations whenever that can help in obtaining its goals and/or provide additional legitimacy to its actions; and it tends to act unilaterally or on the basis of bilateral arrangements whenever it feels this would better serve its interest. Finally, acting as a regional power, Moscow seeks to avoid a situation whereby its own freedom of action is restricted by its neighbour states, or through external international organizations.

All these patterns suggest that the Russian commitment to multilateralism is selective rather than unconditional, varying according to specific issue and geographic areas. This conclusion is supported by the fact that Russia's contributions to diverse multinational activities and operations remain below the level of the responsibility that would usually be expected of a member of the exclusive group of 'leading powers'. Moscow is not only reluctant to spend more on multilateral institutions, but often hesitates to join in multinational efforts, preferring to work though bilateral arrangements instead. This may be in part because Russia seems to believe it lacks the leverage needed within multilateral organizations to avoid undesired outcomes and to promote the realization of those it prefers.

4 Leading in the concert of great powers

Lessons from Russia's G8 chairmanship

Pavel K. Baev

Introduction

The privilege of chairing the G8 was hailed by the Russian leadership as a unique opportunity to demonstrate their country's rising power and re-assert its coveted 'great-power' status. Russian foreign policy from mid-2005 and through most of 2006 was focused on upholding the chairmanship, while Vladimir Putin saw the summit in Strelna, near St. Petersburg, as the crowning moment of his presidency. No expense was spared on staging the 'best summit ever'. The anti-globalization protesters who had made so much trouble at the 2001 Genoa summit and again in Heiligendamm in 2007 were kept on a short leash, and it was only the somewhat disagreeable 'Leningrad weather' that made a slight blemish on the perfectly organized high-profile event. Summing up the achievements of 2006, Foreign Minister Sergei Lavrov praised the 'significant growth of the Russian factor in international affairs', stressing how 'the success of our chairmanship in the G8 had the most profound impact on the global politics'.[1]

With hindsight, we can see that the priority attached by Moscow to the G8 format was blown out of proportion, yet it was consistent with Russia's specific interpretation of multilateralism, as examined by Robert Legvold in his contribution to this volume. In the most general terms, it all boils down to the idea of a 'concert of great powers', demonstrated first of all in permanent membership in the UN Security Council, with the G8 coming as a significant second. Driven by this idea, President Boris Yeltsin made great efforts to secure an invitation to join the G7, which, ever since its inception in the mid-1970s, had been perceived by Soviet leadership as the headquarters of the 'imperialist camp' – even though the G7 had no permanent structures and focused primarily on economic matters.[2] After several trial years in the G7+1 format, Russia was finally accepted as a full member at the 1998 Birmingham summit, only a few months before it was hit by a devastating financial crisis. As a novice in distress, Russia had to accept the agenda set by other members and follow their lead, so its 'institutional power' remained limited even as it recovered from depression and acquired new wealth. The 2006 chairmanship was seen as the opportunity to change this pattern and achieve a higher status than, for instance, that accorded to Canada.

It is even easier to see that ambitions which had been pitched too high were bitterly frustrated, and became transformed into a spiteful desire to avenge perceived rejections and humiliations. Putin's 'landmark' speech at the security conference in Munich, richly coloured by this frustration, was in fact a closing statement for the chairmanship that had jeopardized rather than confirmed Russia's membership in this prestigious Western club.[3] While Putin put the emphasis on disagreements over arms control matters, claiming that the plan for deploying elements of US strategic defence in Eastern Europe constituted a direct threat to Russia's security, his indignation related more to the Western efforts, however inconsistent, to hold Moscow accountable to the normative standards upheld by many multilateral organizations, including the OSCE. Lashing out against US 'imperialism' and UK 'imperial thinking' and denigrating the OSCE as a 'vulgar instrument' of these powers, Putin sought to exempt his regime from democratic norms, and to justify this in terms of asserting Russia's 'sovereignty'.

The persistent emphasis in official political rhetoric on Western hostility to Russia's reclaiming what it considers its legitimate place among the 'great powers' indicates that the Kremlin has not come very far in drawing lessons from the less-than-successful experience in presiding over the G8 proceedings. This learning process is only tangentially related to the record of implementing the promises given and commitments accepted at the various 'club' events;[4] the plain fact that the Russian leadership still tries to deny is that, despite Putin's skilful manoeuvring around the 'round table', he increasingly finds himself in a minority of one. This intransigence inevitably accentuates the implications for the Group that its six founding members (Canada joined in 1976) have to acknowledge and compensate for, collectively and individually.

This chapter will evaluate these implications, seeking to establish whether this pattern of relations is useful or indeed sustainable. It starts with the topic of 'energy security' that constituted the main focus of G8 debates in 2006, and then moves to the security agendas related to the wider Middle East, from Lebanon to Afghanistan. Next it examines the clash of interests centred on democracy development in the no longer newly-independent but still post-Soviet states, not least in Russia itself, and finally attempts to extrapolate existing trends to the near future of the G8 as Russia moves into the uncertain period of Putin's departure from the summit of power.

Energy comes first

Russia's initial plan for the G8 chairmanship was truly complex and multi-dimensional, covering a broad range of 'burning' issues from non-proliferation and counter-terrorism to human security, with 'energy security' proposed as a key but by no means the absolutely central topic.[5] In fact, as practical work on this plan got underway, Russia's inability to contribute to the chosen topics of education and dealing with infectious disease became embarrassingly obvious, not least due to its undeniable mismanagement of the deepening domestic demographic crisis.[6] Moscow's lack of sincere interest in the problems of Africa that had been prioritized by the British G8 leadership during 2005 was rather disconcerting for the partners. On top of that, serious disagreements about dealing with the nuclear programmes of Iran and North Korea were deepening rather than narrowing (see Pikayev's chapter in this volume for more detail), while the sharp escalation of the crisis in Lebanon also saw a lack of coherent response. That left 'energy security' as a far more dominant issue for the G8 deliberations – by default rather than by design.

Besides the obvious preference for playing on its perceived strength in energy-related matters, Moscow had an additional incentive for focusing on energy matters. While global economic trends have traditionally been central to the G8 discussions, the real heart of the 'club' has always been financial interactions and controls – and Russia is still excluded from those, as the finance ministers have retained the G7 format. Moreover, there is also the G20 financial format, where states like Brazil, South Africa and Saudi Arabia are represented. Russia is worried that the model might be adopted for reforming the 'club', so that the core group of five to seven states would be supplemented by some 15 other members – including Russia, but with its privileges seriously diluted.[7] In order to prevent such a belittling reform, Moscow sought to use its new 'petro-roubles' wealth based on huge energy export revenues for claiming a full say on economic matters. Finance Minister Aleksei Kudrin made every possible effort, including paying Russia's external debt ahead of schedule and writing off some hopeless debts for countries like Afghanistan and Syria, in hopes of gatecrashing into the financial G7.[8] These efforts were in vain. Despite the 'economic miracle' so confidently promised by Kudrin, Russia did not receive an invitation from Germany to partake in the meetings of finance ministers in 2007, nor can it expect a more positive attitude from Japan in 2008.[9]

This setback, while upsetting, was still perceived as temporary, since Russia's financial clout was expected to grow in parallel with the size of its hard currency reserves (amounting to some USD 450 billion in autumn 2007). It was also seen as of only secondary importance since the main priority was firmly set on 'energy security'. This grand but vague notion was not only open to different interpretations but indeed had essentially opposite meanings for Russia and its seven partners, with the USA still striving to restore the impossible invincibility of energy independence.[10] Andrei Illarionov, Putin's former economic adviser and the G8 'sherpa', argued that energy security was just a 'phantom' called into existence because of massive state interference into the energy sector. Indeed, that point was perfectly illustrated by the 'gas war' between Russia and Ukraine in winter 2005/2006 that cast a far longer shadow over the high-level politics of energy relations than Moscow had expected.[11]

One distinct goal that the Kremlin pursued by focusing the debates so narrowly on this top priority area was to alter the political discourse on energy matters that had prevailed since the Group was established in the mid-1970s, together with the International Energy Agency (of which Russia is still not a member), largely in order to find appropriate responses to the shocking blackmail by oil producers who had joined forces in OPEC. One part of the discourse 'modernization' suggested by

Moscow was increased attention to the energy needs of the poorest countries that were particularly hard hit by the six-fold increase in oil prices. Formulated by Putin as a condemnation of 'energy egoism', this line of argument appeared impeccably 'politically correct' but proved somewhat uncomfortable for his counterparts, who found themselves under implicit pressure to increase aid and assistance to the 'dispossessed' in order to compensate for a new burden that was not of their own making.[12] Another and a more meaningful innovation in the energy-political discourse was the proposal not to juxtapose but to integrate two opposing analytical schemes – 'security of demand' and 'security of supply'. Besides its strict 'political correctness', this idea appeared to open the way towards harmonizing conflicting interests, while in real terms it meant replacing market mechanisms with a complicated combination of inter-government agreements between key producers and consumers.[13]

The focal point for all these debates and exercises in transforming the discourse was the document 'Global Energy Security', approved by the G8 on the basis of a Russian draft. Some of Putin's ideas (for instance, regarding 'energy egoism') were discreetly dropped, while others were adopted in watered-down form; Moscow could feel satisfied that consumers and producers were treated on equal basis, but its ideology of greater state control over the energy business failed to receive even conditional approval.[14] The main thrust of discourse transformation, however, has been in a direction not quite envisaged by the Russian leadership: the point of departure became the notion of 'diversification' and the main avenue of new thinking was designated as 'climate change'. Moscow had nothing against 'diversification' in the narrow sense as the ability to redirect energy flows from one market to another, but it was caught flat-footed in the newly-energized debate on diversifying away from hydrocarbons – it had nothing to say on alternative fuels, or 'greener' technologies for burning coal, or increasing the efficiency of energy consumption, or even the rehabilitation of exhausted oil and gas fields. The only topic in these debates where Russia was able to make a serious contribution was nuclear energy, but its readiness to dismiss the problematic security aspects of this potentially vast market was rather worrisome for the USA and France (as the main competitors), while Germany remained stubbornly opposed to the revival of nuclear power generation, so the G8 was unable to adopt a meaningful common stance.

The real significance of these somewhat abstract exercises lay in claiming leadership in re-conceptualizing the energy theme in a period of breathtakingly high prices aimed at securing for Russia the role of 'energy security guarantor'. This claim was, however, seen as too ambitious from the rather diverse points of view of the seven counterparts, and so that role was duly denied. One part of this failure was that Moscow, while adopting a globally-grand rhetoric, had in fact a rather narrow geographic focus for its real energy deal. The energy dialogue with the USA, launched amidst great fanfare back in 2002, had been to all intents and purposes wrapped up by the end of 2004 with no practical results – in no small degree due to the Kremlin-led destruction of *Yukos*.[15] Energy relations with Japan had never had a strong foundation, and the *Sakhalin*-2 'affair' undermined it even further. The great promise of energy co-operation with China also remained a matter of declarations and memoranda of understanding.[16] The key content of the 'energy security' concept in the Russian interpretation was the offer to the four European members of the G8 – Germany first and foremost – to integrate their gas distribution networks with GAZPROM's production and transportation assets and thus receive firm guarantees of delivery of agreed volumes on 'reasonable' prices. This offer was presented in an elaborate form during Putin's visits to France and Germany in September and October 2006 – and was unequivocally turned down, to the great disappointment of the Kremlin.[17]

The reasons for that discord were multiple, varying from the consequences of the 'gas war' with Ukraine to the less-than-ideal chemistry between Putin and Angela Merkel, and they are carefully examined in Margot Light's chapter on Russia–EU relations in this volume. What is important to emphasize here is the fact that the key European consumers, and first of all Germany, remained unconvinced of Russia's ability to cover their needs despite Putin's 'word of honour'. That the country was uniquely endowed with hydrocarbons was beyond doubt, but its sustained under-investment in modernizing key assets and GAZPROM's astounding inefficiency in managing the resources placed under its control seemed to indicate clear prospects of an energy crisis spiralling out of control by the end of this decade. The steadily growing internal demand (stimulated by artificially low prices) and the stagnant production inevitably create an export crunch. Even if the most likely victim is to be Ukraine and not West European customers, the political repercussions of this forced reduction in deliveries will necessarily be profound.[18]

Intense energy debates in the G8 did not enhance mutual understanding but clarified for the seven 'fat cats' (Putin's term) the conclusion that Russia could not be a provider of 'energy security'. The technical rationale for this conclusion was the common assessment that, despite being the largest producer and exporter of energy in the world, Russia could not manage the role of a swing producer, delivering additional barrels and cubic meters in situations when supply and demand got out of synch. The bottom line, however, was that Moscow, with its peculiar mix of unprincipled mercantilism and securitized pragmatism, could simply not be trusted to perform the crucial role of controller of energy flows.

Combating terrorism and looking for opportunities in the Middle East

One of the grave concerns in the Kremlin in planning the image-boosting G8 chairmanship was the possibility of a large-scale terrorist attack that could derail the Strelna summit in much the same way as the Gleneagles summit of July 2005 had been disturbed and overshadowed by terrorist attacks in London. Every possible security precaution was taken in St. Petersburg, which – unlike Moscow – had never seen a single deadly explosion. The hunt for terrorists across the North Caucasus was stepped up, yielding the best result imaginable: Shamil Basaev, arch-terrorist and the key figure in the underground networks of armed resistance, found his end in the blast of an explosives-laden lorry in a remote corner of Ingushetia.[19]

With hindsight, we may see that these extraordinary security measures were a case of more than just a desire to eliminate any unnecessary disturbances to the carefully staged summit. Unlike on previous occasions, the Kremlin generally wanted to reduce the salience of the theme of joint efforts in countering the threat of international terrorism.[20] The main reason for downplaying an issue so widely perceived as a key area of co-operation based on common interests was the growing divergence of strategic trajectories in combating terrorism. By the end of 2006, Russia had significantly reduced the smouldering instability in the North Caucasus and eliminated the threat to Moscow;[21] for the West, however, the 'war on terror' was not going well at all: the USA faced a deepening and widening civil war in Iraq, NATO encountered escalating resistance to its state-building work in Afghanistan, and the threat of new attacks in Europe remained alarmingly high. In this situation, the Kremlin saw few benefits in expanding its counter-terrorist co-operation with the West in any format, including the G8, while it was keen to identify and exploit the new political opportunities that were opening due to US and NATO overstretch.

One area where Moscow found expanding space for political manoeuvring was a Middle East hit by a series of shock-waves spreading from the epicentre in Iraq, which attracted volunteers driven by various ideological motives and made them into seasoned guerrilla warriors. While Iraq was off-limits for the G8 discussions, the conflict that required urgent attention at the Strelna summit, cutting short even the 'energy security' debates, was Israel's intervention in Lebanon. Consensus on that burning issue was hard to achieve, and Putin did not see it as a part of his chairman's duties to make extra efforts to hammer it out. Instead, Moscow preferred to emphasize the lack of available capabilities in key Western security institutions and volunteered to send an engineer battalion to Lebanon – but not as an element of the rather feeble joint 'peace operation'.[22] Russia's new trump card in the Middle East, besides its 'friendly' relations with Syria, was its readiness to maintain 'normal' contacts with the Palestinian government formed by *Hamas* even after the start of in-fighting. Seeking to gain some political profile 'on the cheap' but to avoid unnecessary confrontation with the USA, Moscow took care not to overplay that card, assuming that Washington would have to progress through many unsuccessful rounds of 'shuttle diplomacy' performed by Secretary of State Condoleezza Rice before recognizing the dead-end and finally acknowledging the usefulness of Russia's channels.[23]

A theme that was touched on only tangentially in Strelna, although very much a matter of serious concern for most participants (even Japan), was the situation in Afghanistan, where the deterioration in state-reconstruction was becoming undeniable. Moscow refrained from its habitual criticism of NATO's shortcomings in addressing the problem of opium cultivation but took a symbolically important step by discontinuing arms supplies to the government in Kabul. The prevailing assessment among Russian experts was that NATO, despite boldly defining its operation as 'mission possible', would not be able to mobilize sufficient resources to sustain deployment in the face of mounting resistance.[24] Failure was thus only a matter of time, and while Russia had no intentions of being part of it, the prospect of a new Taliban triumph was also not particularly appealing. Preventive damage limitation appears to be the idea behind the low-profile policy of restoring ties with the Tajik and Uzbek factions and reconstituting the Northern Alliance to keep control over Mazar-i-Sharif, Konduz and the Panshir Valley.[25] Throughout 2007, this policy has remained exploratory rather than truly pro-active; however, already its initial settings have proven rather unhelpful for the government of Khamid Karzai.

The most complicated political intrigue in the wider Middle East was spun around Iran, and the Strelna summit saw its fair share of Persian positioning and horse-trading. Since the start of its G8 chairmanship, Moscow, although initially sceptical, had become increasingly convinced that Iran constituted the single most important problem for Washington, and thus assumed that tangible rewards could be extracted by promising every incremental co-operative step. Indeed, Russia held two crucial keys to the problem: its veto-power in the UN Security Council, and the nuclear fuel pledged for delivery to the newly-constructed Bushehr reactor; it also had the additional leverage of exporting to Iran conventional armaments, particularly surface-to-air missiles. The economic interests involved in these nuclear and arms deals with Iran were not especially significant in real terms, so Moscow was free to agree to symbolic UN sanctions and to delay the launch of the Bushehr power plant, thus keeping Washington on the hook.[26]

This intrigue has continued after the end of Russia's year in the limelight. At the G8 summit in Heiligendamm in June 2007, Putin assured Bush that he shared his threat assessments and so suggested jointly use of the early warning station in Gabala, Azerbaijan – but he also confirmed to the Iranian leadership that Russia did not consider Iran as a source of threat.[27] The aim of this manoeuvring was to postpone the moment of truth, so that the hard choices would have to be made by Putin's successor in the Kremlin.[28] Two key considerations for these choices are that Russia would much prefer to live next door to a non-nuclear Iran but would not be really threatened by its nuclear weapons; and that, while peaceful resolution of this crisis is greatly preferable to a US military intervention, the latter could also play into Russia's hands by further undermining the usefulness of US 'hard power' as well as eroding its 'soft power'.

On the whole, Russia managed to score a few points in the great Middle Eastern game by making friends with characters that none of the G7 members wanted to be associated with and by exploiting the vulnerabilities in the West's ambivalent strategy of transforming this explosive region. These inconclusive achievements have been based entirely on political manoeuvring, without involving any real engagement. Consequently, their sustainability remains questionable, while Russia's role in a region sliding to the brink of a major turmoil is in fact rather marginal and could hardly answer to any 'great-power' ambitions.

Democracy matters

Putin was well aware that the position of G8 chairman would expose him to extra scrutiny and pesky criticism regarding the non-democratic direction in the evolution of his regime. The heavy emphasis on 'energy security' and the incremental concessions on the Iranian problem were intended to distract the attention of, respectively, the European 'four' and the USA to some pro forma declarations. In addition, the 'normalization' in Chechnya and the reduction of instability in the North Caucasus were seen as sufficient conditions for closure of the fruitless exchanges on the human rights problems, while the thaw in relations with Ukraine after the March 2006 parliamentary elections should have eliminated this issue from the Strelna discussions, particularly since the question of Ukraine's accession to NATO had been postponed into indefinite future. The Kremlin also carefully gauged the tensions in relations with Georgia, assuming (with good reason) that the EU's lack of readiness to propose a meaningful solution for Kosovo would get Moscow off the hook regarding the (mis)management of 'frozen conflicts'.[29]

Russian experts and commentators were confident that Putin's offers could not be refused and that his defences were unassailable, so Moscow paid scant heed to voices in the USA arguing that Russia should be excommunicated from the G8 and the Strelna summit boycotted. Thus, all the more shocking was the stern speech delivered by US Vice President Richard B. Cheney – a person certainly taken very seriously by the Russian political establishment – at a high-profile policy conference in Vilnius. This speech was described as an 'ultimatum' and as a 'considered nasty provocation': it was only Andrei Illarionov who argued that Cheney actually offered an 'olive branch' by insisting that Russia was not 'fated to become an enemy'.[30] This opinion, however, was not heard in a Kremlin already awash in worries about a possible disastrous fiasco of the summit.

That speech determined the pronounced concentration of Moscow's attention in the following months on relations with the USA, and eventually made the bilateral Putin–Bush meeting into the central event of the Strelna 'gala'. Putin's team carefully prepared a package of bargaining chips, from Iran to new proposals on arms control, fully convinced that human rights issues were in real terms of little importance for 'comrade Wolf'. As Putin pointed out: 'How quickly all the pathos of the need to fight for human rights and democracy is laid aside the moment the need to realize one's own interests comes to the fore'.[31] Sergei Sobyanin, Vladislav Surkov and other members of the presidential administration were busy clearing up the 'misunderstandings', so that the forthcoming tête-à-tête could create an opportunity for a new 'look-in-the-eye' session (similar to the first meeting between Putin and Bush in Ljubljana in June 2001) that would open a new chapter in Russia–US co-operation on an 'equal basis'.[32]

The Kremlin obviously underestimated the significance of the 'normative' dimension of the G8 networking that covered a wide range of democracy/human rights issues, interpreting as its victory the consent of the seven counterparts to participate in all the scheduled activities without any demonstrative gestures. It refused to see the point made in one international media editorial that 'however hypocritical Cheney might be in lecturing anyone about human rights – especially just before heading off to court President Nursultan Nazarbaev of Kazakhstan, hardly a paragon of civic virtue – that does not mean he was wrong'.[33] It also failed to grasp the dynamics of consolidation of the bi-partisan consensus in the USA around the conclusion that a Russia moving away from democracy could not be a reliable partner, and Putin – as ever, confident in his communication skills – failed to understand Bush's personal disappointment in their 'special relations' that were not improved in any significant way by the 'lobster summit' at Kennebunkport in July 2007.[34]

These denials, typical of the hermetically closed system of decision-making atop the enormous bureaucratic pyramid, could not hide for long the plain fact that nothing resembling a new Russia–US deal was to emerge from the summit.[35] However, Putin was not disheartened by that setback, and instead sought to get an even better deal by launching an 'autumn offensive' in Europe aimed at exploiting every crack in the trans-Atlantic alliance that had been opened by the Iraq debacle. The energy wedge was inserted with demonstrative sureness, but Chancellor Merkel refused to yield. Besides European concerns that Russia's politicized gas business had been reduced to stagnation by expanding state control, reservations about the Kremlin's 'gasified' policies of aggressive expansion in the European energy market definitely also played a role in that estrangement.[36] Whereas many Europeans felt uncomfortable at the prospect of external control over vital domestic energy-supply systems, the prospect of control by a Russia that was proceeding along the path of 'enlightened authoritarianism' was outright unacceptable.

Two rather strained EU–Russia summits in Lahti and Helsinki saw disagreements going far deeper than the specific issue of Polish meat products, as the European states laboured to forge a common position on engaging Russia on new terms that would acknowledge Russia's increasing tendency to challenge the norms and rules of 'partnership'.[37] That tendency was highlighted by the murder in Moscow of journalist Anna Politkovskaya on 7 October 2006, which generated a resonance that Putin failed to comprehend; next month, the deadly dose of Polonium-210 administered in London to Aleksandr Litvinenko became the proverbial last drop in the barrel of Western complacence. Russia's chairmanship in the self-appointed club of liberal 'great powers' ended on a sour note indeed.

Conclusions: drawing the 'Munich' line

There was no hiding from the utterly disappointing net results of the Year 2006 for Putin. After holding the position that had seemed to promise so much gain, both Russia's prestige and his personal reputation plummeted.[38] One immediate lesson drawn by the Kremlin was to discard the idea of 'energy super-power' and abandon the theme of 'energy security', since discussions were producing only greater disagreements and demands for Russia to clarify its ambiguous intentions. At the World Economic Forum in Davos, first deputy Prime Minister Dmitri Medvedev still boasted of Russia's prospect of becoming the top oil producer in the world, but Putin in his presumably final address to the parliament merely acknowledged this fact, while placing emphasis on 'innovations' that should secure accelerated growth in industry.[39] Grandiose Soviet-style plans for increasing electricity production and expanding the nuclear industry were elaborated under presidential supervision, while Europe was left to ponder the prospects for developing the Yamal and Shtokman gasfields.

Another sour lesson from the anti-climax of the G8 chairmanship was that there was nothing to be gained by maintaining a co-operative approach to key security matters, whereas a shift to more assertive and even confrontational behaviour could yield dividends both at home and abroad. Now Putin has apparently decided that taking a tough stance might earn him more respect, since his trusted friends have disappeared from the political arena and there is little time to befriend rising new leaders. The occasion for a clear break with the policy of partnership was chosen with utmost care, since the Munich conference was intended to be a no-nonsense event where Putin's complaints and accusations would be taken seriously.[40] The demonstrative unwillingness to take steps towards any compromise was maintained at the two unproductive Russia–EU summits in Samara (May 2007) and Mafra (October 2007).[41] Moscow sought to emphasize that the USA was an 'imperialist' power in decline; and that the Western alliance, rather than holding the line from Afghanistan to Morocco, was in fact in retreat. This assertion helped in explaining away the mounting international criticism as Western vexation over Russia's growing influence; moreover, it allowed the Kremlin to portray Russia as a potentially indispensable power, not only in terms of energy, but also due to the political weight gained and exercised outside the narrow format of the G8.

This desire, or perhaps phantasm, was spelled out not in the elliptic discourse of 'energy security' but in the straightforward vocabulary of 'hard security', exemplified by the moratorium on implementing the Conventional Forces in Europe Treaty (1990/1999) announced by Putin in his April 2007 address to the parliament and executed by the presidential decree of 14 July 2007. While a step of little practical consequence, it was loaded with symbolism and accompanied by loud protestations against the planned deployment in Poland and the Czech Republic of US strategic radars and interceptor missiles.[42] Rejoicing at every arms control argument between Washington and its 'old' and 'new' European allies, Moscow is not afraid to confront NATO head-on, confident that the overstretched and bitterly divided Alliance would not be able to muster any punishing counter-measures. The Kremlin insists that it has no desire to set in motion a new 'Cold War' – and indeed the new division of Europe bears little resemblance to the militarized ideological confrontation some 25 years ago. The 'Fulton' label attached to both Cheney's and Putin's speeches in Vilnius and Munich is certainly a journalistic parabola, but the level of mutual mistrust and the readiness to ascribe to the other side inherently evil intentions seem unpleasantly reminiscent of the poor standards of yesteryear.

Russia's estrangement from the West is not driven by Putin's 'attitude problem', which his hand-picked successor Dmitri Medvedev now tries to overcome. It is the steady drift away from democratic norms and liberal guidelines in state-building that determines the self-assertive confrontational line in Russia's foreign policy, which thus becomes more organic to its domestic policy. Russia's main failure in chairing the G8 lay in the reversal of democratization, which has made its membership in the 'club' both useless and senseless.

5 Russia's attitude towards nuclear non-proliferation regimes and institutions

An example of multilateralism?

Alexander A. Pikayev

Introduction

In its official documents and declarations, the Russian Federation has always expressed its commitment to 'collective' – i.e. multilateral – approaches to settling international problems within the framework of international law. Such expressions can be found in all three official doctrinal papers of the Russian Federation – the Military Doctrine, the National Security Concept, and the Foreign Policy Concept.[1] Although these three documents were adopted as early as 2000, the first year of Vladimir V. Putin's presidency, so far they have not been replaced by any revised versions. Consequently, these documents officially remain in force, even though some of their parts seem to be, at least partially, outdated in practice.

Top officials responsible for the country's foreign policy continue to reiterate Russia's commitment to multilateral action based upon instruments of international law. For instance, on 20 December 2006, Minister of Foreign Affairs Sergei Lavrov stated:

> ...we have, generally, correctly determined prospective trends in world development. First of all, I have in mind...the increasingly collective nature of international relations...we realize more and more – and not only we, but other states as well – that the unilateral use of force may result in expansion of conflict only...No one alone can determine the right prescription for settling any modern problem...[2]

In this chapter, Russia's overarching commitment to multilateralism at the policy/strategic level is examined in relationship to the issue area of nuclear non-proliferation, with a particular focus on the UN as a key locus for multilateral co-operation on this question. First, the extent to which nuclear non-proliferation is a national security priority, and this priority is considered something that to be achieved multilaterally, is examined through a brief review of major policy documents. Secondly, the cross-cutting political and economic interests that shape Russia's commitment to nuclear non-proliferation are described, including the influence of threat perceptions. Subsequently, an individual proliferation case – Iran – is taken up to illustrate how these policy commitments and cross-cutting interests have interacted in shaping Russia's foreign policy stances in the UN and with key partner states. Some of the main features of Russia's multilateral engagement in focus in this chapter include Russia's commitment to working on non-proliferation along with other leading states, such as the USA, and the expectation that multilateral co-ordination that goes against Russian political and economic interests should be acknowledged and duly recompensed.

Nuclear non-proliferation as an important national security priority

Nuclear non-proliferation occupies a prominent place in all three of Russia's main doctrinal statements. According to the National Security Concept, which was approved by Presidential Decree 24 on 10 January 2000, the proliferation of weapons of mass destruction (WMD) and their means of delivery is considered to be amongst the main threats in international relations. Correspondingly, strengthening the WMD non-proliferation regime is noted in the National Security Concept as a main goal of the Russian Federation for maintaining national security. Countering WMD proliferation is presented as an area of objectively overlapping interests between Russia and other states. The document states that Russian foreign policy should aim, *inter alia*, at:

- fulfilling mutual obligations to reduce and eliminate weapons of mass destruction;
- maintaining international export controls on goods and technologies;
- adapting existing arms control and disarmament agreements to new conditions of international relations, and
- facilitating the establishment of zones free from weapons of mass destruction.

Russia's Foreign Policy Concept, which was approved a few months after the National Security Concept on 20 June 2000, further develops and clarifies some provisions of the National Security Concept. In this policy document, the Russian Federation confirms its commitment to working with other states in preventing the proliferation of nuclear weapons, other weapons of mass destruction, and their means of delivery, as well as related material and the associated technologies. It also firmly supports strengthening and developing necessary international regimes; it reiterates the country's commitment to compliance with its obligations under the Comprehensive Test Ban Treaty, and calls on all other states of the world to join the latter.

In particular, the Concept outlines the importance of relations with the United States. Despite serious disagreements, sometimes on very basic principles, US–Russian interaction is seen as a necessary condition for achieving an improved international situation. This interaction is considered especially essential in dealing with problems of disarmament, arms control and WMD non-proliferation.

The Military Doctrine, approved at approximately the same time as the Foreign Policy Concept (21 April 2000), pays less attention to non-proliferation issues. The proliferation of weapons of mass destruction is here not mentioned as a main source of military threats to Russia's national security. However, reference is made to non-proliferation-related measures in a clause devoted to describing steps for maintaining Russian military security. Among them:

- strict compliance with Russia's international agreements on arms limitations, reductions and elimination, facilitating their implementation and maintaining their regimes;
- readiness to further reduce Russia's nuclear weapons supply to minimal levels on a bilateral basis with the United States and on a multilateral basis with other nuclear powers, in keeping with requirements for strategic stability;
- efforts to achieve universal acceptance of the non-proliferation regime for nuclear weapons and their delivery vehicles, to increase of efficiency of the regime by using a combination of prohibitive, control and technological measures and comprehensive prohibition of nuclear tests.

Although non-proliferation is not mentioned as top national priority in any of the three doctrinal papers, it occupies a quite prominent position in all of them. Provisions of the documents underline Russia's strict compliance with arms control and disarmament agreements, the need to strengthen the international nuclear non-proliferation regime, and the desire to work toward that end on a co-operative multilateral basis. It seems especially important that the documents sent such positive signals in 2000, at a time when relations between Russia and the West – primarily with the United States – were still chilled by disagreement over the NATO bombings of Yugoslavia in 1999.[3] This demonstrated that Moscow saw non-proliferation as an important mechanism and value *per se*, and that co-operation in the area was not linked with the status of political relationships with key partner countries or specific diplomatic disagreements. Even against the backdrop of a downturn in Russo–Western relations, the Kremlin signalled its willingness to co-operate, maintaining non-proliferation as a strategic national security imperative rather than as a bargaining chip to be used for practical short-term political gains.

Russia's specific interests in nuclear non-proliferation

Nuclear proliferation among states

Although non-proliferation represents important national foreign and security policy priority, the Russian Federation, like other countries, also looks at the non-proliferation regime through the prism of its specific interests in other areas. These specific interests result from Russia's unique geostrategic position and its international status. Geographically, Russia occupies a huge territory in Europe and Asia, extending through 11 time zones from the Baltic Sea to the Bering Strait.

The perimeter of its borders measures 60,000 km. Despite all recent efforts to improve border control, considerable portions of its borders, primarily to the south, remain porous and ill-protected, leading feelings of vulnerability to both traditional and non-traditional security threats.

This vulnerability makes it natural for Moscow to seek co-operative relations with major powers located to the south of the post-Soviet space, above all with China, India and Iran.[4] Interdependencies with Beijing and Tehran and the need to maintain good political relations with them shape policies in many important areas – from regulating migration to arms sales and non-proliferation as well. This is why it might sometimes seem that non-proliferation values appear somehow muted in connection with Russia's relations to some Asian powers.

A second important factor is the magnitude of Russia's international commitments. In contrast to the United States and NATO, the Russian Federation does not maintain military deployments overseas, with the exception of deployments in states that, until the Soviet collapse, constituted a single country with its capital in Moscow. While the USA and NATO are worried about the threat that new nations gaining nuclear weapons could pose to forward-based forces and the limitations this could impose on freedom of action in remote regions, this is not considered as a challenge for Russia. The Kremlin follows a defensive posture. Its aim is to protect its national territory and to provide security guarantees for several adjacent states, all of which, in the memory of the generation now in power, represent a part of the national territory. Therefore, the potential nuclearization of some new countries is not considered to be any real challenge. Russia remains a nuclear superpower, and its nuclear capabilities will exceed those of potential new nuclear nations for a long time to come.[5]

In other words, the absence of overseas deployments permits the Kremlin to rely credibly on nuclear deterrence in defending its vital security interests against potential state-proliferators. This also means that Russia may not perceive the risks of nuclear proliferation with the same level of urgency as, for example, the USA and some of its allies.

Non-state actors

Moscow is much more concerned about the danger of proliferation among non-state actors.[6] Russia's vulnerability from the South, instability in the Caucasus and large-scale terrorist activity inside the country during the last ten years or so have forced the Kremlin to take seriously risks of nuclearization of terrorist groups. Perhaps, given the 1999 terrorist explosions of apartment blocks in Moscow and Volgodonsk where hundreds of civilians were killed, it was not a mere coincidence that 2000 saw a more active non-proliferation policy. While in the 1990s Russia resisted the idea of imposing restrictions on fuel deliveries to the Bushehr nuclear power plant, which was built in Iran with Russian assistance, by 2001 the policy had changed.[7] Moscow linked deliveries of fresh fuel to the plant with Iranian agreement to return spent fuel back to Russia. That measure would alleviate proliferation concerns about Tehran reprocessing the spent reactor fuel in order to separate weapons-grade plutonium. After long hesitation, Iran had to accept the Russian demands.

Russia's prioritization of the prevention of nuclear proliferation among non-state actors was demonstrated by the promotion of then Convention against Nuclear Terrorism. It became the first international convention to be submitted by the Russian Federation, and was approved by the UN General Assembly in September 2005. The document contained several specific international and national measures aimed at preventing nuclear terrorism.

The US–Russia co-operation that took place during debates around the Convention in the UN continued in 2006. In July 2006, just prior to the G8 Summit in St. Petersburg, the US and Russian presidents adopted the Global Initiative on Countering Nuclear Terrorism.[8] This is a multilateral effort aimed at improving co-operation between the states in fighting against potential nuclear terrorism. The USA and Russia invited founding partners to attend its first meeting and adopted a Statement of Principles of the Initiative. They also invited the IAEA to participate as an observer.

Both presidents stated their intention to invite as many states as possible to participate in the Initiative in order to broadly strengthen national capabilities in countering nuclear terrorism worldwide. They also agreed that informing industry and the wider public is necessary for achieving full implementation of the Initiative.

Co-operation under the Initiative is meant to include the following:

- improving protection, control and accounting of nuclear material and radio-active substances, as well as physical security of nuclear installations;
- detecting and intercepting illegal trafficking and other illegal activities involving nuclear and radioactive material and above all, implementing measures aimed at preventing terrorists from acquiring and using such material;
- responding to acts of nuclear terrorism and neutralizing their consequences;
- developing technical means to contribute towards countering nuclear terrorism;
- ensuring that law enforcement agencies undertake all possible measures to avoid sheltering terrorists who seek to acquire and use nuclear material;
- strengthening national laws in order to ensure efficient prosecution and punishment of terrorists and those assisting them.

The 2005 Convention on Countering Nuclear Terrorist Acts is considered an important, although not exclusive, legal base for implementing the Initiative. Among other documents, the presidents mentioned the Convention on Physical Protection of Nuclear Materials and Facilities, UN Security Council Resolutions 1373 and 1540, and national legislation. Interestingly, Putin and Bush excluded from the Initiative clauses dealing with nuclear weapons, facilities and materials considered legitimate for military purposes under the NPT.

This again demonstrated the unwillingness of these nuclear powers to undertake intrusive non-proliferation measures that might affect their own nuclear arsenals.[9]

Potentially, this might create doubts among some states on accession to the Initiative in the future.

Beyond the 2005 Convention and the 2006 US–Russian Joint Statement, Russia's priorities in countering nuclear proliferation among non-state actors were reflected by its support of UN Security Council Resolution 1540 requiring all UN member states to implement national measures aimed at preventing proliferation of WMD materials and technologies beyond their borders. Other examples might include Moscow's accession to the Proliferation Security Initiative (PSI) in 2004. The accession was met with surprise by many observers from Russia and allied countries,[10] and could represent a gradual retreat from the Kremlin's policy of denouncing the use of force as a mean to reach international objectives, including enforcing compliance with international agreements.

Perceived sources of threat

Like the United States and major European nations, the Russian Federation perceives that terrorist and proliferation threats related to national security are coming from the South and are associated primarily with the greater Middle Eastern area and Islamic fundamentalism. This broad but rough agreement between Moscow and some Western capitals has permitted them to find common ground in addressing controversial issues like the war in Afghanistan, peacebuilding in Iraq, the Palestinian–Israeli conflict and even a response to Iranian nuclear programme. The links between Chechen groups and international Islamic fundamentalists also have contributed to a muting of Western criticism towards Russian operations in Chechnya.

However, the Russian threat perception seems narrower than the US one, and there are also differences between Russia's approach and mainstream European approaches. All three broad Middle Eastern terrorist groups, originating from Sunni and Shia fundamentalism and Arab nationalism, have affected the United States. Countering the spread of Shia fundamentalism from Iran has been one of the major tasks of US diplomacy since the Iranian revolution in 1979. In the 1980s, it was the primary reason why Washington supported Iraq in a war against Iran, which was started by Saddam Hussein and involved the use of Iraqi chemical weapons against Iran.

Arab nationalism has posed a threat for both the United States and Europe. It was their planes and ships that became targets of militant Palestinian and Libyan-sponsored terrorism in the 1970s and 1980s. Most recently, the 9/11 attacks on the United States together with terrorist acts in Madrid and London have focused attention on Sunni fundamentalist groups like al-Qaeda. In the past, however, elements of these groups were considered by Washington to be natural partners in attempts to contain Shia fundamentalism and to push Soviet troops out of Afghanistan.

While the United States sees al-Qaeda as a major threat to its national security, European leaders tend to take a more nuanced approach. There are still debates on sources of the terrorism and methods of countering it. In contrast to the USA,

Europe did not reach a consensus that al-Qaeda was the source of a recent wave of terrorism in Europe. It also seems that European responses are more shaped by a history of terrorist attacks that were motivated by Arab nationalist ideas and took place in Europe or adjacent areas. The history of the Russian experience is different. During the Cold War, various Arab groups were considered to be useful as tools in consolidating Soviet influence in the Middle East. More recently, co-operation with moderate Arab regimes has played a role in cutting off the support that radical Islamic movements provide to the Chechens and Islamic radicals inside and around Russia.

Past and present relations with Shia Iran are more complicated. In the 1980s, the Soviet Union was concerned by the behaviour of Iranian radicals, but focused instead on the positive aspect of the tacit co-operation of pro-Iranian groups in Afghanistan in the 1980s. Today Moscow denounces Iranian escapades against Israel, but capitalizes on co-operation with Tehran in settling some regional conflicts, as in Tajikistan, and, until recently, Afghanistan.[11]

Terrorism supposedly supported by international Sunni fundamentalism is considered a real and present danger. Indeed, in three major terrorist attacks alone – the 1999 explosions in apartment blocks in Moscow and Volgodonsk, the 2003 siege of the theatre in Dubrovka, Moscow, and the 2004 seizure of a school in Beslan, North Ossetia – more than a thousand people were taken hostage, and almost that many were killed. This has deeply affected Russia's foreign policy and security perceptions, including its attitude towards non-proliferation. Now, like the Bush administration, the Kremlin tends to look at many international developments in terms of the need to 'fight international terrorism' – a Russian term similar to Washington's 'war on terror'.

Therefore, both Moscow and Washington pay close attention to countering terrorism originating from Sunni fundamentalist groups. This represents an important area of overlapping interests. In late 2001, it led to unprecedented co-operation between the two powers during the Afghan war. Later, however, priorities diverged somewhat. The USA became increasingly involved in fighting Iraqi insurgents only partially linked with al-Qaeda, while Russia concentrated on settling domestic problems in the North Caucasus.

In sum, in terms of terrorism/proliferation threat perceptions in the Greater Middle East, the United States faces challenges posed by the widest possible spectrum of various Islamic fundamentalist and Arab nationalist groups. For its part, Europe seems most concerned about Arab nationalists, and more recently, Sunni radicals. For Russia, countering terrorist groups of Sunni origin represents the priority, while attitudes towards Shia fundamentalists and Arab nationalists remain far less negative.

These gradations in attitudes create differing emphases in the policies of these three major players, both in the region of primary concern and in nuclear non-proliferation activities. Consensus on a Sunni fundamentalist threat triggered close co-operation in the ongoing war in Afghanistan. As an important consequence of that shared engagement, the United States, Russia and EU countries have similar positions on Pakistan. All three share concerns about Pakistan's nuclear arsenals, but remain very cautious in pressing Islamabad to roll back because of the need to win Pakistani support for stabilization efforts in Afghanistan.

In the 2003 Libyan case, the United Kingdom – the country most heavily affected by the Lockerbie terrorist attack in 1980s sponsored by the Libyans – played a key role in convincing the nationalistic Quaddafi regime to denounce its WMD-related programmes. Here London relied upon the support of another power suspicious of Arab nationalist regimes – the USA. However, Russia demonstrated little interest in the case, since Moscow did not perceive a proliferation threat to be coming from Tripoli.[12]

Similarly, the 2003 US-UK led invasion of Iraq was, at least in rhetoric, explained as motivated by the risk posed by the supposed WMD acquisition of Saddam Hussein's nationalistic and secular regime (which brutally oppressed radicals of both Sunni and Shia origins). Again, Washington and some European countries were so concerned at the prospect of an anti-Western Arab nationalistic government gaining nuclear weapons that they decided to start a risky ground military operation with the real possibility of becoming embroiled in a counter-guerrilla war. By contrast, Moscow showed a milder attitude, reasoning that the issues raised by an Iraqi WMD programme, if such existed, could be solved by diplomatic means.

Washington has traditionally taken a hard line on Iran, as Tehran has for a long time been perceived as one of the major regional opponents – perhaps *the* major one – to US interests. Nuclear weapons in Iranian hands are evaluated as a serious threat for the US military deployments in the region, which, if successfully targeted, could fatally neutralize the US conventional superiority in the region. As a result, Iran might gain much broader capabilities to exert influence around its borders, and could dramatically shift the regional balance of power against the United States and its local allies.

By contrast, most Europeans states and Russia followed much a milder policy until 2005, trying to convince Iran to dismantle the most controversial elements of its nuclear programme by offering various carrots. Even since mid-2005, when Iran withdrew its self-imposed ban on uranium enrichment, Moscow and the E-3 (France, Germany and the UK) continued diplomatic dialogue with Tehran, while the United States observed from a distance.

One proliferation case: Iran

Dependence on Iran in 1990s

Since the mid-1990s, Russia's attitude towards Iran has been a main point of disagreement between Moscow and Washington. The United States quite aggressively demanded that the Yeltsin administration cut off its co-operation with Iran in the sphere of peaceful nuclear technology and arms sales. Moscow, which at that time was considerably dependent on the assistance from the West, partially accepted the US requirements. In 1995, the Russian Ministry of Atomic Energy refused to sell uranium enrichment centrifuges to Iran. At that time, the Gore–Chernomyrdin Memorandum was also signed, whereby Moscow committed itself to forgo new arms sales contracts with Tehran, while the Clinton administration accepted that previous arms deliveries contracts would have to be honoured.[13]

Russian sources claim that the United States insisted on halting only the most controversial aspects of the Russo–Iranian nuclear co-operation, and, in exchange for that, hinted at its willingness to accept the continuation of the construction, with Russian assistance, of Iran's Bushehr nuclear power plant. However, the United States continued to press Russia to withdraw from Bushehr as well. At this, Moscow drew the line and decided to move forward despite Washington's objections. Later in 2000, in keeping with the general deterioration in US–Russian relations, the Kremlin denounced the Gore–Chernomyrdin Memorandum.

Russia's choice to resist US pressure could result from disappointment with developments on another non-proliferation battlefield – the Korean peninsula. In 1993, the International Atomic Energy Agency discovered that the North Koreans had violated their safeguards agreement with the Agency. At that time, Russia's nuclear industry was still engaged in implementing earlier contracts on constructing a civilian reactor in North Korea.[14] Moscow – in strict compliance with its international non-proliferation obligations – decided to halt all peaceful nuclear co-operation with Pyongyang. President Yeltsin issued a decree ordering all Russian nuclear experts to return home and all Russian entities to stop any further nuclear co-operation with the Democratic People's Republic of Korea (DPRK). As a result of the Yeltsin decree, all Russian nuclear assistance stopped.

However, in 1994 the United States signed an agreement with Pyongyang, known as the Agreed Framework, or Framework Agreement, according to which the US-led group of countries promised, *inter alia,* to help the DPRK in building a light-water energy reactor as compensation for freezing the country's nuclear programme. Neither Russia nor China was invited to participate in the international body – the Korean Energy Development Organization – established to carry out this project.

As a result, Russia found itself punished economically and politically for its commitment to non-proliferation values. The rapid response to North Korean violations led to the exclusion of Moscow from the DPRK nuclear energy market. In broader terms, Russia had lost its seat at the table where peaceful settlement of the Korean conflict was discussed. For the Kremlin this was especially painful, as North Korea was a direct neighbour of the Russian Federation, and the community of ethnic Koreans in Russia occupied a prominent place in the economic and political life of the country.

After these developments, Russia generally responded to US arguments to halt the Bushehr project in the following way: why should the Russian light-water reactor in Iran be seen as a danger to nuclear non-proliferation, while a similar US reactor in North Korea was considered as consolidating the non-proliferation regime? The situation contributed to the development of an idea that gained currency in Russia: the USA was using the non-proliferation regime for dishonest competition in order to squeeze out Russian nuclear industry from its traditional markets. Needless to say, this notion was not conducive to the promotion of non-proliferation values amongst Russia's political and business class.

Beyond the trauma imposed by the Agreed Framework (described above), Russia's firm commitment to continue co-operating with Iran in the 1990s can be understood as a mixture of economic and political factors. In a period of radically declining investments in its own nuclear industry, foreign contracts came to be seen as the only source of income that could ensure the survival of this critical branch of the Russian economy. In the 1990s, Bushehr was one of Russia's three contracts for building foreign reactors, the other two being projects in China and India. Only one new reactor was under construction in Russia itself.

A similar situation existed for Russia's defence industry as well. In the 1990s, due to minuscule procurement by the Russian armed forces, the defence industry also became dependent on foreign sales. Primary destinations for Russian arms deliveries were China and India, and Moscow wanted to diversify and expand its markets. Iran seemed a potentially lucrative market, capable of absorbing significant sales. Therefore, despite strong US pressure, Russia continued to co-operate with Iran in peaceful nuclear applications, and defence. For Moscow, this represented not only a welcome opportunity to raise several hundred millions of dollars annually, but more importantly a way to maintain two key sectors of the economy critical to national security and to retaining the nation's status as a developed economy and a great power.[15]

The political role of Iran was even greater. Moscow and Tehran possessed important and overlapping interests in Caucasus and the Central Asia. In the1990s, Tehran significantly contributed to the de-escalation of the civil war in Tajikistan, convincing Islamist opposition to halt armed resistance and participate in intra-Tajik dialogue. Furthermore, both Russia and Iran provided considerable assistance to the Afghan Northern Alliance, the then internationally recognized government of Afghanistan, which was fighting against the fundamentalist Taliban and desperately needed international support. In late 2001, the forces of this Northern Alliance, with Russian help, significantly aided the United States in ground operations against the Taliban and, independently, managed to occupy Kabul.

Both Russia and Iran were concerned at Turkish, and later US, activities in the South Caucasus and Central Asia. Moreover, Iran represents the sole alternative land route from Russia to Armenia and a source of energy supplies for Armenia (Russia's only ally in the South Caucasus) should Georgia interrupt Russian military and energy transit through its territory.

Iran, via the Caspian Sea, also provides Russia with the most direct access to the Indian Ocean, which is important both geopolitically and economically. In the early 2000s for the first time Tehran granted Russian strategic bombers flyover rights, enabling them to participate in military manoeuvres in the Indian Ocean.

Changing realities in a new millennium

In the 2000s, the situation started to change. Russia's economic recovery led to increased national military procurement and ambitious plans for developing nuclear energy. This greatly enlarged domestic market has made Russia's nuclear and defence industries less dependent on exports. For instance, over the next decade Russia will commission one or two commercial nuclear reactors a year.[16] Beyond that, Moscow is receiving more contracts in China and Central Europe, and might gain access to Indian markets if the Nuclear Suppliers Group removes restrictions on nuclear co-operation with New Delhi. Despite vague notions of signing new contracts with Iran, the Russian nuclear industry is now becoming much less dependent on Tehran.

Politically, the relative calm in Tajikistan and the fall of the Taliban regime greatly alleviated pressure on Russia's Central Asian allies. This has removed, at least temporarily, the need for co-ordination between Moscow and Tehran on two issues that had greatly shaped bilateral relations in 1990s. Moreover, Russian–Turkish rapprochement might also be foreseen, since Turkey is seen as a potential alternative transit route for Russian hydrocarbon resources to the West.

Decreasing Moscow's dependence upon Iran has meant increased freedom of action for Russian diplomacy. Co-operation in the nuclear and defence areas has changed from purely commercial ventures into a more stick-and-carrot approach. In 2005, Moscow announced that a deal had been reached with Tehran on deliveries of Thor tactical air defence systems, greatly needed by Iran to counter the real risk of US or Israeli air raids against its nuclear assets. However, there was no delivery of these systems in 2005, nor in 2006. Most probably, Russia delayed deliveries in order to maintain the risk of air strikes as a credible threat to Iran, in light of its reluctance to accept restraints on its nuclear programme.

A similar situation might apply in the Bushehr case, where completion of reactor construction and deliveries of fresh fuel for the power plant have also been delayed. As these delays cannot be explained by technological reasons, perhaps they too may be associated with Russia's desire to maintain pressure to get Iran to freeze its nuclear programme. In autumn 2006, under pressure from Tehran, Russian authorities had to state a deadline for completion of the reactor building and deliveries of the fresh fuel. Moscow had to promise that fresh fuel would be delivered in spring 2007 and the reactor completed by September 2007. However, fresh fuel was not delivered in 2007, and the deadline for completing the plant was again extended for another year. The official explanation cited delays in payments by Iran, although many observers explained it by Iran's inability to accept the demands of the international community regarding its nuclear programme.

Russian officials dealing with Tehran have almost unanimously expressed misgivings in their interactions with Iran. They claim that the Iranian side has never been sincere in its promises that the country's nuclear programme was of a completely peaceful nature. In a long interview provided for a Russian weekly, Sergei Lavrov expressed his disappointment in the following way:

> Unfortunately, the reaction of our Iranian colleagues to the efforts made by Russia and other countries does not always seem adequate…It would be more productive if Iran would react more constructively to the Russian and 'group of six' proposals.[17]

2006: Iranian sanctions

Russia's patience towards Iran's behaviour was nearly exhausted by the summer of 2006. Reportedly, during the summit of the Shanghai Co-operation Organization (SCO) in June 2006, President Mahmud Ahmadinejad of Iran promised Putin that he would respond to the offers of the group of six – by the G8 Summit, which had been scheduled to take place in St. Petersburg (Russia) in mid-July. For President Putin, the G8 St. Petersburg summit was an important personal priority and he had high expectations about a positive Iranian response during that meeting. However, soon after the Shanghai SCO summit, Tehran stated that it would not respond to the G6 package until late August. Very likely, the Russian leader felt deceived.

Unsurprisingly, Russia changed its long-time resistance to the idea of adopting an anti-Iranian UN Security Council resolution soon after the St. Petersburg summit. On 31 July 2006, the first such resolution was adopted almost unanimously, with Russian support. This document required Iran to halt all activities on uranium enrichment within one month: otherwise, it could face international sanctions.

Iran decided to ignore the UN Security Council resolution – in violation of its obligations as a member state of the United Nations. Nevertheless, Russia and China urged for another round of negotiations, and the European Union also decided to give Iran another chance. However, talks failed between Ali Larijani, secretary of the Iranian version of the National Security Council, and Javier Solana, EU High Commissioner on Common Foreign and Security Policy.

This posed a challenging dilemma for the Kremlin. As a veto-holding permanent member of the UN Security Council, Russia could endlessly protect Tehran from any UN-sponsored sanctions. Such a choice might be willingly supported by another UNSC permanent member – China, which is planning to invest many billion dollars into the Iranian oil and gas industry. This dual veto would rescue Russo–Iranian relations; moreover, by standing together with China, Russia would not be isolated in the UN Security Council.

On the other hand, Moscow has devoted considerable rhetoric to the necessity of maintaining a central role for the UN in resolving international security conflicts. Therefore, Iran's outright rejection of the UN Security Council resolution would require a strong response. Otherwise, the UNSC – and its permanent members – could lose their credibility as globally legitimate arbiters.

Another motivation to respond to the Iranian position was Tehran's inability to settle its disagreements with the IAEA. In 2002, it was discovered that Iran possessed illegal nuclear programmes which had not been declared to the IAEA, in violation of the safeguards agreement previously signed with the Agency. Since that time, the IAEA has made several attempts to discover the real nature of Iran's past activities, but Tehran has consistently failed to co-operate adequately with Agency inspectors.

This lack of Iranian co-operation with the IAEA was Russia's primary official argument in favour of adopting the UN Security Council resolution containing sanctions against Iran in response to its continuation of suspected illegal nuclear activities. Sergei Lavrov stated:

> ...when the Iranians followed a course aimed at ignoring the IAEA require-ments regarding the measures necessary for clarifying all aspects of the Iranian nuclear programme,...we supported approval of UN Security Council Resolution 1696, which strengthened requirements formulated earlier in a resolution approved by the IAEA Board.[18]

Russia's approval, in December 2006, of the UNSC Resolution containing sanctions against Iran could be considered a sea change in the Kremlin's attitude towards Tehran. As recently as June 2006, no one could have predicted that Moscow would agree to sanctions against Iran. This may have come as a surprise to Iran as well. In 1990s, when Russia was weak, it consistently resisted US pressure to halt its peaceful nuclear co-operation with Tehran. By 2006, however, with the Kremlin feeling strong in its independent foreign policy, it joined a concert of other powers in introducing sanctions against Iran.

Conclusions

Analysing Russia's nuclear non-proliferation policies in the 1990s and the 2000s, it becomes clear that a weak Moscow, despite all its dependency on the West, represented greater problems for nuclear non-proliferation than a Russian leadership which perceived itself to be strong and independent, particularly in terms of economic growth. Despite extensive US pressure in the 1990s, Russia successfully resisted all attempts to halt its nuclear co-operation with Iran, a co-operation that was in many ways driven by the need to maintain a key strategic sector – the country's nuclear and defence industries. In 2006, despite its now much stronger position towards Washington, Moscow itself came to the conclusion that it had to support sanctions against Iran in the UN Security Council. Iran's behaviour challenged the integrity of nuclear non-proliferation regimes and the credibility of important universal institutions, like the UN Security Council and the IAEA. Therefore, Russia's own interests associated with these institutions were seen to be at stake.

Another lesson: When certain leading nations opted for unilateral approaches to solving acute non-proliferation problems and sought to exclude other players artificially, the problems themselves remained unsolved and Russia demonstrated reluctance to help in other cases. In today's world, the major actors possess their own interests, and these may not necessarily coincide with the interests of the other players. However, instead of looking for facile unilateral conclusions, these powers should focus on the commonalities in their broad interests and try to narrow their disagreements through routine mechanisms of multilateral dialogue. The 2006 G6 framework on Iran represents a good example of one such co-operative multilateral approach.

6 Russia and Europe and the process of EU enlargement[1]

Margot Light

Introduction

Russia's relationship with the European Union provides an excellent example of the ambivalence and contradictions that characterize the attitude of the country's leadership towards multilateralism. A consciousness of Russia's European identity and the desire to belong to Europe are contradicted by an increasing stress on Russia's sovereignty, the inviolability of the country's borders and a perception that Russia is a great power and should be treated within the EU with the respect due to a great power. Although in the early years of the relationship, 'horizontal' multilateralism (and the 'low politics' it entails) dominated the relationship, disagreements at the 'high politics' level have increasingly hijacked progress on 'low politics' issues.[2]

Russia's commitment to 'horizontal' multilateralism has also been affected by the eastward enlargement of the EU. First, the Kremlin leadership was extremely reluctant to extend to countries previously in the Soviet sphere of influence the same privileges that it had granted to the original 15 EU members in the Partnership and Co-operation Agreement (PCA). Second, the suggestion in the initial conception of the European Neighbourhood Policy that Russia should be included in that neighbourhood on a par with the EU's other neighbours, offended the Russian leadership's belief that, as a great power, Russia could not be considered in the same category as the EU's other neighbours. Third, the more closely the EU has advanced, through eastward expansion, towards the borders of the former Soviet Union, the more it has been evident that there is a potential conflict between Russia's multilateral engagement with the EU and its multilateral engagement with its 'near abroad' in the Commonwealth of Independent States (CIS). Fourth, together with the heightened emphasis on sovereignty, the Russian leadership has become increasingly hostile to the perceived attempt by the EU to impose 'European' values and norms; EU criticism of Russia's domestic politics is seen as an attempt to intervene in the internal affairs of the country.

The EU–Russian 'strategic partnership' is a highly institutionalized relationship, with a dense network of regular political consultations and economic negotiations, frequently on highly detailed and technical questions. According to the Russian ambassador to the European Communities, 'the Russia–EU partnership…deals with a variety of important pragmatic tasks'.[3] In other words, 'low politics' predominates in the relationship. Although much has been achieved in the past 15 years, the relationship falls far short of what might be expected from a strategic partnership. Russia's preference for bilateral rather than multilateral relations has interfered with the development of its partnership with the EU as a whole. Moreover, the increasing frustration felt by Russians at their inability to set the Russia–EU agenda and their growing resentment of the EU's expectations that, in relation to norms in particular, Russia should be a 'policy-taker' rather than a sovereign policy-maker, have soured the relationship. Indeed, Russian–EU relations have deteriorated in recent years to the extent that Russian EU experts talk of a 'systemic crisis' in the relationship and call for a new type of agreement to replace the PCA when it expires in 2007.[4] The EU appears equally disappointed, as evidenced by a 2004 report by the Commission drawn up at the request of the European Council because 'relations have…come under increasing strain with divergence between EU and Russian positions on a number of issues'.[5] As a result, there has been little combined effort to manage the process of EU enlargement. Indeed, EU enlargement is one reason why the relationship has deteriorated, since it has led to a growing determination to re-establish and preserve Russia's sphere of influence in the former Soviet space.

In general, Russians believe that theirs is a European country and they see themselves as European. They are, by and large, well disposed towards the European Union and have never perceived it as a threat to Russia. Although analysts and academics who focus specifically on the EU have long been anxious about the consequences for Russia of EU enlargement and about the impact of the imposition of the Schengen visa regime, they also see enlargement as 'a natural and objective process contributing to the enlargement of the zones of stability and economic prosperity on the European continent'.[6] They believe that the potential benefits of enlargement will outweigh the initial negative impact on Russian trade.

Given the extent to which Russian political elites identify themselves and their country as European, and their predominantly positive perceptions of the EU and of the benefits to Russia of good relations with the EU, it may seem surprising that the relationship between the two has run into difficulties. This chapter endeavours to identify the causes of the deterioration that has occurred since Putin became president of the Russian Federation. We begin with a short account of Russian–EU relations.[7]

A brief history of Russian–EU relations

The EU concluded a ten-year PCA with the Russian Federation (RF) in June 1994 'founded on shared principles and objectives' which included the promotion of international peace and security, support for democratic norms and for political and economic freedoms. Russia's PCA was more than an ordinary treaty on political and economic relations, since the aim of the EU was to support the reform process in Russia and create the conditions necessary for the establishment of a future free trade area between it and Russia. Because of the first war in Chechnya, member states delayed ratifying the PCA, and the agreement came into force only on 1 December 1997. The RF had already begun to receive economic and other forms of support from the EU through the TACIS programme (Technical Assistance to the Commonwealth of Independent States), the purpose of which was to support the process of transition to a market economy and democratic society. In all €1,573.5 million – almost half of the total TACIS bilateral aid to the former Soviet states – was committed to the Russian Federation between 1991 and 2002.[8]

In June 1997, the EU signed a new inter-governmental agreement, the Amsterdam Treaty, which established a new policy instrument called 'common strategies' which were intended to commit EU members to co-operate on policy towards a particular area or country where they had important interests in common. The first such strategy to be adopted was the Common Strategy on Russia, approved in June 1999. It committed the EU to assist in establishing a 'stable, open and pluralistic democracy in Russia'. Four areas of action were defined: consolidation of democracy, the rule of law and public institutions; integration of Russia into a common European economic and social space; stability and security; and common challenges on the European continent. The EU would focus on these areas in order to 'strengthen the strategic partnership between the Union and Russia'.[9] In October 1999, Moscow responded to the Common Strategy with its own 'Medium-Term Strategy for the Development of Relations between the Russian Federation and the European Union (2000–2010)' which elaborated Russia's goals for its relationship with the EU.[10] It set out ten spheres of co-operation between Russia and the EU and listed various ways in which administrative support, co-ordination and the use of specialist groups would be improved within Russia to facilitate implementation of the Strategy and further the EU–Russia strategic partnership.

By then the European Council had also agreed to expand its common foreign and security policy (CFSP) in order to give the EU 'the capacity for autonomous action, backed up by credible military forces'.[11] Moscow did not appear to perceive this as a threat to Russian security. The Common European Security and Defence Policy is not mentioned in Russia's National Security Blueprint, which was adopted in January 2000, for example, nor is it listed as a potential threat in the new military doctrine adopted in March 2000.[12]

Although both the EU and Russia sometimes expressed disappointment at the slow progress in implementing the PCA and the strategies, a dense network of political and economic consultations was established. The senior civil-servant level Co-operation Committee established by the PCA met frequently, while various subcommittees brought Russian and EU experts together. EU–Russia summits at the highest level took place at regular six-monthly intervals, interspersed by meetings between the EU Troika (the head of the country holding the Presidency of the Council, the High Representative for the CFSP and a representative of the EU Commission) and their Russian counterparts. There was also a steady flow of high-level visits between Moscow and various other European capitals.

Trade relations between Russia and the EU expanded rapidly. The value of EU–Russia trade increased from €38 billion to €85 billion between 1995 and 2003, making Russia the EU's fifth largest trading partner and the EU Russia's largest trading partner, accounting for nearly 40 per cent of its foreign trade by 2003. Energy supplies predominated in Russia's exports to the EU, accounting for about 57 per cent of exports in 2003. An 'energy dialogue' was instituted in October 2000 which aimed to work towards an EU–Russia Energy Partnership.[13]

The Russian–EU relationship continued to develop smoothly until the second Chechen war began in 1999. The Council of the EU condemned the bombardment of Chechen towns and the treatment of internally displaced people, and briefly limited TACIS assistance to priority areas such as human rights, the rule of law, support for civil society and nuclear safety.[14] Russian officials took offence at EU demands that, in their view, related to 'domestic' matters.[15] Despite the strain that this put on the relationship, President Putin appeared to remain committed to closer links with 'Europe' more broadly, and with the European Union in particular. In his annual address to the Federal Assembly in April 2001, for example, he listed integration with Europe as 'one of the key areas' of Russian foreign policy.[16] Not long afterwards, however, Russia's relations with the EU began to falter.

Causes of the deterioration of Russian–EU relations

The deterioration in the Russian–EU relationship in the last few years is the result of domestic developments in Russia, resentment of the EU's normative agenda, as well as reactions to the enlargement of the EU. Lately, energy issues have also caused problems; but behind these recent difficulties, there are some longer-standing structural problems that result from the very different ways in which the Russia and the EU operate. I begin with a brief analysis of the structural incompatibilities, before turning to the difficulties that have arisen because of the direction in which Putin has led Russia, and as a result of EU enlargement.

Structural incompatibilities

Two structural incompatibilities, in particular, have led to problems in the relationship between Russia and the EU. The first is their respective bureaucracies; the second is the preference on the part of both Russia and of many EU member states for bilateralism, which serves to undermine the EU's attempts to implement a common strategy.

The complexity of the Brussels bureaucracy, on the one hand, and the absence in Russia of suitably qualified administrative support or co-ordinating mechanisms to deal with the EU, on the other, complicate Russian–EU relations. EU members themselves frequently complain about the EU bureaucracy. Russians also complain about it; they do not understand how it works and they rail bitterly against its 'rather woolly decision-making procedure'.[17] They do not accept the EU's inflexibility and its reluctance to compromise, for example about the Schengen regime. The EU Commission, in turn, criticizes the lack of co-ordination within the Russian government. Russians themselves are even more critical of the inadequacies of their own bureaucracy, pointing out, for example, that there were too few experienced negotiators in the Ministry of Trade to deal with the economic consequences of enlargement.[18] Russian EU specialists argue that '[Russian] policy towards the EU suffers...from a weakness of bureaucratic support', and insist that 'official bodies engaged in routine interaction with the EU need seriously to improve their work'. They suggest that this might be done either by assigning the role of co-ordinating Russian policy to an existing institution, or by establishing a special agency to 'co-ordinate efforts to work out and advance a single Russian position on all aspects of relations with the European Union'.[19] One Russian specialist on the EU has proposed that the PCA should simply be extended when it expires in 2007 because 'the catastrophic shortage of qualified experts, in addition to the marked disunity among government agencies, makes it very difficult to form an efficient task force' to negotiate a new agreement.[20]

This lack of capacity has two consequences that have a negative effect on the relationship. First, Moscow rarely puts forward its own initiatives; instead it confines itself responding to policy proposals emanating from Brussels. This in turn gives rise to complaints that the EU treats Russia as the 'junior partner'. A second consequence is that, during Putin's presidency, progress on anything substantive has increasingly depended on agreements at very high levels – and, since summits have been infrequent and liable to getting hijacked by broader problems in the Russia–EU relationship (that is, by issues of high politics), progress in matters of low politics has faltered.

The second structural incompatibility – the preference for bilateralism – afflicts both Russia and the EU. On the Russian side, the preference for bilateral rather than multilateral relations predates the Putin presidency. It was a prominent feature of President Boris Yeltsin, who liked to refer to 'my friend Bill' and 'my friend Helmut'. Indeed, it could be argued that this preference for bilateral relations has been inherited from the Soviet leadership; the ostensibly multilateral Warsaw Treaty Organization, for example, was in fact underpinned by a series of bilateral treaties between the Soviet Union and the other member states. In the case of Russia's relations with the EU, the preference is compounded by the personal relationships that President Putin has established with individual European leaders (for example, Chancellor Gerhard Schröder, President Jacques Chirac and Prime Ministers Tony Blair and Silvio Berlusconi) and by attempts to use these relationships to exploit differences of opinion between member states. Russian experts warn that these relationships are becoming less and less effective.[21] Now Schröder, Berlusconi, Chirac and Blair are all out of power, so Putin has lost key allies in his bilateral diplomacy.

The blame is not entirely on the Russian side, however. European leaders themselves cultivate these personal relationships to raise issues on a bilateral basis, even when the EU as a whole could or should address the issues. In the process they sometimes undermine EU policy.[22] The Common Strategy was intended to ensure co-ordination between EU and member-state policy towards Russia. One reason for undertaking a review of EU policy in 2004 was the recognition that this goal had not been achieved. According to one analyst, the problem is that several member states consider Russia to be too important a global player to let the EU take the lead in relations with it.[23] As we will see, this is an issue that has become particularly important in connection with the EU's dependence on Russia for energy supplies.

The preference for bilateral relations and the attempt to use these relationships to exploit differences of opinion between member states reflect the current predominance of geopolitical realism in Moscow's official foreign policy thinking which, in turn, explains Putin's tendency to conduct the Russian–EU relationship at the level of high politics. The problem is that geopolitical realism and a preference for high politics do not easily incorporate the soft security concerns and cross-border co-operation which are the prime focus of such EU initiatives as the Northern Dimension and many of the border issues that fall within the domain of co-operation in the area of freedom, security and justice.

Putin's domestic policy

Since his inauguration as Russian President in 2000, Vladimir Putin has introduced a series of measures that make Russia, at best, a 'regulated democracy'. It is not difficult to see why he has felt this necessary. First, the 1993 constitution gave the predominance of political power to the president but this did not prevent constant strife between the Duma on the one hand, and the president, his administration and his government. There was also strife between the president and his government – the country had five different prime ministers between March 1998 (when long-serving premier Viktor Chernomyrdin was dismissed) and August 1999 (when Putin became Prime Minister, at the same time becoming Yeltsin's designated successor). Putin saw it as essential to bring an end to the conflict between the legislature and the executive and to ensure stability of government.

The second reason why Putin held that centralization of power and authority was necessary was that he believed that the RF was on the brink of disintegrating. Russia is a multinational federation consisting then of 89 federal units. Although there is a federal treaty binding the units to the centre, many of the units had signed separate treaties with the central government in the 1990s, arrogating political and economic power to the regional government. The result was a highly asymmetric federation and an impoverished central government. Despite the great constitutional power accorded to the president, therefore, the central government became weaker and weaker between 1993 and 2000 in relation to the power of the federal units. Putin believed that unless power was returned to the central government, the RF would disintegrate, as the Soviet Union had done a decade before.

His political programme focused, therefore, on constructing a strong state (or, in Putin's terminology, re-establishing the 'power vertical') and a 'managed democracy'. A main element consisted of establishing a strong 'party of power' – now called United Russia – to support presidential policies. It currently holds 310 of the 450 seats in the Duma and can count on the co-operation of two or three of the smaller parties. The Duma has, in effect, become a 'pocket parliament'. Putin also changed the composition of the Federal Council, the upper house of parliament. It had previously consisted of the governors/presidents and the heads of the legislatures of the 89 federal units. In the name of separating legislative and executive power, Putin changed its composition. Two representatives of each federal unit now serve in the Federal Council, one chosen by the governors/presidents, the other by the legislatures. In an attempt to ensure that central laws were implemented across the country, Putin also established seven federal districts encompassing the 89 federal units, each presided over by a governor-general representing the president. Putin also clamped down on the media – particularly the electronic media critical of the government.

These changes caused some concern in the EU. Then, in the wake of the Beslan tragedy in September 2004,[24] President Putin introduced two more changes that were far more serious in their impact on Russian democracy. First, the governors/presidents of the 89 federal units, previously elected by popular vote, would now be nominated by the president and elected ('confirmed' might be a more accurate term) by the regional legislature. Second, Putin changed the electoral law. In the 2007 parliamentary election, the Duma was elected entirely on the basis of proportional representation of political parties (previously half the deputies were elected from single-mandate constituencies). At the same time, the threshold for parties for representation in the Duma has been raised from 4 to 7 per cent, and smaller parties can no longer form electoral alliances to enable them to win seats in the Duma. This effectively prevents the smaller political parties from gaining any seats whatsoever.

There is no doubt that these political measures have created a 'power vertical'. But they have also reduced the political choices open to citizens, have made it more difficult for a plurality of opinions to be heard and have reduced the possibility of the political opposition influencing policy. The resulting decline in democracy has caused considerable disquiet within the EU. At a practical level, Putin's measures have had a negative impact on particular aspects of EU policy. 'Strengthening the power vertical', for example, is incompatible with the regional interdependence and cross-border co-operation explicitly fostered by the Northern Dimension. More generally, Putin's perceived retreat from democracy has given rise to considerable criticism by the EU which, in turn, has provoked a steadily increasing resentment in Russia of the EU's normative agenda.

Russian rejection of the EU's normative agenda

It is clear from the aims of the PCA and the Common Strategy that the promotion of democratic values and the rule of law are very prominent aspects of the EU's policy towards Russia. It is not surprising, therefore, that Russia's growing hostility to the intrusive nature of EU policy and to its imposition of Western values and norms has become an impediment to deepening relations. Particularly since the beginning of Putin's second term as president, Russian officials have made clear that regardless of what they signed up to in Russia–EU documents and communiqués in the 1990s on 'common European values', they no longer accept the incorporation of such values into the Russia–EU relationship, since they perceive these values as determined exclusively in the EU and simply proclaimed by EU officials for Russia to adopt.

By 2004, the official Russian position was that Russia would participate in European affairs 'not as an object of "civilizing influences" on the part of other states or groups thereof, but precisely as an equal among equals'.[25] Although Putin still claims that shared values determine Russia's democratic and European choice, he and other officials often qualify this with the assertion that values such as democracy should reflect Russian traditions. The term 'sovereign democracy', recently proposed and promoted by Putin's deputy chief of staff, Vladislav Surkov, appears to embody this conviction that Russians should define their own democracy and protect themselves from values exported from outside.[26]

EU members have expressed growing concern about the extent to which political and security developments within Russia represent a rejection of European values. In fact research has shown that not only does this apply to Moscow's official policy – these values are not firmly rooted in Russian society either.[27] By 2004 the European Parliament Committee on Foreign Affairs, Human Rights and Common Security and Defence Policy had become forthright in its criticism of Russian over human rights.[28] Despite this unpromising situation, the promotion of common values is referred to in the EU–Russia Road Maps for the Common Spaces, although *what* or *whose* values remain undefined.[29]

Hostility to the EU's normative agenda has been reflected in the dismissal of European anxiety about Putin's political reforms as well as in resentment of the EU's reaction to Russia's policy in Chechnya and how it deals with terrorism. The Kremlin has accused the EU of double standards in refusing to label Chechens as international terrorists. Putin was extremely angry, for example, when the Danish and British courts refused to extradite Akhmed Zakaev, President Maskhadov's envoy, to Russia, and then when the British courts granted him political asylum in November 2003.[30] Russian resentment of the EU's response to Chechen terrorism became far sharper in September 2004, after the Beslan siege, when Dutch Foreign Minister Bernard Bot (the Netherlands held the EU presidency at the time) said that although the EU was fully sympathetic, it 'would also like to know from the Russian authorities how this tragedy could have happened'.[31] This tactlessly phrased request for further information caused outrage in Russia, and the Foreign Minister, Sergei Lavrov, called the remarks 'profane'.[32] However, this diplomatic row was smoothed over rapidly, and the Russian government agreed to an EU proposal to establish regular consultations on human rights, the first of which took place on 1 March 2005.[33] Nevertheless, resentment at what are perceived as attempts to interfere in Russia's domestic affairs continues, as do Russian objections to EU 'double standards'. Recent reflections of the hostility towards (or fear of) the export of European values include the controversy over the role of the EU and the USA in democracy promotion and the 'colour revolutions' in Georgia, Ukraine and Kyrgyzstan, and the Kremlin's latest measures for preventing similar incursions into Russian politics – such as the new law on NGOs.[34]

Post-socialist states and EU accession

Two sets of problems arose in Russian–EU relations in 2003 and 2004 as a result of the imminent accession of the post-socialist states of East-Central Europe to the EU. The first concerned the countries that would now form the neighbourhood of both Russia and the enlarged EU, while the second centred on Russia's relations with the acceding states themselves.

As EU enlargement loomed closer, the European Commission began to think about the effect that enlargement would have on the countries that would find themselves on the external borders of the enlarged EU: the Western Newly Independent States (NIS), as the Commission calls the former Soviet states of Belarus, Moldova, Russia and Ukraine, and the Southern Mediterranean. Although there was no intention of granting them accession to the EU in the foreseeable future, they were perceived as the EU's 'essential partners'. The attainment of security, stability and sustainable development *within* the EU was deemed to require political reform, social cohesion and economic dynamism *outside* it, in particular in its new eastern neighbourhood. The European Commission proposed 'a differentiated, progressive, and benchmarked approach' to its new neighbours, among which was Russia.[35] Kremlin officials were shocked to discover that the EU appeared to put Russia in the same category not only as Belarus and Moldova, but also as the states of North Africa. This did not accord with their perception that Russia is a great power and should be treated within the EU with the appropriate respect. Sergei Yastrzhembsky, presidential representative in charge of Russia's EU policy, complained that 'The offered suit is too small for us. It is not the right size for Russia's shoulders', while Deputy Foreign Minister Vladimir Chizhov stated categorically that 'Russia does not regard itself either as an object or subject of this policy. Our relations with the EU are built on principles of strategic partnership'.[36] Russia was left out of the European Neighbourhood Policy; instead the EU and Russia decided to develop their strategic partnership through the creation of four common spaces.[37] In effect, this meant that the EU had acquiesced to Russia's ideal form of multilateralism – that is, co-operation around key issues. Additionally, it showed recognition that the European neighbourhood was also Russia's neighbourhood; in other words, this was a shared neighbourhood in which Russia and the EU would have to co-operate. It is in this shared neighbourhood that some of the most serious difficulties in EU–Russia relations have arisen.

The second problem that emerged as enlargement grew closer concerned Russia's relations with the acceding states themselves. In early 2004 the question arose about the status of the PCA after enlargement. The EU apparently expected that Russia would automatically extend it to all ten new members prior to the EU enlargement on 1 May 2004. On 30 January 2004, however, the ambassadors of the EU member states were invited to the Russian Ministry of Foreign Affairs, where Chizhov announced that 'the issue of extending the PCA is not merely a technical procedure that can be implemented automatically'. He handed them a document listing Russian concerns. Although most of the 14 points on the list involved trade and tariff issues, concerns about access to Kaliningrad and the status of ethnic Russians in Latvia and Estonia were also included. The EU's response was curt: unless the PCA was applied to the EU-25 'without pre-condition or distinction by 1 May 2004', there would be serious repercussions on Russian–EU relations.[38] The Russians were outraged. Here again, the perception that their country is a great power and should be treated within the EU with the respect due to a great power was offended. Chizhov declared that Russia expected to participate in European affairs as an equal partner, while Mikhail Margelov, chairman of the Foreign Affairs committee of the Federal Council, accused the EU of using 'the language of sanctions'. Dmitry Rogozin, chairman of the Duma International Relations committee, announced that 'Russia is not about to act on orders from Brussels'. Since the Council meeting which issued the EU's response was attended by representatives of the acceding states, Moscow was convinced that its fears that the former socialist states would turn the EU against Russia were confirmed.[39]

Despite the harsh rhetoric, both sides seemed to recognize that compromise was essential. Russia signed a protocol extending the PCA to the new members on 27 April. Attached to it was a joint statement listing 'outstanding issues' that both sides undertook to address.[40] The compromise was contained in the joint statement which noted some of Moscow's concerns (including goods transit between Kaliningrad and Russia) and provided for a transitional period during which the terms of some existing bilateral agreements would continue to operate. Nevertheless, the conviction that the new member states are turning the EU against Russia has continued to produce discord.

Energy security

A new problem arose in Russia–EU relations in 2006: energy security, an issue which Russia had placed first on its agenda for its G8 chairmanship in 2006 (see Baev's chapter in this volume for a detailed discussion of Russia's G8 chairmanship). As a result both of EU enlargement and of increasing consumption, the proportion of Russian energy in the EU's total energy imports rose from 24 per cent in 2001 to 27.5 per cent in 2005, of which gas imports increased from 41 to 50 per cent.[41] At present, Russia is as dependent on the European market as the EU is on Russian supplies; although there are potentially huge markets in the Far East, Russia's oil and gas pipeline networks run from east to west and it will take years to construct pipelines from Russia to China or the Pacific coast.

European fears about Russia's energy policy were sparked off by the arrest and trial of Mikhail Khodorkovsky, head of Yukos, then Russia's largest oil company, and the completely opaque take-over of Yuganskneftegaz, the most valuable Yukos asset, by state-owned Rosneft in December 2004. They were exacerbated in October 2005 when Gazprom, the 51 per cent state-owned gas monopoly, bought up Sibneft, the country's fifth largest oil firm. This consolidated Gazprom's position as a global energy giant and provoked anxiety in Europe that Moscow was seeking to return a major part of Russia's energy resources to state control and would attempt to use energy as a political lever.

These fears appeared justified when Gazprom raised the highly subsidized price at which it sold gas to Ukraine to the world price level, effectively quadrupling Ukraine's costs, without any transition period. There were sound market reasons for the price increase – world energy prices had risen massively and Russia had been subsidizing Ukrainian gas ever since the disintegration of the USSR. Nevertheless, the timing of the rise (the Ukrainian parliamentary election campaign had just begun) and the fact that Putin himself became involved in the dispute suggested that political motives were at least as important as economic factors. The Russian government had supported Viktor Yanukovych in the presidential elections in 2004 and was alarmed by the pro-Western foreign policy pursued by President Yushchenko after the 'Orange Revolution' – a policy which included the publicly announced determination to join NATO and the EU.

When the negotiations over the price Ukraine would pay for gas in 2006 broke down without any agreement, Gazprom cut off Ukraine's gas supply. Some 80 per cent of the gas supplies from Russia to Europe is transported by pipelines that pass through Ukraine, and during the dispute supply to the EU was briefly disrupted – according to Gazprom, because Ukraine was siphoning off gas.[42] The EU became highly alarmed, called on Russia and Ukraine to resolve the dispute and launched a debate on the need to diversify EU energy supplies. The European media, by and large, accused Russia of launching a gas war, while remaining silent about Ukraine's role in the dispute. The Kremlin was deeply offended and insisted that Russia was a reliable supplier.[43]

An energy dispute, involving both gas and oil, with Belarus a year later, at the beginning of 2007, seemed to give credence to the Russian argument that increases in the price of energy were based on market principles rather than political factors. The gas dispute was resolved two minutes before the expiry of the previous contract, and the threat to supplies via the Yamal network (which transmits about a fifth of the gas Russia exports to Western Europe) was averted. The oil dispute proved trickier to resolve. It was caused by Russia imposing a duty of US$ 180 per ton on crude oil exported to Belarus, and Belarus retaliating with a transit fee of US$ 45 per ton on Russian crude oil in transit to the West through Belarus. It resulted in a brief interruption to the flow of oil to Europe, affecting supplies to the Czech Republic, Germany, Hungary, Poland, Slovakia and Ukraine. Although the disruption was caused by Belarus siphoning off oil, in response to which Transneft had shut off the taps, it produced an unprecedented outpouring of Western sympathy for President Lukashenka. By 11 January the dispute had been resolved and the oil flow through Druzhba pipeline, which crosses Belarus, had reached full volume. By then, however, Russia's tarnished reputation as a reliable energy supplier had deteriorated still further, and there were renewed calls for the EU to diversify its energy sources.

In February 2006 Gazprom appeared to be interested in acquiring Centrica, Britain's largest utility company. The negative response to this news prompted Alexei Miller, Gazprom CEO, to say that unless Europe was more responsive to Gazprom's ambitions to acquire downstream assets within the EU, Gazprom would take its business to China and North America. EU anxiety was further raised when

Semyon Vainshtok, head of Russia's oil pipeline monopoly Transneft, announced a few days later that the projected East Siberia–Pacific Ocean oil pipeline system would enable Russia to cut supplies to Europe. Since then more than 100 kms of pipe have been laid and 330 kms prepared for pipe installation.[44]

There have also been problems with the three production-sharing agreements made in the mid-1990s with Royal Dutch Shell, ExxonMobil, and Total SA under which, in lieu of taxes, Russia receives part of the oil and gas produced, once the investors' costs are covered. In the case of Shell, which announced in 2006 that the costs of its Sakhalin-II project had doubled, the Russian Ministry of Natural Resources threatened to suspend its licence in Sakhalin because of alleged environmental violations. In December 2006 Shell agreed to sell a majority share in Sakhalin-II to Gazprom. Exxon Mobile and Total have apparently infringed technical provisions in their contracts, and their licences too may be revoked. A BP joint venture (TNK-BP) to develop a vast gas field in Siberia also came under attack, and in June 2007 TNK-BP was forced to sell a 62.9 per cent stake in the Kovykta field to Gazprom.[45] In all cases, Western analysts believe that the real problem is that Russia wants to regain state control over its oil and gas industries.[46] Europeans fear that the Russian will use that state control as an instrument of foreign policy.

The EU's fears have persisted despite several multilateral initiatives that focus on Russian–EU energy security. For example, a Russian–EU Energy Dialogue was established in 2000 to deal with problems of security of supply, including 'rationalization of production and transport infrastructures, European investment possibilities, and relations between producer and consumer countries'.[47] More-over, energy co-operation at the inter-governmental level was supplemented in October 2005 by the establishment of a Russia–EU Energy Forum, a platform for the business community to discuss energy co-operation.[48] There is also an international Energy Charter Treaty (ECT), established on the initiative of the European Commission in 1994 as a legally-binding multilateral instrument to deal with inter-governmental co-operation in the energy sector. It sets out a sectoral legal framework for energy; comprising some fifty articles, it deals with issues pertaining to investment, trade, transit, competition and environmental concerns.[49] Russia signed the treaty but has not ratified it.

Russia's reluctance to ratify the ECT is a clear example of the changes that have occurred in its attitudes towards multilateralism. Russia signed the ECT at a time when its economy was extremely weak. However, as the economy recovered (in large part because of huge rises in the world price of energy), Moscow officials began to display a new assertiveness in the pursuit of domestic and foreign policy goals, and to give precedence to national interests over the multilateral interests which the ECT was intended to serve. International agreements like the ECT, and the 'horizontal' multilateralism they represented, were no longer to be permitted to impinge on Russia's domestic affairs. Putin has insisted that the ECT must be amended to take account of Russian interests before it can be ratified. He objects, in particular to the Treaty's requirement that Russia should open up access to its pipelines currently under the monopoly control of Gazprom and Transneft.

Since this objection coincided with demands that European states should open up their downstream operations to enable Gazprom to buy into their distribution and retail natural gas infrastructure, it reflected poorly on Russia's understanding of the reciprocity implied in multilateralism.

Paradoxically, just before the Russia–Ukraine gas dispute, Russia and Germany had reached agreement on a major new project to build a pipeline under the Baltic Sea. The 1200 km-long North European Gas Pipeline will link Vyborg in Russia with Greifswald in Germany via the Baltic Sea, making it possible for Russia to supply gas to Germany and the rest of the EU without relying on gas transit via Poland and Ukraine. It is also likely to increase the EU's dependence on Russian gas, despite the former's policy debate about the need to diversify its energy supplies.[50]

Both the 2006 Russian–Ukrainian gas dispute and the North European Gas Pipeline deal draw attention to a problem that the EU has in co-ordinating policy towards Russia. It is in relation to energy issues, in particular, that the preference of some EU leaders (especially those of the larger member countries) for raising important issues on a bilateral basis rather than resolving them multilaterally is most evident. On questions of energy, EU member states retain national control and they tend to follow their national interests, even if these conflict with the interests of the EU as a whole or with the interests of other members. But whatever their divergent national interests, these developments also highlight apprehensions that are generally shared within the EU. Apart from a general disapproval of the Russian state reclaiming control of the country's energy assets and anger that Russian pressure was creating difficulties for Ukraine, a favoured EU protégé, the gas dispute served to remind EU members that since Europe is dependent on Russian energy, it is potentially vulnerable to the same kind of pressure that Ukraine experienced. Moreover, since Gazprom is widely held to be synonymous with the Kremlin, its possible acquisition of downstream assets within the EU conjures up a vision of Kremlin control over European domestic gas markets.

Conclusion

What do these problems suggest about the future of Russian–EU relations? None of the difficulties are likely to be overcome in the foreseeable future. In the longer term, Russia's understanding of the EU will improve and so will its administrative capacity – but in the immediate future, inadequate administrative support or the absence of co-ordinating mechanisms seem likely to continue to hinder progress. It is also likely that the centralization of power in Russia, and the concentration of decision-making at the top of the 'power vertical', will remain permanent features of Kremlin politics. As a result, the tendency to wait for summits to resolve problems will continue, and difficult issues will continue to be politicized.

Given the predominance of geopolitical realist thinking in Russia, the preference for bilateral relations and the use of those relations to bypass or undermine EU policy is unlikely to change. Geopolitical realism also means that Russia will persist in perceiving the shared neighbourhood in zero–sum terms, as an area of struggle for influence rather than as opportunity to co-operate.

Although Putin rejects the depiction of Russia as an 'energy superpower' (it is deliberately used, he claims, to evoke associations with the Soviet Union), Russia's claim to great-power status which seemed so hollow in the 1990s has acquired substance since energy prices began to increase. There is a clear correlation between Moscow's increasingly independent foreign policy stance and the growth in the Russian economy that has resulted from the rise in world oil prices. Russia has acquired considerable international clout through its energy resources, and this seems both to have undermined its commitment to moving closer to the EU and the EU's ability to design a co-ordinated strategy that can harmonize EU and member-state policy. Russian resistance to the export of EU values will continue. Thus it seems that Russian–EU relations are more likely to progress if they can be based on an understanding and acceptance of shared interests, rather than on values. While it is perhaps too dramatic to argue that Russia–EU relations are experiencing a 'systemic crisis', it is clear that concerted efforts will be required from both sides if there is to be effective multilateral co-ordination between them.

7 Inside or outside? Russia's policies towards NATO

Hannes Adomeit

Russia closely follows the process of NATO transformation and counts on the complete removal of direct and indirect components of its anti-Russian orientation from military planning and the political declarations of the member countries of the alliance.

(Russian Defence Ministry)[1]

We are concerned over the process of NATO expansion. This organization has been and remains a military and political bloc with all the set of threats that any formation of this type involves.

(Putin)[2]

Is it possible that Russia will ever join NATO?' Putin: 'Why not? I do not rule out such a possibility. I repeat, on condition that Russia's interests are going to be taken into account, if Russia becomes a full-fledged partner.

(Putin)[3]

Can Russia's policies towards and role in NATO be regarded as part of a comprehensive transformation of Russian foreign policy – away from policies of confrontation and competition, to co-operation with the West? Is it correct to consider Russia's relationship with NATO a convincing example of 'multilateralism' in the sense of that country working constructively both with and within established Western institutions?

Judging from official pronouncements at NATO headquarters in Brussels and some in Moscow, the answer to both questions is an unambiguous yes. The two actors point out that since the 1997 NATO–Russia Founding Act on Mutual Relations, Co-operation and Security, which still provides the formal basis for NATO–Russia relations, Russia's status and role in NATO have significantly changed. That country is no longer a *partner* in the bilateral framework of the Permanent Joint Council (PJC) established in May 1997, but an ordinary *member* of the NATO–Russia Council (NRC), founded in May 2002, in which 26 NATO countries and Russia meet as equals (NATO 'at 27'), that is, with the same rights and responsibilities.

The latter body is described as the main mechanism for consultation, consensus-building, co-operation, joint decision and joint action between the two entities. A constructive political dialogue is said to be taking place there. Issues discussed are reported to include the situation in Afghanistan, Serbia (Kosovo) and Montenegro, Bosnia and Herzegovina, the southern Caucasus (notably Georgia) and the 'Greater Middle East'. Practical co-operation, directed by the NRC and developed through various subordinate working groups and committees, is regarded to have generated benefits for all participant countries in several important areas. These include the fight against terrorism, crisis management, non-proliferation, arms control and confidence-building measures, theatre missile defence, logistics, military-to-military co-operation, defence reform and civil emergencies.[4] However, unofficially at NATO and both informally and publicly in Moscow, different and less favourable views of the relationship obtain.

At NATO, there is disappointment that much of the co-operation has remained at the technical and 'low-politics' level, that it has assumed a largely symbolic quality, and that it has failed to change the relationship at the 'high politics' and strategic levels. After the foundation of the NRC in 2002, there were hopes at NATO that co-operation would produce spillover effects to the domestic political realm in Russia, strengthen military reform efforts, enhance transparency in defence decision-making, contribute to the creation of a civil society, and internationally help to solve 'frozen' conflicts. Such hopes were dashed. Current perceptions are that Russia has become a much more difficult partner, that the Kremlin, riding high on a wave of apparent domestic political stability, high oil prices and attendant high economic growth rates, is pursuing 'great-power' policies in ever more problematic and unacceptable ways. Whereas Russia can no longer be considered an adversary, it can also not be regarded as a strategic partner.

In Russia, conversely, the foreign and defence establishment still appears to be suffering from the trauma of the collapse of both the Warsaw Pact and the Soviet Union, and to resent that the Western alliance has not been dissolved but has attracted more and more members. At the very least, in its view, the basic character of NATO as a military alliance should have been changed to become more of a 'political organization'. Resentment is running particularly high on the issue of NATO enlargement – 'expansion' in the Russian understanding. In the negotiations on German unification in 1990, so the argument runs, Western negotiators had given binding assurances that NATO would not move 'one inch farther to the east' of a unified Germany. Yet NATO has moved east nevertheless – first to include three former members of the Warsaw Pact, and then four more East-Central and Southeastern European countries plus three former republics of the Soviet Union, thus bringing the alliance and its military infrastructure 'right up to the Russian borders' – a potential instrument for rolling back Russian influence in the neighbouring countries.

Such disappointments were voiced, for instance, by Russian Foreign Minister Sergey Lavrov in December 2006.[5]

> In the Russia–NATO Council', 'we are accumulating the potential for practical co-operation in the struggle against common security threats and challenges.

But, he went on to say,

> we firmly raise questions about the transformation of NATO, the alliance's plans for enlargement, the reconfiguration of the US military presence in Europe, the deployment of elements of the American missile defence system here, NATO's refusal to ratify the CFE Treaty, ... and we would like to see how Brussels will react to our proposal concerning engagement with the CSTO [Collective Security Treaty Organization] in regard to the threats emanating from the territory of Afghanistan.[6]

The enumeration of such disappointments sounds reasonable enough and conveys the impression of a constructive attitude. However, Russia's approaches to multilateralism have generally been limited by a strict adherence to traditional notions of sovereignty, combined with the rejection of Western ideas and the practice of supra-national integration. In domestic politics, the strong emphasis on traditional concepts is reflected in such (theoretically incongruous) constructs of the current system as 'sovereign democracy'.[7] From this perspective, yielding parts of sovereignty in the sensitive matter of security must appear as a particularly novel and problematic concession to the international community.

The question arises, therefore, whether multilateralism in organizations such as NATO can have anything but a strictly limited quality. Might it be that Russia in NATO, rather than aiming at enhancing the viability and effectiveness of the organization, simply wants to make sure that no decisions are taken that are detrimental to its own interests? To that extent, multilateralism would primarily mean damage-limitation rather than constructive engagement. And rather than multilateralism, the primary approach to current international politics would still be the concept of 'multipolarity' as advanced by then foreign minister Yevgeny Primakov, of developing and strengthening power centres that would balance each other as in the traditional concert of powers that arose in Europe after 1815.

In order to comprehend the Russian approaches, to assess the current and likely future extent of NATO–Russian co-operation and competition, and to judge the degree to which Russia is pursuing foreign policy goals through multilateral or through unilateral approaches, first, the *evolution* of the relationship will be reconstructed in this chapter. The period and issues to be covered range from President Yeltsin's 20 December 1991 letter to NATO on Russian membership in the Western alliance as a foreign policy objective, to the recent deterioration of the relationship after Putin's speech at the 43rd Munich International Security

Conference on 10 February 2007. Second, on that basis, the main *forum* of NATO–Russian multilateralism, the NRC, will be analysed as to functions and significance as well as the major current dimensions or *key areas* of co-operation. Third, there follows a critical assessment as to the actual significance of the various declarations, agreements and projects, and the likely *future direction* of the relationship.

Evolution of Russia's relationship with NATO

A few days before the formal dissolution of the Soviet Union and the first-ever meeting between NATO foreign ministers and those of the former Warsaw Pact, President Yeltsin of Russia wrote a letter to the Secretary General of NATO. Russia, he wrote, wished to develop a dialogue between former adversaries 'both on the political and military levels', and continued: 'Today, we are raising the question of Russia's membership in NATO regarding it, however, as a long-term political aim'.[8]

Foreign Minister Andrei Kozyrev explained in a radio interview that Russia no longer regarded NATO 'as an aggressive military bloc' but viewed it 'as one of the mechanisms of stability in Europe and in the world as a whole. Our desire to co-operate with this mechanism and to join it is therefore natural'. He advocated the creation of a 'zone of security and co-operation from Vancouver to Vladivostok' in which NATO would 'play a role that is positive and by no means insignificant'.[9]

Academic specialists provided further arguments in support of such views. Thus, according to Sergei Karaganov, a weathervane of the Russian security and defence establishment, the danger of Russia's 'military-political isolation' in Europe had to be avoided. Such a danger now existed, as the new democracies of East-Central Europe were gradually aligning themselves with NATO. Until quite recently, he noted, Russian policies designed to suppress the extension of [NATO] guarantees and bloc structures to Central and Eastern Europe had been quite appropriate, but today such measures of demarcation were neither possible nor necessary. Furthermore, like Spain after Franco, Russia after the coup had an interest in 'including the [Russian] military in common European security structures'.[10] Another specialist even went as far as to assert: 'The North Atlantic alliance is now the guarantor of our security, and if we could now join it, this would be the best way for us to ensure that security'.[11]

Even before political developments in Russia undercut the basis for such dreams, more sober voices raised questions about the country's relations with NATO that are pertinent also today. Alexei Arbatov,[12] another specialist of renown, pointed out that a simple question had to be asked: 'In what capacity does Russia intend to join NATO?' He distinguished three possibilities. First, Russia could join as a guarantor of the security of Western Europe. The West Europeans, however, would most likely say 'No, thanks'. For the foreseeable time it suited Western Europe perfectly well to have the United States as their defender, rather than an unstable Russia. Second, it had been said that NATO was set up not only to deter the Soviet Union but also to control Germany. So why not involve Russia in this task? This idea, too, was unrealistic, because the West 'will probably reach some kind of *modus vivendi* with Germany'. Furthermore, it might be appropriate 'to ask the Germans whether they would mind being controlled with the help of Russia, which receives most of its economic aid from Germany'. Third, 'if one supposes that the United States or Western Europe would guarantee Russia's security', this too is unrealistic: 'With its armed forces of three million men and tens of thousands of nuclear warheads, Russia faces no serious military threat from the outside, neither from the Muslim world, nor China, nor the Ukraine or any other CIS state, nor any other country'. In any case, Atlanticism à la Kozyrev was not to last. As early as the autumn of 1992, it was swept away by a confluence of powerful forces and currents of all sorts – 'Eurasianist', conservative, nationalist-chauvinist and orthodox Communist. President Yeltsin failed to counteract these currents. He himself proclaimed that 'Russia was and continues to be a great world power' that should not 'shy away from defending our own interests', even if such action were to be criticized as 'imperialist'.[13]

Anti-NATO rhetoric and campaigns under Yeltsin

As part of the shift away from Atlanticism, the Russian government revised its attitudes and policies towards NATO. In November 1993, a widely publicized study by the Russian Foreign Intelligence Service (SVR), then headed by Yevgeny Primakov (who was later to become foreign minister and prime minister), characterized NATO as the 'biggest military grouping in the world that possesses an enormous offensive potential'.[14] Calling the alliance an organization still wedded 'to the stereotypes of bloc thinking', the study charged that NATO wanted to remain a 'military alliance' rather than embark on the 'creation of a mechanism for the support of international security'. It was clear what the Russian intelligence service would prefer: a system of 'collective security that would somehow range between NATO on the one hand and the CSCE and the United Nations on the other'. The authors of the study were emphatic in their opposition to NATO membership for the countries of Central and Eastern Europe. Reacting to Lithuania's official request to join NATO, Yeltsin's press spokesman even warned that the expansion of NATO into areas in 'direct proximity to the Russian border' would lead to 'military-political destabilization of the region'.[15]

As for Russia's possible participation in NATO's Partnership for Peace (PfP), its stance was characterized by ambiguities and contradictions. Thus, on 31 March 1994, the president's press spokesman stated that Russia would not be ready to join the PfP for at least six or seven months. This was flatly denied by Kozyrev, who said that the PfP would be signed later in the month, but he reversed that announcement after demonstrative NATO air strikes against selected Bosnian Serb gun positions near Gorazde. In June 1994, Russia finally did sign on to the PfP.[16] However, more serious than those oscillations were the massive verbal attacks against NATO in connection with its role in the Balkans.

In September 1995, NATO had conducted air strikes against Bosnian-Serb positions after mortar-shell explosions in the Sarajevo market the preceding month. Reinforcing the currents of pro-Serb, pan-Slav and pan-orthodox agitation in Russia, Yeltsin went as far as to accuse NATO of conducting a campaign of 'genocide against the Serbs' and 'conjuring up the flames of a new world war in Europe'.[17] These diatribes, however, did not prevent Russia from endorsing the Dayton Peace Accords. Starting from 1996, it even actively helped in their implementation by participating in the NATO-led Implementation Force (IFOR) and Stabilization Force (SFOR) in Bosnia and Herzegovina, and from 1999 in the Kosovo Force (KFOR). Russian peacekeepers deployed to Bosnia and Herzegovina constituted the largest non-NATO contingent, and, according to NATO as well as independent reports, served well alongside their allied counterparts.

Co-operation coincided with domestic political changes: the assumption of power positions by the 'oligarchs' and their participation in domestic and foreign policy decision-making aimed at altering the Kremlin's approach to NATO. Yeltsin's new entourage recognized more clearly the counter-productive nature of the campaign against NATO enlargement and the necessity of reaching a *modus vivendi* with the alliance. As a result of these developments, on 27 May 1997, the NATO–Russia Founding Act on Mutual Relations, Co-operation and Security was signed – which, as noted, still provides the formal basis for NATO–Russia relations. It expressed the common goal of building a lasting and inclusive peace in the Euro-Atlantic area and set up the Permanent Joint Council (PJC) as a forum for regular consultation on security issues of common concern, aimed at helping to build mutual confidence through dialogue.

This approach, however, was abruptly abandoned during the resurgence of violence in the Balkans in 1998. In the controversy over Kosovo, Russia again sided with Serbia and refused to sign the Rambouillet Accords, arguing that Belgrade would not consent to their implementation by a NATO-led force. Following the NATO air attacks against Yugoslavia on 25 March 1999, Moscow suspended its participation in the PJC and reverted to anti-NATO hyperbole. Standard phraseology was that of NATO 'aggression in violation of international law'. Officials asserted yet again that the alliance was committing 'genocide' against the Serbs; the Defence Ministry announced that Russia's forces were being brought up to combat readiness; and the president was reported to have said that Russian nuclear warheads were being re-programmed to cover targets in NATO countries.

Yet the pattern of Russian behaviour and its consequences basically followed that of the war in Bosnia-Herzegovina: Moscow voted for UN Security Council Resolution 1244, thereby *ex post facto* sanctioning the 'illegal aggression' against Yugoslavia. It decided yet again to participate in an international stabilization force, KFOR.

As with the first round of enlargement, Russia's vitriolic anti-NATO rhetoric served to accelerate rather than break the momentum towards the second round of enlargement. The Kremlin's recognition of its inability to stop the process reinforced 'if you can't beat them, join them' rationale. President Putin proved the foremost advocate of this practical argument, often speaking up against the recalcitrance and opposition found among security and defence officials and officers. In the self-proclaimed spirit of 'professionalism' and 'pragmatism', he set out to review five major positions on the Western alliance.

Review and revisions under Putin

First to be abandoned was the utilization of imagined or real differences between the United States and Europe as a principle of foreign policy. This principle had been a basic feature of Soviet foreign policy ('utilization of contradictions between the power centres of imperialism') and, in essence, had been continued by Yeltsin after he had turned his back on Kozyrev's Atlanticist approach. Russia's 'medium-term strategy' for the development of relations with the EU, a document delivered by Putin (in his then capacity as prime minister) to the EU 'troika' in Helsinki in October 1999, still contained the traditional approach. Russia, it is stated there, welcomed the European Security and Defence Policy (ESDP) in order to limit 'the United States and NATO and their dominance on the continent' and 'to counter-balance NATO-centrism in Europe'.[18] However, even before the 9/11 terrorist attacks on the USA in 2001, President Putin had signalled a desire to improve Russian–US relations. The attacks gave him the opportunity to do so and in that context to abandon the policy of attempting to drive wedges between the United States and Europe inside and outside NATO.

A second Soviet argument repeated (as noted) by Yeltsin's Russia after 1992–1993 was the idea that, after the end of the Cold War and the collapse of the Warsaw Pact, NATO basically had no reason and no right to exist. Later, with the signing of the Founding Act and Russia's participation in the Permanent Joint Council and then, under Putin, in the NATO–Russia Council, that argument was to fade into oblivion.

The third component of Russian attitudes concerned the geopolitical reach of NATO. The air campaign against Yugoslavia had clarified that NATO was prepared to engage itself 'out of area'. In that context, Russian diplomats had conveyed the view that NATO's 'aggression' was illegal because NATO had violated not only the UN Charter but also its own treaty provisions. Yeltsin, however, as noted, had *de facto* ratified NATO's intervention in Yugoslavia by endorsing the UN mandates for peacekeeping in Bosnia-Herzegovina and Kosovo; moreover, Putin, in the interest of fighting 'international terrorism', had consented to a US military presence in Central Asia and the leading role of NATO in the International Security Assistance Force (ISAF) in Afghanistan. The Russian Foreign Ministry had even welcomed the 'decisive role that NATO is playing in Afghan affairs'.[19] Thus, for Russia under Putin, the 'out of area' problem, too, became relegated to history. Opposition to 'humanitarian intervention' without a UN mandate, however, has remained unchanged.

A fourth component concerned, and still concerns, NATO enlargement. On this issue there have only been superficial changes. Publicly voiced resentment regarding the entry of previous Warsaw Pact members and former Soviet republics into NATO is often muted. Obviously, Russian spokesmen realize that raising the issue in strong terms can only refuel suspicions among the new members and rub in the point about how Russia failed to stop them from joining the alliance; but enlargement is still regarded by the security and defence establishment as 'a big historic mistake'.[20] As Russian attitudes and policies vis-à-vis Ukraine, Moldova and Georgia clearly underline, resentment against NATO moving ever 'closer to Russian borders' and 'encircling' the country is still strong. Moscow sees enlargement, encirclement and the creation of new US or NATO bases in East-Central and Southeastern Europe as part of Washington's strategic design to roll back Russian influence in the neighbouring countries. Logic would have it that any member of an international organization should have an interest in its viability and effectiveness, as well as in the improvement and enlargement of its functional and geographic scope, but Russia is not a member of NATO – it is only associated with it through the NRC. Limitation rather than expansion of its relevance, scope and functions appears to be one goal of Russian participation in the NRC.

This holds true also concerning the fifth issue, which is intimately related to enlargement: the very character and purpose of NATO. Disregarding the fact that NATO has always been both a military and a political alliance, Moscow has continued to call for a change in its structure, from a military alliance to a political organization. The Kremlin's operative term for such a process is that of 'transformation'. Gorbachev's consent to a unified Germany was, *inter alia,* predicated on such a demand. Yeltsin tied it to his grudging acceptance of enlargement and so did Putin. If NATO became 'more political than military', he claimed before the accession of the seven new members in the second round of enlargement, 'that would change things considerably'.[21] He then went on to say that if NATO took on 'a different shape and were to become a political organization, of course, we would reconsider our position with regard to [NATO's] expansion'. That change was not to take place. Therefore, after the second round, the Foreign Ministry lamented the 'mechanistic' character of the enlargement process: it would have been better if NATO had 'transformed' itself first, and only then enlarged. The reversal of the sequence had contributed to the fact that relations with NATO continued to be associated with 'negative images' in Russia.[22] Putin has agreed with such assessments and stated apodictically: 'The manner in which the Baltic states joined NATO is sheer boorishness'.[23]

The problem with 'transformation', Russian style, is that if it were put into practice, the character of NATO would be changed from a military alliance to something akin to a debating club without military clout, perhaps another collective security organization along the lines of the OSCE. Russia's preferred model or vision of common security appears to be based on three convergent processes: 'transformation' of NATO; development of ESDP; and deepening of US and European co-operation with Russia.[24]

Russia has failed thus far to achieve these objectives. Although NATO prepared and held its summit in Riga in November 2006 with a primary focus on 'transformation', the term means something entirely different than when used by

Russian representatives – indeed, the very *opposite* of what Russian officials have in mind. Transformation in NATO's understanding should contribute to increasing the military effectiveness of the alliance. Envisaged are further improvements in NATO's command structure, as well as more flexible, more interoperable, more technologically advanced and more readily deployable forces, like the now-constituted NATO Response Force (NRF). Russia failed in its purposes also because what the new members wanted was the 'old' NATO: a military alliance with military muscle and safeguards against any resurgence of Russian great-power or neo-imperialist ambitions.

What, then, are the likely reasons for Putin's shift in the direction of a more co-operative stance towards the Western alliance? In NATO portrayals, they are to be found in the terrorist attacks on the United States of 11 September 2001.[25] As evidence, NATO sources point to the fact that Russia opened its airspace for the international coalition's campaign against the Taliban and al-Qaeda in Afghanistan, and that it shared intelligence to support the war as well as anti-terrorist operations worldwide. Such facts, however, testify to the manifestations of the shift, not its underlying rationale. The latter is to be found in decisions taken *prior* to the events of 9/11 to re-orient Russian policies towards the West – towards both the United States and European countries and, institutionally, towards NATO as well as the EU. The terror attacks merely reinforced a policy shift already decided upon in order to spur modernization of the Russian economy and increase the country's status, prestige and role in international affairs. The likelihood of success for the new course appeared high, given US perceptions that Russia was sorely needed in the struggle against 'international terrorism', as well as the (vain) hopes that in the UN Security Council Russia would endorse coercive measures against Iraq, or at least abstain when it came to the vote.

There is also a Western – US and European – rationale for the joint declaration on NATO–Russia Relations of 28 May 2002, and the establishment of the NATO–Russia Council. This is encapsulated in a term used (for obvious reasons) primarily for internal consumption rather then in negotiations with Russian diplomats: *compensation*. Western negotiators realized that a face-saving device had to be found so as to make it possible for Putin, at home and abroad, to abandon the 'red line' argument – the seemingly inalienable opposition to NATO enlargement across the borders of the former Soviet Union. 'Participation' with NATO in a 'joint' format on an 'equal basis' was the rationale found for justifying the end of Russia's open opposition to enlargement.

What, then, are these new institutional arrangements? How do they work, and what have they achieved?

NATO–Russia institutional links: Roles and rationales

The first formalized institutional tie beyond Russian participation in PfP programmes was created in April 1994, when diplomatic representation was opened in Brussels, in the form of the Russian ambassador to Belgium acting simultaneously as 'liaison ambassador' to NATO. Vitaly Churkin of the Foreign Ministry was the first Russian representative, followed by Sergey Kislyak, from the same ministry. Later, the appointment of Lieutenant-General and head of the border guard service, Konstantin Totsky, in March 2003 increased rather than decreased the status of the representation, since the appointment conformed to the Putin-era pattern of *siloviki* (members of power ministries and agencies) being elevated to important positions in government and the economy.

The second major institutional arrangement was made in the military sphere. Since 1996, the Russians have had a permanent military delegation at SHAPE headquarters in Mons, Belgium. The same year saw the first major example of close military co-operation in the form of Russian participation in the NATO implementation and stabilization force in Bosnia and Herzegovina. SACEUR maintained operational control through a Russian general who served as deputy at SHAPE but was empowered only to 'advise' the supreme commander on all operational matters pertaining to the use of Russian forces in SFOR. Within the theatre to which the brigade was allocated, the US commander retained exclusive tactical control.

As for the Kosovo operation (KFOR) that began in 1999, the modalities concerning the participation of Russian forces seem less restrictive on the surface. SACEUR was not directly empowered to assign tasks and missions to the Russian peacekeeping contingent: Russian soldiers came under the tactical control of the KFOR commander and the respective brigade commanders with whom they were deployed. The Russian commander could be requested to perform a mission, but he could decline. In practice, however, little had changed since, as in SFOR, the Russian peacekeepers agreed to work under the NATO operational plan.

In KFOR, in the seven years of its participation, Russia for a time provided the largest non-NATO contingent to the peacekeeping forces in the Balkans – at the peak of their strength 4200 troops (1200 officers and men in SFOR and 2000 in KFOR). When it withdrew both its SFOR and KFOR troops in summer 2003, the Russian Defence Ministry claimed that a military presence was no longer necessary – a bold assertion, considering the actual state of affairs in the Balkans. It is unclear why Moscow – to the regret of Brussels – embarked on this step, essentially scuttling the one and only major example of NATO–Russia military co-operation. The most likely interpretation is that the Kremlin still resented the unilateral NATO military intervention of 1999 and the SFOR/KFOR operational arrangements which in its view amounted to a thinly veiled subordination of Russian forces to NATO headquarters.

The third and, according to NATO's official portrayal, the principal structure and venue for advancing the relationship between NATO and Russia at the political level has been the NATO–Russia Council. It is described as a mechanism for consultation, consensus-building, co-operation, joint decision and joint action, in which the individual NATO member states and Russia work as equal partners on a wide spectrum of security issues of common interest.[26] The NRC, established at the NATO–Russia summit in Rome on 28 May 2002, replaced the Permanent Joint Council (PJC) created by the 1997 NATO–Russia Founding Act on Mutual Relations, Co-operation and Security. Under the NRC, Russia and NATO member states meet as equals 'at 27' – instead of within the bilateral 'NATO+1' format under the PJC.

Meetings of the NRC are chaired by NATO's Secretary General and are held at least monthly at the level of ambassadors and military representatives; twice yearly at the level of foreign and defence ministers and chiefs of staff; and occasionally at summit level. One important institutional innovation has been the creation of a preparatory committee, at the level of political counsellors, which meets at least twice a month; it provides a forum for regular, relatively informal exchanges of views on political issues and practical co-operation. A total of 17 subordinate committees, working groups and expert groups, as compared with only two for the PJC, has been formed – a fact that testifies to the breadth of issues addressed by the NRC.[27] Also the spirit of meetings, as portrayed by NATO, has 'dramatically changed' for the better.[28]

What, then, are the issues dealt with in the NRC's working groups and committees? The list of activities is impressive.[29] It covers the most important security problems from terrorism to environmental protection. 'Hardly a day goes by without an NRC meeting at one level or another', surfers on NATO's home page are told; but sober questions also need to be asked. For instance: Is there a gap between conferences, meetings and seminars on the one hand and practical results on the other? Are there no discrepancies between plans, projects and programmes and their realization? Also, what is the trend line: Is Russia's participation and integration in NATO, the promotion of mutual trust and the importance of the relationship for European security increasing, or decreasing?

The Riga Summit Declaration of 29 November 2006 provides some answers. The 'NATO–Russia partnership' is mentioned behind the 'NATO–Ukraine Distinctive Partnership' and the 'Intensified Dialogue with Georgia' as item number 40 (of 46) in the enumeration of the document. The signatories, it is stated there, 'believe that the co-operative agenda set forth in the May 2002 Rome Declaration has not yet achieved its full potential. Much work remains to be done to this end, and we call on Russia to join us in enhancing our co-operation on key security issues...'[30]

That assessment of the Russian dimension and its placement after Ukraine and Georgia would indicate that, after some promising beginnings, the establishment of trust has given way to disappointment and new suspicions. Between Russia and NATO, a widening gap has developed between the pragmatic and professional attitudes, pleasant atmosphere and the solution of some practical problems at the at NRC level ('low politics') and the general political and diplomatic levels ('high politics'). Furthermore, a closer look at the 'key areas of co-operation' yields the conclusion that the results achieved thus far are more marginal and symbolic rather than substantive and significant.

Struggle against terrorism and new security threats

Joint assessments of terrorist threats in the Euro-Atlantic area are fine, but central questions remain. These concern the role that the military (rather than law-enforcement agencies) ought to have in combating threats. If military instruments were to be used, where are the geographic regions or specific countries where NATO and Russia could conceivably act jointly? The initial co-operation in the war on Afghan soil in all likelihood ran its course shortly after the defeat of the Taliban. Furthermore, neither Russia nor NATO shares the US view that the war in Iraq is part of the struggle against international terrorism.

However, Russia's participation in *Operation Active Endeavour* is a specific example of military-to-military co-operation in the struggle against international terrorism as well as a successful example of intelligence sharing.[31] Formally, NATO's operation began in October 2001, and from the start, Russian participation was desired and, in principle, agreed to by Moscow, but typically for NATO–Russia co-operation, even when there is agreement in principle or on paper, implementation is painfully slow. As late as April 2006 NATO Secretary General Jaap de Hoop Scheffer was only able to announce that 'we are now reaching the final, what I would call, pre-deployment stage for the Russian contribution to the operation' and that a Russian ship was 'about to undergo interoperability tests with NATO ships'.[32] Starting in September 2006, finally, the Russian frigate Pitliviy did participate in the operation. Since then, informally, Russia's participation has been lauded at NATO headquarters as the 'flagship' of practical NATO–Russia co-operation.[33]

Joint manoeuvres and the status of forces agreement

Other examples of military-to-military co-operation are training programmes and military exercises. Several NATO–Russia manoeuvres have been held, including one naval manoeuvre, and some between Russia and individual NATO countries. Furthermore, in April 2005, NATO and Russia signed a Status of Forces Agreement (SOFA) under PfP auspices. This was considered to be another sign of progress, since the agreement makes it easier to conduct joint training exercises in Russia or in NATO countries and for NATO to transport troops, equipment and supplies to Afghanistan. It was also heralded as a sign of normalization of the relationship, since all NATO countries have such agreements with each other. The Duma, however, despite its character as an acclamation body for Kremlin policies, for quite some time failed to ratify the agreement. Thus, at the 42nd Munich International Security Conference on 5 February 2006, Defence Minister Ivanov still only believed that the Status of Forces Agreement would 'lend additional impetus to further co-operation in joint training and exercising, to command staff and troops field exercises to be held at training centres located upon national territories' – he did not say when ratification might occur.[34] Two months later, in Sofia, 'allied ministers were stressing how important it is that we'll see ratification of the so-called SOFA agreements by the Russian Duma',[35] but the NATO appeal, too, went unheard. Furthermore, the 'Torgau' US–Russian military manoeuvres, scheduled for the end of September 2006, were cancelled by the Russian Defence Ministry. The US side was asked to consent to a later date for the manoeuvres until after ratification of the Status of Forces Agreement by the Duma.[36] The cancellation, Russian defence experts thought, was related to the anti-NATO demonstration on the Crimea against the 'Sea Breeze' exercises (see below).[37] In May 2007, the Duma finally ratified SOFA. The whole process thus demonstrated how difficult it is to negotiate agreements with Russia on military issues, then see them ratified and implemented effectively.

Theatre missile defence (TMD)

The working group on TMD has explored prospects of interoperability among the theatre missile defence systems of Russia and NATO member states. Three command post exercises have been held, most recently in Moscow in October 2006, to examine and test by means of computer simulation a jointly developed, experimental TMD concept of operations. Obviously, Russia would like to see NATO use Russian missile defence systems (S-300, S-400), which it considers to be not only on a par with but superior to the most advanced US systems (Patriot PAC-3), but such hopes or expectations may prove unfounded. US military-industrial corporations have been notoriously unwilling to yield significant parts of the business on the Euro-Atlantic arms market even to European defence industry, let alone to Russian firms. Furthermore, the degree of trust among NATO members in Putin's Russia and that of his still-unknown successor has not at all developed far enough to contemplate any sort of dependency on Russian components in NATO weaponry. Ample proof of this was provided, for instance, by the stir created among defence officials and the arms lobby when it was reported that Russia, through its Vneshtorgbank, had quietly been buying stock in the European Aeronautic Defence and Space company – even though the share purchase amounted to only 5.02 per cent of the total stock, which does not entitle Vneshtorgbank to board representation and thus does not give the Bank a voice in EADS company policy.

The issue of joint theatre missile defence has been further complicated by the negotiations with Poland and the Czech Republic, which started in January 2007, on the stationing of components of the US global anti-missile system in these two countries. Although these are bilateral negotiations, Russian opposition to the US plans has led to demands among European governments that the issue should be discussed in NATO, including the NRC. If in fact such discussions take place, they will most likely not affect the US plans for a global system but at best generate ideas how to link the US global system to European TMD.

Non-proliferation

Co-operation between the Western alliance and Russia against the proliferation of nuclear weapons and the spread of ballistic missile technology has intensified, according to NATO. The biggest danger in that respect, as both NATO and Russia verbally agree, is Iran. Unofficially, NATO officials aver that Tehran's nuclear ambitions are discussed in the NRC; however, the main forum for tackling the problem is not NATO but the UN Security Council. Second, there are significant differences in approach between the USA and some European countries, on the one hand, and Russia, on the other, how to deal with Iran. Russia is prepared to exert a modest amount of diplomatic pressure on Tehran and has even agreed to some symbolic sanctions. It will not, however, be party to a stiff sanctions regime that might be able to persuade President Ahmadinedzhad to change course. Third, common positions with the West notwithstanding, Russia co-operates with Iran in the economic and civilian nuclear spheres and has continued to supply the country with weapons.

Defence reform

Despite substantial reductions in the size of the Russian armed forces after the collapse of the Soviet Union and 15 years of talk about 'military reform', the structural changes that have occurred have only scratched the surface. With its 1.1 million men in the forces of the Defence Ministry and another 600,000 in 'other' forces (*drugie voiska*), Russia's military is still too big to be well trained and equipped with modern weaponry. Its force structure is still wedded to fighting a large-scale conventional war. It is also badly led, since it lacks a corps of experienced non-commissioned officers. Hazing shows no signs of abatement, and the quality of a shrinking pool of conscripts keeps declining. Service is to be cut from 24 months to 12 months by the end of 2007, but how this is to be achieved by sticking to the goal of 1.1. million men is a mystery. Hundreds of Russian military officers have participated in various NATO and individual NATO member countries' 'exchange' – essentially one-way programmes, training courses and exercises. Yet the impact on the outlook of the officers and the armed forces appears marginal. To this day, the military in Russia remains a closed system, and one that shuns transparency even more than the 'managed' political institutions of the Putin system.

Energy security

This can be considered to be one of the new security threats. However, NATO and Russia are, as Pavel Baev discusses in this volume, at loggerheads over this issue. This was clearly reflected in US Senator Richard Lugar's opening speech at the Riga Summit. 'NATO must determine what steps it is willing to take if Poland, Germany, Hungary, Latvia, or another member state is threatened as Ukraine was', he said in obvious reference to Russia. An attack using energy as a weapon could, in his view, 'devastate a nation's economy and yield hundreds or even thousands of casualties'. For this reason, NATO should 'avow that defending against such attacks is an Article Five commitment'.[38] Although the summit declaration did not take up Lugar's allusions to Russia as a threat to NATO's energy security, many participants in the hallways of the conference agreed with their thrust.[39]

Crisis management

Under this heading, in NATO's enumeration of co-operative ventures with Russia, the two actors want to develop 'a generic concept for joint peacekeeping operations...aimed at ensuring smooth, constructive and predictable co-operation between NATO allies and Russia in case of such an operation'. However, peacekeeping is something entirely different from crisis management. Focusing on the former rather than the latter, the positive experience of NATO–Russian peacekeeping in the Balkans (SFOR, KFOR) is unlikely to be repeated soon: The 1990s under Yeltsin were a period of Russian disorientation and weakness; the current period under Putin, in contrast, is characterized by genuine (or staged) self-confidence of the 'energy superpower' that explicitly rejects integration into Western institutions and refuses to surrender its freedom of action and sovereign decision-making.[40] Thus, it is hardly conceivable that Russia would agree to a repetition of any thinly veiled subordination to NATO as was presumably evident in the Balkan peacekeeping operations in the 1990s. Corroborating evidence for this proposition can be found in the fact that Russia chose not to form part of the UN peacekeeping mission in Lebanon in the summer of 2006, sending instead, as Andrei Zagorsky discusses in this volume, merely an engineering battalion for a limited period of time, and under its own flag.

The same scepticism is warranted concerning prospects for crisis management in the true sense of the word. For instance, the 'frozen conflicts' in Moldova (Transnistria) and Georgia (Abkhazia and South Ossetia) can be considered to be latent crises that need to be addressed and solved. There seems scant likelihood of that occurring under NATO–Russia auspices with Moscow, in essence, consenting to NATO taking an active role in the solution of these conflicts. Multilateralism stops here. This has much to do with the fact that the post-Soviet geopolitical space is primarily an area of Russian–NATO (and Russian–EU) *competition* rather than co-operation – a fact that deserves to be analysed in greater detail.

NATO–Russia rivalry in the post-Soviet geopolitical space

The reasons for the competitive nature of the relationship are persistent Russian notions of international relations as a zero–sum game, and the unmitigated importance of competition, conflict and the 'balance of power' in international affairs. On this basis, Putin like Yeltsin before him has advanced the claim that the post-Soviet space is or should be a Russian sphere of influence. This is reflected, for instance, in his statement that 'no vacuum' could exist in international relations and that if 'Russia were to abstain from an active policy in the CIS or even embark on an unwarranted pause, this would inevitably lead to nothing else but other, more active, states resolutely filling this political space'.[41]

Putin also has called the dissolution of the Soviet Union a 'national tragedy of immense proportions' and the 'greatest geopolitical catastrophe of the twentieth century'.[42] Although he hastened to add that this did not mean that Russian policies were directed towards the reconstitution of the USSR, he has nevertheless proclaimed the deepening of integration in the CIS, in the framework of the Common Economic Space (CES), and the Eurasian Economic Community as having 'top priority' in Russian foreign policy.[43] Not only economic but also military integration in the post-Soviet space remains an important goal. This is underlined, for instance, in the April 2003 upgrading of the treaty on collective security to the Organization of the Collective Security Treaty (OCST) – a 'Eurasian NATO' of sorts.[44] The fact is that US and NATO ideas of a 'Europe whole and free', the EU's concept of a wider Europe and the European Neighbourhood Policy (ENP), and the 'common vision' of the countries loosely allied in the Community of Democratic Choice are in conflict with notions of a Wider Russia.[45] Western (including NATO) and Russian perceptions and policies are at odds with each other in the whole area stretching from the Baltic states via Belarus, Ukraine and Moldova to the northern and southern Caucasus. For this reason, both past and possible future NATO 'expansion' remains a major issue in the NATO–Russian relationship.

In fact, at the 43rd Munich International Security Conference in February 2007, Putin linked US plans for stationing components of its planned global anti-missile defence system in Poland and the Czech Republic, US military facilities in Romania and Bulgaria, and the failure of the NATO member states to ratify the adapted Conventional Forces in Europe (CFE) Treaty, to the enlargement of NATO.[46] To him, NATO expansion has represented a 'serious provocation'.[47]

Furthermore, given Russia's deviation from universal principles of democracy and its policies directed against the spread of democratic principles and practices to neighbouring countries, it is difficult to conceive how the resolution of 'frozen' and other conflicts could be achieved within a multilateral framework.

The validity of this proposition can be illustrated by the clash of NATO positions and policies in each of the countries and sub-regions of the post-Soviet space, from the Baltic to the Black and the Caspian Sea, and to Central Asia.

The Baltic states

After the Russian foreign and security establishment had grudgingly come to accept the planned accession of Poland, Hungary and the Czech Republic to NATO, President Yeltsin, at the Birmingham G7 (plus Russia) summit in May 1998, drew on the geopolitical map of Europe a 'red line' which NATO was not supposed to overstep. That line ran along the borders of the former Soviet Union. In the then circumstances, it meant that Estonia, Latvia and Lithuania should be prevented from joining NATO.[48] After the three Baltic countries nevertheless were invited at the Prague NATO summit in November 2002 to join and become members in February 2004, the Russian foreign and defence establishment refused to reconcile itself to that fact. Deputy Foreign Minister Vladimir Chizov lamented: 'I can tell you quite frankly and unmistakably that this [the accession of the Baltic States to NATO] does not please us'.[49] Putin, too, could not hide his disappointment and complained, as noted above: 'The manner in which the Baltic States joined NATO is sheer boorishness'.

The fact that Russian and NATO policies toward the Baltic republics run at cross-purposes manifests itself time and again. Russian government officials, presidential advisors, Duma deputies and military leaders have stated that it would be 'very negative' if NATO forces or equipment were to be stationed in the Baltic states. In fact, 'any footprint, as small as it may be' would be unacceptable.[50] In particular, they have voiced their objection to the integration of the three countries into NATO's common air defence. They have, for that reason, opposed NATO's F-16 air patrols over Baltic territory and criticized AWACS reconnaissance flights over Baltic air space. Yury Baluevsky, then Deputy Chief of General Staff, even hinted at 'adequate countermeasures' if NATO were to 'exacerbate the situation in the proximity of Russia's borders'.[51] Similarly, another military spokesman stated that Russia would station S-300 air defence missiles at the western borders of Belarus so as to bolster the joint Russian–Belarus air defence.[52] The Russian government has also complained about the transit regime between the Russian mainland and the Kaliningrad exclave, including military transit, which it considers to be too restrictive and cumbersome.[53]

Part of the Russian opposition to NATO 'footprints' in the Baltic is the demand that Estonia, Latvia and Lithuania sign and ratify the CFE Treaty with its 1999 Istanbul adaptations. Failure to do so, the argument runs, would create some sort of 'strategic grey area' in which NATO could station aircraft, tanks, artillery and nuclear weapons without verification rights for Russian inspectors. Whereas, theoretically, Russia's demand for CFE ratification (and further revision of its provisions) could be taken as proof of a multilateral approach to the management of military issues in the Baltic and beyond, the severe pressure on Estonia in the controversy over moving a Soviet war memorial from the centre of Tallinn to a military cemetery outside the city in May 2007 demonstrated that compliance with unilateral Russian demands rather than multilateral accommodation are the rules of the game in the nexus Russia, NATO and the Baltic states.

Belarus

The threat of stationing S-300 air defence missiles in Belarus mentioned above points to the fact of close Russian–Belarusian military co-operation. This concerns above all air defence but also border protection. Russian interests in the past years have extended also the military-industrial complex, with attempts made to gain control of the viable parts of the Belarusian defence industry. Co-operation in the military sphere is but one indication of the support Russia has given to Belarus even though Lukashenka is *persona non grata* in the NATO area and his regime is regarded by NATO members as the 'last dictatorship in Europe'.[54] The support over the past 15 years also took the form of preferential prices for gas and deliveries of crude oil without customs duties to Belarus refineries for the export of refined products to European countries, the subsidies amounting to an estimated volume of more than US$ 2 billion annually. Since the beginning of 2007, the subsidy regime has ended. However, this change has nothing to do with a policy change in Moscow that would aim at a multilateral approach with the United States and Europe, inside or outside of NATO, to persuade Lukashenka to change course and move in the direction of democracy, a law-based state, a market economy with fair competition and a civil-based society. Rather, it is connected with a change in what Russia sees as its self-interest.

Moldova and Transnistria

Adherence to traditional unilateralist approaches, application of pressure and opposition to external 'interference' in the management of bilateral relations are evident also in the case of Moldova. Given constitutional restrictions, Moldova is not aiming at NATO membership. It has, however, been actively working together with NATO under the Partnership for Peace Programme. Its Western orientation has also included co-operation with the EU and its Neighbourhood Policy (ENP).

The main problem the country is facing is the loss of control over the Moscow-supported separatist entity of Transnistria. Russia is firmly opposed to multilateral efforts to reduce its role as 'guarantor' of peace – any role that NATO might conceivably play and any joint peacekeeping operation with the alliance. This unilateralist approach became evident in the 'Kozak plan' of November 2003, which provided for wide 'autonomy' of the Moscow-supported separatist entity of Transnistria in a reunited Moldovan state, but also entailed the continued military presence of Russia in its eastern part.

Moldova's rejection of the plan and the country's pro-NATO and pro-EU foreign policy reorientation have had harsh consequences. In January 2006, the state-controlled Russian energy giant Gazprom cut off gas supplies to Moldova to gain acceptance of its price demands (see also below, Ukraine). Starting from March 2006, Russia stopped the import of wine and spirits and certain agricultural products from Moldova (see also below, Georgia). And in the controversies over the certification of exports of commodities from Transnistria, Moscow firmly supported the authorities in Tiraspol.

Top Russian officials stringently deny that they are exerting any sort of pressure on Moldova, or that they are clinging to spheres-of-influence notions, but representatives at lower levels of the establishment are less discrete. Thus, one has written with disarming frankness:

> The Russian army will remain in the region as a stability factor. Moscow needs guarantees that the Moldovan leaders sincerely want to become a strategic partner within the Commonwealth of Independent States. ... *Chisinau [must] realize that if it tries to sit on two chairs – European and Russian – it will fall to the ground.*[55]

In other words, Moldova faces a stark choice: It must either give up its NATO (and EU) orientation, or it will continue to suffer economic and political consequences.

Ukraine

Ukraine has closely worked with NATO within various frameworks and institutional arrangements. Co-operation takes place in the NATO–Ukraine Commission, the Joint Working Group on Defence Reform, the Partnership for Peace Programme and the Trust Fund. The Intensified Dialogue and the Membership Action Plan (MAP) in conjunction with the 'Orange Revolution' of autumn 2004 appeared to set the course firmly towards NATO membership; the November 2006 NATO summit in Riga appeared as a realistic date for an invitation to that effect.

Such notions dissipated in the months before the summit, notably during and after the March 2006 parliamentary elections. Even then, the goal of NATO membership appeared unrealistic, as public opinion polls prior to the elections revealed that only 22 per cent of the population supported it and none of the political parties, including those under the 'orange' flag, campaigned on a platform of accession.[56] The outcome of the elections, with significant losses for the political parties that could be expected to work with NATO to ensure changes in public opinion more favourable to NATO, and the later appointment of the loser in the fraudulent 2004 elections, Viktor Yanukovich, to the post of prime minister in August 2006, essentially halted the move towards membership.

Speaking shortly before the Riga summit, the NATO Secretary General still optimistically asserted that

> NATO allies will soon begin drafting exact language on a signal we want to send to countries who aspire to NATO membership. How exactly that signal will look like is a bit difficult to say, but I think I'm not far off the mark if I say it will be an encouraging signal to them.[57]

At Riga, however, the signal sent to the aspirants was discouraging. The summit declaration read:

> We reaffirm that the Alliance will continue with Georgia and Ukraine its Intensified Dialogues which cover the full range of political, military, financial and security issues relating to those countries' aspirations to membership, without prejudice to any eventual Alliance decision.

The alliance would 'meet next in Spring 2008 in order to assess progress, and give further direction to NATO's ongoing transformation, including our enlargement process'.[58]

Transferring the Ukrainian membership issue to the indefinite future serves Russian interests and policies as seen by the Kremlin security and defence establishment. As the Defence Minister pointed out, yes, Ukraine, did have the right to join NATO. However, 'for Russia, the accession of Ukraine…would be especially sensitive', because Ukraine 'has formed a single whole with Russia for centuries' and because 'shared historical and cultural values, the unity of interests and numerous family ties give a special character to relations between our peoples. The attempt at a sharp and hardly justified switchover to Western values may become a serious destabilizing factor *[sic]*, primarily for Ukrainian society itself'. Furthermore, 'the majority of Ukrainians do not want to integrate with NATO, while part of the political elite does not wish to exacerbate relations with Russia'.[59] In other words, Russia is decidedly against membership of Ukraine in NATO. The same applies to Russian attitudes and policies concerning Georgia.

Georgia

At the 21 September 2006, meeting of NATO foreign ministers in New York, Georgia was formally offered the instrument of Intensified Dialogue.[60] Russian interpretations and reactions to that step have interacted with a general deterioration of Russian–Georgian relations. In keeping with diplomatic caution, the immediate reaction of Defence Minister Ivanov to the NATO decision was that he was 'bored by the Georgian question'. The impression was being conveyed that Georgia was of no great importance for Russia in international politics, but this impression did not conform to fact. Belying this interpretation, Ivanov went on to say that two brigades of Russian forces had been deployed at the borders with Georgia, and as a result the accession of the country to NATO would not be detrimental to Russia's military security.[61]

Less than a week later, NATO defence ministers met in the seaside town of Portorož in Slovenia to prepare the alliance's summit in Riga. The council meeting was overshadowed by yet another crisis in Russian–Georgian relations, prompted this time by the arrest of Russian officers of the GRU military intelligence. Before his departure to Portorož, for a concurrent 'informal' meeting of the NRC, Ivanov said that 'banditry' in Georgia had become government policy; the situation in the country was 'reminiscent of 1937'.[62] Putin took up this theme, charging that that the Georgian leaders were adopting a policy of 'state terrorism'[63] and 'both inside the country and in the international arena, are following the policy of [Stalin's secret police chief] Lavrenty Pavlovich Beria'.[64] In rapid succession, Russia started taking steps and adopting postures usually associated with impending military intervention – including the withdrawal of embassy staff; closure of state borders; severing of road, rail, sea and air communications; stop of postal services and money transfers; orders of 'shoot to kill' to Russia's remaining military forces in the country; and the announcement of large-scale naval manoeuvres off the Georgian coast.

Significantly, Russian Foreign Minister Lavrov linked the Georgian moves to NATO, saying that 'the latest [Georgian] provocation and latest statements with regard to the Kodori Gorge, which are in conflict with all existing accords, followed close on the heels after the NATO countries' endorsement of the policy of intensified co-operation with Georgia'.[65] He also voiced suspicion that Georgia wanted to instrumentalize NATO for a military solution to end the 'frozen conflicts' in its breakaway provinces of Abkhazia and South Ossetia: 'A lot of questions arise over the matter', Lavrov said. 'For example, who is the threat to Ukraine or Georgia? Why does Tbilisi aspire to accede to NATO as soon as possible: to contribute to NATO activity in regional security or to solve present-day tasks in bilateral relations with Russia?'[66]

To return to Portorož and the 'informal' NRC meeting, the official report mentioned that the meeting had focused on two main issues: 'NATO–Russia practical co-operation, which is going well; and the current tensions in Georgia, where information was shared by minister Ivanov on this *bilateral issue* between Russia and Georgia'.[67] Moscow, in other words, did not welcome any external involvement but preferred to rely, as vis-à-vis other weak newly independent states, on *unilateral* pressure to achieve compliance.

Conclusions

The multilateralism practised by Russia inside and in relation to NATO is not one that aims at constant improvement of organizational viability and effectiveness, or supports broadening of its membership and geographic scope of activity. Russia wants to have a voice in NATO deliberations and, to the extent possible, influence NATO decisions. However, as these are often prejudged outside NATO and the alliance has built up a kind of protective wall around its core, invisible to the uninitiated but real and effective in insulating its decision-making on important issues from Russian influence, Russian multilateralism has generally had a *symbolic and demonstrative* rather than substantive quality. Its purposes would seem to be, first, to underline that Russia should not and cannot be excluded from any important international organization and, second, to support the claim advanced by the Kremlin administration and the government that Russia is a responsible partner in international affairs. To the extent that the co-operation is substantive, it is *à la carte*. It pertains to matters where Russia has a material interest – as, for instance, on theatre missile defence, if it were able to persuade NATO to buy and use Russian TMD technology.

Multilateralism is to be distinguished from *multipolarity*. It is the latter that still has priority in Russia's foreign policy thinking and practice. This approach consists in the attempt to build and strengthen several centres or poles of power (e.g. China, India, Japan and the EU, perhaps Iran) to counter-balance US influence; and on strategic nuclear questions, multipolar thinking yields to traditional (Soviet) bipolar approaches, the main point of reference still being the United States and Russia's elusive goal of parity.

Evolution of the relationship

Russia's attitudes and policies towards NATO after the creation of the Russian Foreign Ministry in June 1990 have evolved in three phases. A first phase, ranging from June 1990 to autumn 1992 or spring 1993, was characterized by 'Atlanticist' approaches under Foreign Minister Kozyrev. Membership in NATO was proclaimed to be a long-term objective of Russian foreign policy. A second phase extended from 1993 through the 1990s. This was the period in which nationalist, communist, chauvinist, 'Great Power' and 'Eurasianist' forces combined to dismantle the Euro-Atlantic orientation and portray NATO and its eastward enlargement as threats to Russian security. The third, current, phase under Putin consists of a series of contradictions – between:

- Russia's participation in NATO practices and procedures and decreasing trust in the country's political evolution;
- the Kremlin's verbal adherence to European or Western values and its deviation from these values in practice – in fact, the consideration of these values as a potentially 'serious destabilizing factor';
- the conceptual and the operational level in the NATO–Russia Council – or, put differently, between the many NRC conferences, meetings, seminars, plans, and projects on the one hand, and practical results on the other;
- the congenial atmosphere at the NRC, the constructive attitude and professional engagement of Russian officers and officials in the numerous working groups and expert committees of the NATO–Russia Council, on the one hand, and, on the other hand, significant disagreements between NATO and the Kremlin on major international issues, first and foremost, concerning ordering principles in the post-Soviet geopolitical space.

No 'entirely new quality'

It follows from the previous proposition that it was premature to claim that, at the 2002 NATO–Russia summit in Rome, a 'dramatic breakthrough' in the relationship had occurred and an 'entirely new quality' been achieved. Particularly in compassion with the second of the three periods outlined above, some changes have indeed occurred. However, Putin's Euro-Atlanticism is of a different quality than that of the first phase under Kozyrev. Putin's objective is not rapid integration with Western institutions, including NATO. He deals with them, certainly with NATO, as facts of international life that cannot be ignored. And since Yeltsin-style attacks against the Western alliance led nowhere and even (concerning NATO enlargement) proved counter-productive, the operative principle now appears to be the belief that it is better to be associated with that institution and to work with and within it, rather than to confront it. Thus, in addition to its symbolic quality, Russian multilateralism also has a *tactical* dimension.

Enlargement

One reason why it is safe to conclude that Russia's relationship with NATO has as yet not assumed an 'entirely new quality' as compared with the Yeltsin era is the fact that the Kremlin under Putin, too, remains opposed to any third round of including countries of the post-Soviet geopolitical space. This stance was reiterated clearly by Foreign Minister Lavrov in December 2006:

> We remain convinced, that the inertial expansion does not have any just reason and does not promote the strengthening of security in any of the states entering NATO, the organization itself or, of course, Russia. In other words, NATO expansion is a huge mistake by those who invented and implement it.[68]

The significance of 'practical co-operation'

NATO and some Soviet portrayals have it that there may be differences at the political level, still to be ironed out through an increase in 'dialogue', but that 'practical co-operation' has significantly increased in both volume and quality, so that the differences at the political level will narrow over time. A critical assessment of that co-operation, however, reveals many shortcomings. Much has remained at the level of dialogue (e.g. TMD, Challenges of Modern Society). Other practicalities have not been implemented even though they were agreed on long ago (e.g. SOFA, still lacking Duma ratification; cancellations of manoeuvres for that reason). Other practicalities have been implemented in diluted form and later rescinded (the participation of Russian vessels in Operation Active Endeavour). Many other practical steps have foundered on the rocks of Russian domestic politics (defence reform) and diametrically opposed NATO and Russian interests (resolution of 'frozen conflicts' and NATO–Russian joint peacekeeping in the post-Soviet geopolitical space).

Change through rapprochement?

Extending the previous argument, according to one strand of integration theory the increase of 'low-politics' communication and co-operation will ultimately affect the 'high-politics' level. That would mean that the many projects and programmes agreed with Russia – notably the work of the NRC in various working groups and at various levels, with by now hundreds of Russian officers and officials from a range of ministries and agencies who have been exposed to NATO practices and procedures – will eventually result in transforming Russia from a difficult interlocutor to a strategic partner. The EU has laboured along similar lines and so has the planning staff of the German Foreign Ministry with its concept of *Annäherung durch Verflechtung* or 'rapprochement through interlinkage'. Thus far, however, the validity of that assumption has not been borne out.

Perceptions and mutual trust

As a result, expectations connected with 'change through rapprochement' – that the Russian engagement in NATO would contribute to the development of mutual trust – also have proven unfounded or at least premature. The kind of 'managed' and 'sovereign democracy' practised at home and the pretensions of 'energy superpower' abroad have refuelled suspicion among NATO's members. Conversely, suspicion remains unabated in Russia's foreign and defence establishment that NATO (with the United States allegedly behind it) is aiming, after the dissolution of the Soviet Union, at the weakening of Russia and a roll-back of Russian influence on post-Soviet space.[69]

8 Russia and the OSCE

From high expectations to denial?

Jakub M. Godzimirski

Introduction and outline

In 2005, Europe celebrated the thirtieth anniversary of the adoption of the Helsinki Final Act that established the Conference on Security and Co-operation in Europe (CSCE). At its 1994 Budapest meeting, the CSCE was transformed into the Organization for Security and Co-operation in Europe (OSCE). The CSCE was the most visible institutional manifestation of the spirit of détente that resulted in closer co-operation between ideological, political and military rivals and a group of non-aligned countries in Europe for the benefit of all of them. Although there had been several setbacks in this co-operation and in the early 1980s it could seem that détente was in retreat, the ascent to power of Mikhail Gorbachev in 1985 contributed to reversing this negative trend and helped to revitalize co-operation across the ideological dividing lines in Europe. Gorbachev's policy was also to bear some unexpected fruits, the most important – and least expected – of which was the collapse of the Soviet project and the complete redrawing of the political map of Europe. By the end of 1991 Europe was no longer divided into two competing ideological and military blocs. The Soviet empire – both Inner and Outer – was no more, and this fact would have major implications for the development of a new security architecture in Europe.

When a new Russia emerged as an independent international actor, the country had to redefine its international role and find its place in the rapidly transforming security landscape in Europe. The main long-term declared goal of the newly launched Russian state project was to transform the country into a normal Western-style democracy with a functioning market economy. In other words, Russia was to become an integral part of the West and the country had to relate to the existing organizations, secure a new place to itself at the existing institutional tables and forge new relations with the most important international players.

One of the most interesting elements of the existing institutional landscape and most promising arenas for co-operation between Russia and its new and old partners was the Conference for Security and Co-operation in Europe (CSCE), the most inclusive of all political institutions existing in what might be termed the broader European space, stretching from Vancouver to Vladivostok. Up until the end of the 1990s Russia had viewed the CSCE/OSCE as the major tool of European collective security and had wanted to make the organization into the main forum for policy- and decision-making in dealing with conflicts and other security-related problems on the European continent.[1] Now it seems, however, that Russia has lost interest in the OSCE and treats it as far less relevant for the realization of its own long-term strategy.

This chapter aims to show how Russian attitudes towards co-operation with the CSCE/OSCE have evolved over the past 16 years. In the first section we look at the basic set of rules that were to regulate Russia's relations with its partners within the CSCE/OSCE. In the second we examine the evolution of Russian thinking about the role of the OSCE in the new European security landscape under Yeltsin and Putin. The third section focuses on interpreting the evolution of Russia's approach to the OSCE. Moscow's policy towards the OSCE will be placed in the broader context of the evolution of the debate on the place of Russia in the international system, so as to reveal more about Russia's approach to multilateralism in general.

A useful theory framework is the Regional Security Complex Theory (RSCT) proposed by Barry Buzan and Ole Wæver in their 2003 book.[2] Their proposal combines a power-based approach, rooted to a certain extent in the realist paradigm, with constructivism, in which the actions of international actors are seen as a function of their identities. Since the most important single factor shaping Russia's new international identity has been the visible tension between the country's own reading of itself as one of the two global superpowers and its rapidly shrinking capabilities, the RSCT approach seems particularly suitable. After all, ever since the collapse of the Soviet Union, Russia has been very much preoccupied with its own search for a new international identity and more power and influence.

Post-Soviet Russia and the OSCE: basic parameters

By the time the Soviet flag was lowered for the last time over the Kremlin in December 1991 the CSCE had also changed. It was no longer an *ad hoc* forum for discussing various aspects of developments in a deeply divided Europe, but an organization equipped with a number of permanent institutions to help its member states to cope with new kinds of problems and challenges. In November 1990, the recently signed *Charter of Paris for a New Europe* declared that 'the era of confrontation and division of Europe has ended', and that relations among countries were to be 'founded on respect and co-operation'. According to the text of the Charter, Europe was 'liberating itself from the legacy of the past'. The same document identified the main factors that contributed to this profound change, to the opening of what was described as 'a new era of democracy, peace and unity in Europe'. The factors listed included 'the courage of men and women', 'the strength of the will of the peoples' and 'the power of the ideas of the Helsinki Final Act'.

After this profound change – which was to become even more dramatic than anybody could have foreseen, when the Soviet Union crumbled only 13 months after the signing of the Charter of Paris – relations among the states-signatories to the document were to be regulated by the Ten Principles of the Final Act that were to guide them into an 'ambitious future'. The future of the new Europe in the making was to be characterized by a 'steadfast commitment to democracy based on human rights and fundamental freedoms; prosperity through economic liberty and social justice; and equal security for all our countries'.[3]

Already at its initial stage, when the CSCE was to address various challenges in a still-divided Europe, three areas had been singled out as core areas of the CSCE activity, or 'baskets'. They were the politico-military dimension, the economic and environmental dimension, and the human dimension, often described as a 'third basket'. The ten principles listed in the Final Act that were to regulate for relations among the signatories were as follows: sovereign equality and respect for the rights inherent in sovereignty; refraining from the threat or use of force in solution of disputes; inviolability of frontiers and the territorial integrity of states; peaceful settlement of disputes; non-intervention in internal affairs; respect for human rights and fundamental freedoms, including the freedom of thought, conscience, religion or belief; equal rights and self-determination of peoples; co-operation among states; and last but not least, fulfilment in good faith of obligations under international law.[4]

In a situation where the new Russian authorities were declaring that the main goal of their post-Soviet policy was to see their country included in the broadly understood European family of nations, this set of principles and rules could seem highly attractive indeed. The CSCE was the most inclusive of all the political organizations operating on the European continent, and the Kremlin believed that Russia could use this organization in order to achieve its own goals – which in this new post-Cold War situation were expected to overlap with the goals set by most of the European countries and their trans-Atlantic partners.

However, looking back at the 16 years of Russia's interaction with the OSCE, we may find that these hopes have not materialized, and that Russian ruling elite has changed its attitude towards the OSCE as a multilateral arena. During the first years of independent Russian statehood, expectations as to the future role of the CSCE/OSCE ran rather high. However, the situation in 2007 is characterized by what could be – perhaps too dramatically – described as Russia's denial/active undermining of this multilateral organization.

Some possible explanations for this negative trend have been provided by a recognized Russian expert in the field, Sergei Karaganov. In his view, Russia has become more reluctant towards the OSCE because 'its functions can be performed by other organizations' and because the OSC is 'an inefficient organization which is also used quite often unilaterally against political adversaries'.[5] In addition, Karaganov claims that the West wanted to use the OSCE to weaken the Communist system by focusing on the third-basket issues, while the Soviet Union was interested in this form of co-operation because it provided it with extra security (first basket) and paved the way for closer economic co-operation with the West (second basket).[6]

OSCE and Russian policy

There are many ways to understand what has been the importance of the OSCE to Russian political community and in actual foreign policy making. A good starting point could be to see what leading Russian experts say of role the OSCE has been ascribed in Russian policy. The most comprehensive (four-volume) analysis of Russian foreign policy from 1991 to 2002 prepared by a team of leading scholars from MGIMO[7] contains an extensive chronological overview of the major events in Russian foreign policy in that period. While the USA is mentioned in this overview no less than 45 times, there are only three references to the OSCE – December 1994, when the CSCE was transformed into the OSCE; December 1997, on the occasion of the organization's summit in Lisbon; and 19 November 1999, briefly summing up the results of the OSCE summit in Istanbul. Surely this is a rather low score for an organization that the Russian elite had defined in the early 1990s as the most central institutional element of the emerging post-Cold War security architecture in Europe.

The OSCE in Russian doctrines

In order to understand the linkage between Russia's ideas on the role of the OSCE in the new European security architecture and its policy-making in that area we will analyse the Kremlin's official approaches towards the OSCE and then take a look at actual Russian policies towards the organization.

We will start this journey into the OSCE–Russia landscape by looking at how Russia's attitude towards the OSCE has evolved in a series of doctrinal documents. This set of official documents should not be taken as literal guidelines for Moscow's policy-making but rather as an expression of a collective institutional identity and the elite's representation of the problems and challenges faced by Russia and ways of addressing them.

The 1993 Foreign Policy Concept of the Russian Federation (1993 FPC) was the first of the 'doctrinal' coherent official documents outlining the new Russia's goals on the international arena. The CSCE is referred to in various contexts. In the CIS context, the CSCE was to sanction Russia's bilateral efforts in conflict settlement and prevention and peace-making[8] and help Russia to protect rights of Russian citizens living outside the country's borders. Russia also wanted to be able to use the CSCE in case of unilateral actions by other countries that threatened Russia's interests.[9] The CSCE was also to play an important part in arms control and international security: it was to contribute to 'achieving greater openness in the military sphere, including in regard to defence budgets' and development of 'measures of stabilization, trust and transparency'.[10] The CSCE was also seen as a useful and important tool in dealing with the deteriorating situation in Yugoslavia: here the organization was expected to play a part in peace-making efforts.[11]

A more detailed and comprehensive outline of Russia's expectations with regard to the CSCE was provided in a special subchapter on the CSCE.[12] The Helsinki process was described as 'the central channel for providing broad involvement of Russia in European affairs as well as in the formulation of the European-Atlantic and Eurasian communities'. Russia called for continued institutionalization of the CSCE and for its 'transformation into a fundamental element of the formulated new architecture of the international community'. The CSCE was to facilitate Russia's integration into the common European space, and to assist Europe in coping with emerging instabilities. The CSCE was to help Russia to bring 'its legislation up to world standards' in human rights and the rights of national minorities. Five specific policy goals were listed for Russia's co-operation with the CSCE: strengthening of the institutional dimension of the organization; utilization of the CSCE potential for settling crisis situations and upcoming conflicts; bringing the CIS countries up to the European level in matters of protection of human rights and basic freedoms, especially in situations when the Russian and Russian-speaking minorities needed protection; the process of settling conflicts in the former Soviet Union; and finally, the CSCE was to assist in transforming the Russian economy into a market economy.

Russian Military Doctrine 1993 (MD 1993)[13] regarded the CSCE as an important regional organization through which Russia could work together with all states whose policies do not harm its interests and do not contravene the UN Charter in 'the matter of maintaining international peace and security and preventing wars and armed conflicts'[14] and as an important framework within which Russia bears 'responsibility for the material/technical supply, instruction, training, planning, and operational command of the Russian contingents' fulfilling their duties'.

The *National Security Concept of 1997* (NSC 1997)[15] dealt with the OSCE in an only marginal manner. The OSCE is mentioned only three times: as a regional organization that had not yet developed 'various multilateral peacekeeping and security mechanisms' that are effective enough; as an important multilateral and collective organization that may help Russia in its efforts to assist in 'the settlement of regional and local conflicts through peacekeeping activities'; and as an organization expected to play a co-ordinating role in an entirely new system of European and Atlantic security based 'on the principles of equality and indivisible security for all'.

In the *National Security Concept 2000* (NSC 2000),[16] the OSCE had become an endangered species: one of the fundamental threats in the international arena was described as 'the desire of some states and international associations to diminish the role of existing mechanisms for ensuring international security, above all the United Nations and the OSCE'. The OSCE was to provide aegis – together with the UN and the CIS – for Russia's engagement 'in settling conflicts, including peacekeeping activities'.

The *Russian Military Doctrine 2000* (MD 2000)[17] had a similar view, but in addition the OSCE was seen as an important rule- and standard-setter, as indicated by the following: 'the Russian Federation carries out rear and technical support, training and preparation of Russian contingents, the planning of their utilization, and operational command and control in line with the standards and procedures of the United Nations, the OSCE, and the Commonwealth of Independent States'.

In the *Foreign Policy Concept 2000* (FPC 2000)[18] the OSCE is mentioned only twice. Firstly the OSCE was described as an important regional organization that was to assist Russia in realizing its goals in Europe where Russia 'is interested in the further balanced development of the multi-functional character of the Organization for Security and Co-operation in Europe (OSCE)'. However, it was noted that Russia strongly opposed 'the narrowing down of the OSCE functions, specifically the attempts to redirect its specialized activities to the post-Soviet space and the Balkans'.

What can we learn from these doctrinal documents about the Kremlin's official approaches to the OSCE? First of all, we clearly note a diminishing interest in this multilateral organization. While in the FPC 1993 the CSCE is mentioned 13 times, the later documents mention the OSCE no more than three times each. We can also see changes in the role assigned to the organization. While in 1993 co-operation with the CSCE was seen as almost a panacea for all the problems facing Russia after the collapse of the Soviet Union, in later doctrinal documents the organization is assigned much less prominence. It is given a limited and barely 'legitimizing' role, is seen as an institution that sets rules of behaviour to be followed by Russia, as a technical facilitator for the realization of Russian foreign policy, especially in conflict settlement, and as a structure that is to form the core of new system of collective security in Europe based on the equality of its all members.

We discover a clear distinction – the documents published before 2000 do not contain any critical passages on the OSCE, while the FPC 2000 openly criticizes the OSCE for its attempt to narrow its activity only to the western Balkans and the post-Soviet space. Another important feature of the Russian official discourse on the OSCE is its general focus on military security, i.e. first-basket issues, and after 1993 no focus at all on issues subsumed under the second basket (economic) and third basket (humanitarian). Does this focus on traditional hard-security matters mark only a discursive shift, or does it also reflect a change in the pattern of Russian interaction with the OSCE? To answer this question we need to look not only at the Russian discourse but also at how it has been translated into actual policy towards the OSCE.

Russia and the OSCE: Yeltsin's years

In 1994 Andrei Kortunov published an article on the CSCE which was later reprinted in the second volume of the MGIMO anthology.[19] As his views are representative of Russian thinking about the organization in that period, his text provides useful insights. He underlines that its pan-European character gives it higher legitimacy compared with NATO and makes it an important mechanism for improving collective security in Europe. This should transform the OSCE into the most important European security organization, and one that should decide on the use of NATO's military assets when addressing first-basket issues, i.e. political-military relations.

Although Kortunov envisaged an important role for the organization, he recognized its weaknesses and saw its failure to cope with real problems in

Europe. He tried to present a broader picture of the CSCE and its potential role in the creation of a pan-European system of collective security, but his conclusions were pessimistic – given the circumstances, Russia should strengthen its co-operation with other institutions and contribute to gradually turning the CSCE into a more efficient organization by prompting it to embark on deep organizational reforms.

Another important and representative text is Kirill Benediktov's analysis of Russia's relations with the OSCE.[20] In his understanding, Russia was from the outset interested in transforming the OSCE into 'a powerful organization that would be able to independently conduct security policy on the European continent'.[21] Although this policy was from the very start torpedoed by the West – especially by the USA – which was more interested in what Benediktov terms a 'NATO-centric' European security system, in 1992 Russia managed to convince the West that strengthening the OSCE would be in its own interest as well. This Western consent was a reward for Russia's pro-Western policy conducted by A. Kozyrev, but Benediktov holds that it was the opposition between the Russian plan to transform the OSCE into a pan-European collective security organization and what he labels 'NATO-centrism' that has contributed most to the shaping of Russian – and Western – policy towards the OSCE. A major and imminent challenge facing Russia in the months after the dissolution of the Soviet Union was the need to find a new framework for conflict prevention and management in the turbulent post-Soviet space. As Russia had declared that it wanted to join the West and behave in a civilized way, it was important to get CSCE /OSCE sanction for its peace-making and peace-keeping efforts in the post-Soviet space. The 1992 CSCE Helsinki Document titled *The Challenges of Change* contained precisely such a provision:

> CSCE peacekeeping activities may be undertaken in cases of conflict within or among participating States to help maintain peace and stability in support of an ongoing effort at a political solution. In this respect, we are also prepared to seek, on a case-by-case basis, the support of international institutions and organizations, such as the EC, NATO and WEU, as well as other institutions and mechanisms, including the peacekeeping mechanism of the CIS.[22]

Benediktov interpreted the fact that the CSCE agreed to give the CIS right to conduct its own peacekeeping missions as a victory of Russian diplomacy.

All in all, during the first years of the new Russia's co-operation with the CSCE, the Russian elite had an overly optimistic vision of the future of the organization, but already at the 1994 Budapest summit some serious problems emerged. Russia's proposal on the role for the 'third force' in the settlement of regional conflicts was rejected by the other CSCE members. As Benediktov puts it, 'for the first time in the history of the Helsinki process Russia was completely isolated'.[23]

Notwithstanding opposition from Russia's Western partners, Moscow policy-makers continued to insist that the OSCE should become the main pillar of the new European security system. In order to achieve this goal Russia proposed that a new document outlining the basic principles of security co-operation in Europe – a *Charter for European Security* – should be prepared. At its Ministerial Council in Budapest in December 1995 the OSCE established the Security Model Committee that was, *inter alia*, to intensify focused discussion on all aspects of a new common and comprehensive security model for Europe for the twenty-first century.[24]

The OSCE Lisbon Summit in 1996 took place at a time when Russia's relations with the West had worsened due to the latter's plans for enlarging NATO. Russia tried to get the other OSCE members to support its plan for transforming the OSCE into Europe's main pillar of security. The OSCE was deemed the best instrument for remodelling the European security architecture because 'all the countries have the same status and decisions are based on consensus which makes it possible to defend Russia's interests in relevant documents and decisions'.[25] The Lisbon Summit adopted the *Lisbon Declaration on a Common and Comprehensive Security Model for Europe for the Twenty-First Century,* presenting the main principles of security co-operation and again confirming the importance of the 1990 Conventional Forces in Europe (CFE) Treaty in that area (see below).

It should have been clear to Moscow's policy-makers that the West would not give in and accept the Russian proposals on assigning the OSCE the role of 'controller' of its own security structures. And yet, Benediktov notes, even 'the most sober Russian politicians claimed that the OSCE had the sufficient potential to play the role of co-ordinator of all European security organizations including NATO, WEU, CIS and others'.[26]

At the Copenhagen Ministerial Summit in December 1997 the OSCE adopted the *Common Concept for the Development of Co-operation between Mutually-Reinforcing Institutions,* which was intended to help the organization to achieve a Platform for Co-operative Security 'to strengthen the mutually-reinforcing nature of the relationship between those organizations and institutions concerned with the promotion of comprehensive security within the OSCE area'.[27] Adoption of this document, which reflected Moscow's positions, was seen by Benediktov and by Russian officials as proof that, for the first time since Budapest, Russia had managed to achieve a breakthrough in its relations with the OSCE. The Kremlin's official comment on the results of the Copenhagen summit underlined that Russia's views on the central role to be played by the OSCE had been practically supported.[28]

Although Russia had been insisting on rapid preparation of the Charter of European Security, it took five years to reach agreement on the final draft before it could be finally adopted at the OSCE summit in Istanbul in November 1999. This summit was described as 'a hard ordeal for the Russian diplomacy', but in the end it proved satisfactory to all parties.[29] On the one hand, the West persuaded Russia to include a special paragraph (no. 23) on the activity of the OSCE Assistance Group in Chechnya, but Russia could also claim 'victory' because it managed to prevent the inclusion of special paragraphs on the importance of human rights, and got the rest of the OSCE to 'fully acknowledge the territorial integrity of the Russian Federation and condemn terrorism in all its forms'.

The summit took place at a very difficult time in Russian–Western relations. The Western intervention in Kosovo had enraged Russia, while the beginning of the second Chechen war occasioned Western criticism of Russia.

By the end of the 1990s it had become clear that there were certain issues which in the longer run could sour relations between Russia and at least some other OSCE members. The final statement of the 1997 Copenhagen Ministerial Council noted 'with deep concern that a bilateral agreement between Russia and Moldova of 21 October 1994 to withdraw all Russian forces from Moldova and the expectation in the Lisbon Document of early, orderly and complete withdrawal of the Russian Troops are still far from fulfilled, in particular as regards munitions'. The statement continued: 'Ministers expected the withdrawal of Russian military forces from Moldova to be continued and completed in the near future in accordance with the commitments undertaken at the Lisbon Summit' and warned that 'the OSCE will continue to follow the issue closely'. Also the situation developing in Chechnya was viewed with some concern, although the 'the Ministerial Council praised the valuable work done by the OSCE Assistance Group to Chechnya notably during the elections in January 1997'. The document also contained statements on the situation in the conflict zones in the CIS, acknowledging the efforts of Russia as facilitator.[30]

The meeting of the Ministerial Council in Oslo in 1998 produced similar critical statement on the withdrawal of Russian troops from Moldova. It called for 'full implementation of the relevant OSCE decisions' and expressed 'concern over the lack of progress in the withdrawal of Russian troops currently stationed in the Republic of Moldova, with the understanding that the removal of Russian armaments, military equipment, ammunition and other ordnance from Moldova should be the primary step in this direction'.[31]

However, it was the Istanbul Summit in November 1999 that was to become the major watershed event in Russia's relations with the OSCE. Long-dormant but tense issues such as questions of separatist and military conflicts both inside and outside Russia's borders came to the forefront. When preparing for this summit, Russian diplomats were aware that the West would use this forum to criticize Russia's handling of the Chechen problem. However, Kremlin policy-makers interpreted this as nothing more than a 'shell game' aimed at shifting the focus from the Western aggression against Yugoslavia to Russia's problems in the Caucasus.

At the meeting, the delegation led by President Yeltsin tried hard to prevent Russia from being condemned for its action in Chechnya. Yeltsin delivered an impassioned speech on 18 November in which he defended Russian policy on Chechnya and accused the West of employing double standards – a clear reference to the Western action in Kosovo.[32] Despite the Russian outbreak of rage and the clear message that Russia would not allow any interference in its own matters and that the fight against 'bandits and terrorists' would continue, Western condemnation notwithstanding, the Russian delegation signed all the prepared documents of the OSCE Summit.

The meeting issued a rather 'soft' statement on Chechnya, underlining the organization's acknowledgement of the territorial integrity of the Russian Federation and condemning terrorism in all forms. The final declaration called, however, for alleviation of the hardships of the civilian population of Chechnya, and for the creation of appropriate conditions for international organizations to provide humanitarian aid. It stressed the importance of a political solution, and offered the assistance of the OSCE in this field. The final statement also welcomed the agreement reached between the organization and Russia allowing a visit by the Chairman-in-Office to the region, and reaffirmed the existing mandate of the OSCE Assistance Group in Chechnya.

The Istanbul summit also addressed several other issues where Russia's positions differed quite significantly from those of the West. Russia's attitude towards conflicts in the post-Soviet space[33] and the issue of the adoption and ratification of a new version of the CFE Treaty, discussed further below, became especially important bones of contention in Russia's relations with its Western partners within the OSCE.

Concerning the Transdniester conflict, the final declaration from the summit stated that it recognized the positive role of the 'peacekeeping' forces in the region, Russian–Ukrainian mediation as manifested in the document on normalization of Moldova–Transdniester relations from 16 July 1999[34] and the Oslo Ministerial meeting.[35]

The 1999 Istanbul OSCE Summit also unanimously adopted a statement on the situation in Georgia. The organization reaffirmed its strong support for the sovereignty and territorial integrity of Georgia and stressed the need for solving the conflicts regarding the Tskhinvali region/South Ossetia and Abkhazia/Georgia – particularly by defining the political status of these regions within Georgia.[36] The solution should be based on respect for human rights and the development of joint democratic institutions as well as the prompt, safe and unconditional return of refugees and internally displaced persons.[37] The OSCE also welcomed the progress in negotiations on the reduction of Russian military equipment in Georgia reached at this summit, lauded the progress that had been made towards solving the conflict between South Ossetia and Georgia, expressed its support for the leading UN role in Abkhazia, condemned the acts of ethnic cleansing in Abkhazia, and branded the 1999 presidential elections and referendum in Abkhazia as 'unacceptable and illegitimate'.[38]

Work on the enhancement of the 1990 Conventional Forces in Europe (CFE) Treaty was a major point on the hard-security agenda in the late 1990s. In Istanbul an amended version of the treaty was signed, reflecting the changes in Europe since the signing and implementation of the original CFE nearly a decade earlier. According to Zdzislaw Lachowski of the Stockholm International Peace Research Institute (SIPRI), the most important changes to the treaty were the following:

> It discards the principle of balancing armed forces of two hostile politico-military blocs, and instead emphasizes individual country rights, limits and obligations. In place of rivalry and division, the principle of a common and

indivisible security space is underscored. The balance of power is replaced by peaceful security co-operation. Finally, the exclusive bloc-related character of the treaty is to be changed: the European conventional arms regime is declared open to other European countries.[39]

Before the amended version of the treaty could be signed at Istanbul, however, the parties had to settle a series of problems linked with the emergence of the completely new situation in the European security architecture. The dissolution of the Warsaw Pact and of the Soviet Union itself made partly obsolete the whole philosophy of the CFE, as it had reflected the clear bipolarity previously existing in Europe. Recent developments on the former Soviet territory, with many local conflicts and uncontrolled and partly 'forced' deployment of units and hardware, and the debate on NATO enlargement, followed by the implementation of this plan in early 1999 – all these contributed to the re-thinking of the basic ideas behind the treaty, to the redistribution of limited quotas of military hardware and not least to hard bargaining on the basic principles for a new settlement.

In the case of Russia, three issues appeared central in this bargaining process. The first was the redistribution of quotas on former Soviet territory, where the Russian military presence in the region would have to be taken into consideration. The second issue was the question of deployment in the northern and southern flank zones. The third was the problem of maintaining a strategic balance between a weakened Russia which had lost much of its CFE-limited quotas and a still coherent and even enlarging NATO.[40]

Russian analysts described the signing of the new renegotiated CFE agreement as one of Russia's most important achievements at the Istanbul Summit.[41] *Nezavisimaya Gazeta*'s political commentator Dmitrii Gornostayev concluded that the new version of the CFE treaty re-established a more just distribution of forces in central Europe by getting Belarus, the Czech Republic, Germany, Hungary, Moldova, Poland, Russia, Slovakia and Ukraine to sign additional documents adjusting their national limits to the new geopolitical realities.

One possible negative side of the new arrangement was, according to Gornostayev, the proposed solution to the problem of the Russian military bases in Georgia and the Russian military presence in Moldova. According to agreements reached between Russia and the two countries, Russian forces were to withdraw from two Georgian bases – Vaziani and Gudauta – by late June 2001, while treaty-limited equipment was to be withdrawn from these bases by the end of 2000. Talks on the two additional Russian bases in Georgia – Akhalakalaki and Batumi – were to be conducted in the following year.[42]

The signing of the amended CFE Treaty demonstrated the will of the parties to make it more suited to new post-Cold War realities. Originally designed for coping with conventional weapons in a bipolar Europe, the CFE Treaty proved flexible enough to become a useful tool also in the new situation where one of the original military blocs had been dissolved and the other had decided to enlarge. Much of Russia's official opposition to NATO enlargement had been rooted in the geopolitical paradigm with its focus on balance of power and the issue of what

Moscow perceived as the emerging 'imbalance of power' in relations between Russia and the enlarging NATO. Thus, the OSCE's ability to forge a new formal basis for further discussion on conventional forces in Europe should be viewed as a major achievement for an organization otherwise often unable to deliver what was expected of it.

Russia's fatigue with the organization was demonstrated by Moscow's reactions when other OSCE members condemned its actions in Chechnya, its role in conflict settlement in the post-Soviet space, its inability or unwillingness to withdraw troops from Moldova and Georgia, combined with its accusing the West of artificially linking the withdrawal of Russian troops with ratification of the adapted CFE Treaty. Although the OSCE had played positive roles – for example by alleviating the situation of the Russian minority in the Baltic republics, and engaging in work on peaceful solution of existing conflicts (as in Chechnya, where the organization's representative contributed to brokering a peace agreement in 1996) – Kremlin officials had begun showing signs of dissatisfaction with some 'anti-Russian' or even more generally 'anti-Eastern' features of the organization and its work.

The Istanbul Summit was important also for another reason – it was the last one attended by the ailing Russian president Boris Yeltsin, who only few months earlier had appointed a new prime minister, Vladimir Putin. Only six weeks after the Istanbul summit, Putin was anointed Yeltsin's heir-apparent, and in spring 2000 he was elected president in the first round and by a clear majority of Russian voters. This chain of events opened what has come to be known as the 'Putin era' in recent Russian history. During Putin's years at the helm, several important reforms have been implemented in Russia; the economy has rebounded, and Russia has adopted a more assertive attitude in its relations with the outside world. These changes have also put their mark on Russia's relations with the OSCE.

Russia and the OSCE 1999–2006: Putin's team in action

It was under Putin that Russia decided to torpedo the work of the OSCE by making use of its procedures that require the consensus of all member states. Between 2000 and 2006, five out of seven Ministerial Councils were unable to produce a final document on which all member countries could agree – mainly because of Russia.

To understand Russian policy towards the OSCE under Putin we start with a brief presentation of Putin's own views on the organization, and follow by listing the main Russian grievances.

One of the first public mentions of the OSCE made by Vladimir Putin came after his meeting with OSCE head and Austrian foreign minister, Benita Ferrero-Waldner in April 2000. On this occasion he said that he would like to see the role of the OSCE enhanced to 'deal not only with the problems of European provinces but with Europe itself', and suggested that the OSCE might play a more prominent role in the former Soviet republics and in Kosovo.[43]

Later, however, Putin showed considerable reluctance towards addressing the issue of Russia's relations with the OSCE. In all his State of the Nation speeches from 2000 to 2007, at his major open press conferences with Russian and foreign journalists and in his live conversations with Russian voters in the same period, the OSCE is mentioned only five times.

At a 2004 press conference he criticized the OSCE for not been willing to monitor elections in Chechnya – and thereby legitimize Russian policy in that war-torn region. He accused the West of double standards, because election observers had been sent to Afghanistan, Kosovo and even Iraq – but not to Chechnya. In the same statement he accused the West of applying double standards with respect to the situation of ethnic minorities: the West had pressured Macedonia to accept special rules for ethnic Albanians in Macedonia where they formed 20 per cent of the population, but turned a blind eye to the situation of Russians in Riga, where ethnic Russians comprised a full 60 per cent of the population. At the same event he reminded a US journalist that the OSCE had uncovered deficiencies not only in Ukrainian and Afghan democracies but also in the USA: 'the OSCE criticized American organizers for preventing monitors from visiting some polling stations. There were even instances of voter intimidation'.[44]

In his speech to the nation in 2007 Putin had a longer statement on the role of the OSCE, one that could be interpreted as calling for greater role for this organization in security-related matters:

I also call your attention to the fact that elements of US strategic weapons systems could be deployed in Europe for the first time. It is clear that the US plans to deploy a missile defence system in Europe is not just an issue for bilateral Russian–American relations. This issue, in one way or another, affects the interests of all European countries, including those in NATO. In this respect, this subject should be, and I would even say must be, discussed in the Organization for Security and Co-operation in Europe as part of this organization's political and military dimension. It is time for us to give the OSCE real substance and have it address the issues of genuine concern to the peoples of Europe rather than just hunting for fleas in the post-Soviet area.[45]

The list of Russia's main grievances was presented by the Deputy Minister of Foreign Affairs responsible for relations with the OSCE, Yevgenii Gusarov, in a lecture given at the Russian Diplomatic Academy in Moscow on 15 June 2000.[46] One of his important points was that, due to the dissolution of the Warsaw Pact and the former Soviet allies' rapprochement with the West, the internal balance in the OSCE had changed – in Russia's disfavour. The 'new majority' was trying, according to Gusarov, to impose not only its own views but also ideas and approaches that Russia was not always interested in supporting. He claimed that the OSCE had become an instrument of Western policy towards the former Soviet area. By establishing 'missions', 'information centres', 'presence' and 'working groups', the OSCE was now working as a Western bridgehead in the area defined by Russia as important to the country's national interests – including Chechnya, the

Caucasus, Central Asia and the Balkans. Gusarov was highly critical of the OSCE's focus on 'third-basket' issues like human rights, legal protection of minorities etc., and accused the organization of not paying enough attention to matters of politico-military, economic and environmental security. He accused the OSCE of 'double standards', and sarcastically labelled it the Western 'democratizator' of the European peripheries.

Gusarov outlined the main five points of Russia's new strategy towards the OSCE:

1   Russia should actively embark on a policy of using the OSCE as an instrument for promoting Russian national interests, such as protection of Russian compatriots abroad and co-operation with the OSCE in regions like Tajikistan, Nagorno-Karabakh and Transnistria.
2   Russia should try to reduce the geographical and functional disparities in the organization. One such measure is Russia's focus on the problems in the western part of the European continent and even in the USA (Northern Ireland, Corsica, law enforcement in the USA). He said that Russia would request the creation of a Special Commissioner for Western European and American issues.
3   The OSCE should focus on inter-governmental and inter-state relations, not on the domestic affairs of its members. The ideas of 'humanitarian intervention' and 'limited sovereignty' should not be used as guidance for OSCE activities.
4   Russia should work for the strengthening of the OSCE, making it a fully fledged organization capable of implementing its policies. Decisions taken by the OSCE should be based on consensus reached by all member states.
5   Russia should delegate its own diplomats and promote their candidatures in the OSCE, since Russian representation in the central organs of the OSCE is today too weak and does not correctly reflect the country's international weight.

Some five months later, Moscow was able to demonstrate its willingness to implement this new strategy. At the Vienna Review Conference in November 2000, Russia showed considerable resistance when faced with what it saw as unfair criticism on the part of the majority of the OSCE members. In the final statement Russia was criticized for lack of co-operation with the OSCE on the return of the Assistance Group to Chechnya, for its unilateral introduction of a visa regime for citizens of Georgia and for a possible differentiated application of the regime to the population in border areas (Abkhazia and South Ossetia), for lack of progress in the withdrawal of Russian troops and armaments from Moldova,[47] and finally for not reducing equipment levels in the flank region.[48]

The Russian side saw the adoption of resolutions criticizing Russia as a manifestation of the new negative trends in the OSCE, and even as OSCE interference in the domestic affairs of a sovereign state.[49] Above all, the criticisms were seen as unfounded. In an interpretative statement, the Russian delegation claimed that the propositions and conclusions produced by the meeting were not legally binding, as they were not supported by all participating states:

> The propositions and conclusions contained in the statement on a whole range of questions connected with the OSCE's activities and the assessment of the situations in various participating States do not correspond to the actual circumstances and fail to reflect the entire spectrum of opinions of OSCE participating States. These propositions and conclusions are not in line with the understandings negotiated by all participating States and, consequently, are not based on the consensus principle. The Russian Federation does not consider itself bound by any of the conclusions or recommendations contained in the statement. Equally, it does not consider it possible for the said conclusions and recommendations to be taken into account in the future work of the Organization and its bodies.[50]

The Russian delegation blocked the adoption of these resolutions, and the Vienna meeting failed to produce a final communiqué. This ability to resist pressure and make effective use of the 'consensus paragraph' proved – at least in the eyes of Moscow's policy-makers and analysts – the usefulness of Russia's new strategy towards the OSCE and towards the West, which Russian policy-makers accused of using the OSCE to promote its own interests.[51]

At the Ministerial Councils in Bucharest (2001) and in Porto (2002), Russia did not invoke the consensus paragraph. These meetings produced final declarations and several other official documents, especially on combating and preventing terrorism, but also on such non-divisive issues as human trafficking. This lack of Russian opposition to the work of the OSCE in this period was due to several factors, the most important being: the lessening intensity of the conflict in Chechnya, the 9/11 terrorist attacks on the USA in 2001 and Russia's reactions to those tragic events, Russia's rapprochement with the West and the formation of a Russian–Western anti-terror coalition and, last but not least, a new opening in Russia's relations with NATO, symbolized by the establishment of the NATO–Russia Council (NRC) in 2002.

However, this new honeymoon in Russia's relations with the OSCE lasted only until the 2003 Ministerial Council in Maastricht, where the Russian delegation again invoked the consensus paragraph. It issued a statement explaining the Russian positions as follows: 'the Russian Federation cannot, however, agree with a number of positions and conclusions, first and foremost those referring to Russia's so-called Istanbul commitments'. In the view of the Russian negotiators, these assessments by the Chairmanship did not correspond to the understandings agreed at Istanbul by the participating states and, consequently were not based on consensus. For that reason, the delegation underlined that Russia did not 'consider itself bound by the evaluations, conclusions and recommendations contained in these assessments'. In addition, it expressed regret that 'owing to the position of certain States it was not possible to arrive at an agreed text of the Ministerial political declaration and regional statements on Georgia and Moldova'. Russia also strongly criticized certain states for 'linking the so-called Istanbul commitments with the ratification of the adapted Treaty on Conventional Armed Forces in Europe (CFE Treaty)'. It warned that this approach had 'led to the dangerous erosion over the last four years of the arms control regime in Europe' and that Russia could be compelled to 'seek alternative ways of maintaining a sufficient level of national security and of developing its defence potential'. This harsh statement on the CFE Treaty was Russia's response to the declaration of the majority of ministers who gathered in Maastricht and declared that the Treaty on Conventional Armed Forces in Europe (CFE) 'continued to make a significant contribution to security and stability and remained a cornerstone of European security' – however, linking its ratification with the fulfilment of 'commitments made at the 1999 Istanbul Summit on Georgia and Moldova'. In the view of those countries, only 'their fulfilment, without further delay, would create the conditions for States Parties to move forward on ratification of the adapted CFE Treaty'.[52]

Similar declarations of disagreement on the CFE were made in the statements attached to the final documents of the three next Ministerial Councils – in 2004 in Sofia, in 2005 in Ljubljana and in 2006 in Brussels. In addition to this disagreement on whether CFE ratification should be linked with the fulfilment of Istanbul commitments, the final documents from these three summits contained separate statements explaining Russia's positions and reasons why Russia did not give its consent to the texts of the final documents.

What have been the divisive issues – in addition to the lack of ratification of the adapted CFE Treaty – that prevented Russia from endorsing the text of the final conclusions in 2004, 2005 and 2006 and from helping the OSCE to survive? In December 2004 in Sofia, Russia expressed deep regret because 'it was not possible to reach a consensus on such a pressing matter as the improvement of election practices'. At the same time, however, Russia expressed the hope that 'next year the OSCE will be able to conduct a comprehensive analysis of election laws in the participating States and to draw up unified standards, common criteria and a methodology for objective election monitoring and unbiased evaluations of election results' for use in assessing the state of democracy in all OSCE states. Russia held that such an evaluation should be used to 'judge the effectiveness of the activities of the Office for Democratic Institutions and Human Rights and the OSCE as a whole'. Furthermore it expressed regret that 'the initiatives proposed by the countries of the Commonwealth of Independent States for improving the state of affairs within the Organization' had not received appropriate attention. The Russian delegation warned that 'the thematic and geographical distortions persisting in the work of the Organization and the widespread application of "double standards"' might call into question 'the usefulness of the OSCE and its ability to respond appropriately to modern-day challenges and to meet the real interests and needs of the participating States'.[53]

In 2005 in Ljubljana, Russia expressed regret that it had 'proved impossible to reach consensus on the document on Moldova'. One of the reasons, in the opinion of Russian delegation, was that several ministers 'insisted on formulations that simply contradicted the facts', as they proposed supporting solutions which would rule out the possibility of an agreement being reached between the government of Moldova and Transnistria, and which called for a settlement to be sought without the involvement of Transdniestria. Russia was similarly unhappy that it had been impossible to adopt a document on Kosovo, and accused some delegations of refusing 'to back up our common adherence to the Helsinki Final Act'.[54] Another important issue discussed in Ljubljana was the question of reform of the organization. It seems that the main goal of this reform, at least as seen from Moscow, would be 'to minimise the influence that the OSCE has on the situation in the CIS and to prevent the Organization from acting as a "transmission belt" conveying democratic values to the area'.[55]

In 2006 in Brussels, CFE ratification remained the main bone of contention. The group of Western countries reaffirmed their 'commitment to the CFE Treaty as a cornerstone of European security and to the early entry into force of the adapted Treaty, which would permit accession by new States Parties', but continued to link it with 'fulfilment of the remaining Istanbul commitments on the Republic of Georgia and the Republic of Moldova', calling upon Russia to resume and complete its withdrawal from Moldova as soon as possible.

Moscow's response to what it interpreted as unfounded accusations was swift, and came in the form of a statement pointing out that Russia had 'honoured all of the Istanbul agreements relating to the Treaty on Conventional Armed Forces in Europe without exception' and had ratified the Agreement on Adaptation. The statement also declared that 'the fate of the Treaty now depends entirely on our partners'.[56] In addition to these statements on the CFE, Russia also expressed support for Kazakhstan's bid for the OSCE Chairmanship in 2009 and warned against 'attempts to establish any conditions for determining the Chairmanship of the OSCE', as that could 'undermine the fundamental principles of the sovereign equality of the OSCE participating States'.[57]

Conclusions – or, how to read Russia's relations with the OSCE?

What were the reasons for this toughening of tone vis-à-vis the OSCE? Many factors, both domestic and international, have influenced Moscow's policy towards the OSCE. The evolution of Russia's approach to co-operation with this most inclusive European and trans-Atlantic organization has been intimately linked with the country's evolving self-understanding of its own international role, with the way Russia's leaders have defined the long-term strategic goals of their grand strategy, with the evolution of the CSCE/OSCE, and, importantly, with Moscow's understanding of the 'utility' of this multilateral organization for the grand strategic designs of Russia.

As noted above, the Regional Security Complex Theory (RSCT) proposed by Buzan and Wæver provides a useful approach to reading Russia's relations with the OSCE.[58] According to Buzan and Wæver, relations among states – and security complexes – can range from conflict formation, through construction of a security regime to security community. In all these contexts, the existence of multilateral institutions may play a positive role in conflict prevention, conflict mitigation and conflict solution. And this is probably the role that the Russian leadership has been assigning to the OSCE throughout the various stages of building the new Russia's relations with its surroundings.

Within this theoretical framework the OSCE could be seen as a multilateral organization that was to help Russia, in the immediate post-Soviet years, to manage its dealings with two most important remaining security complexes that Russia had to relate to – one European, one North American. The OSCE also could serve as a facilitator for Moscow's policy within the Russia-centred security complex made up of the former Soviet states, especially in Russia's attempts at finding solutions to the conflicts emerging in this space and in dealing with the issue of Russian and Russian-speaking minorities in the former Soviet republics. In addition, the CSCE/OSCE could be seen as having a certain role in alleviating the pains of Russia's transformation by helping it to address its domestic social, political and economic vulnerabilities and, finally, could be seen as a useful tool for managing a weakened Russia's relations with other global centres of power, especially the USA.

When Russia emerged as an independent actor in late 1991, the country's international surroundings appeared highly anarchistic. What was perhaps the most important feature in Russia's closest environment was the rapidly developing power vacuum caused by the unexpected collapse of the Soviet Union, a fact described later by Vladimir Putin as 'the greatest geopolitical catastrophe' of the past century. Russia had to relate to 14 newly independent states established on the post-Soviet territory and build new types of relations with its former enemies in the West. The Russian elite's outlook of the international system was a mixture of Marxism and hard-core realism[59] where international relations were perceived as a predatory zero-sum game.

Under these circumstances it was understandable that the political elite saw the CSCE/OSCE as an institution that could help a weakened Russia to survive in this dangerous environment. At that stage, Russia was interested in transforming its relationships with other actors, from being based on a Hobbesian logic, to either a Lockean – or if possible – Kantian logic. According to Alexander Wendt, states do not need to be concerned only with their own security and behave in an inherently egoistic manner, as international 'anarchy is what states make of it'.[60] In a more recent work, Wendt introduces the above-mentioned triad and claims that the Hobbesian logic entails 'a distinct posture or orientation of the Self toward the Other' in which the Other is defined as enemy; in the Lockean culture, the Other is seen as rival and competitor, while in the Kantian logic the Other is seen as friend and partner with whom you can settle disputes without resorting to violence and with whom you can co-operate to face common challenges and threats.[61] In Russian designs of the early 1990s, the CSCE/OSCE was to be used as a vehicle for transforming the logic of the system surrounding Russia. Moscow expressed both the will to and the interest in rejecting the Hobbesian logic that had governed the Soviet Union's relations with the West, and declared that it wanted Russia to become a full-fledged member of the Western security community based on the Kantian logic. As a step towards realizing this ambitious goal, a collective security regime was needed, and the CSCE/OSCE was to become its institutional basis.

In a situation when the choices made by the Kremlin political elite and the country's increasing weakness and vulnerability put Russia on a pro-Western, liberal course, the Russian leadership could believe that the CSCE/OSCE could provide various opportunities. As stated in the 1993 FPC, the CSCE was to help Russia (re)join Europe by assisting it in democratizing the political system; it was to secure a weakening Russia against external threats by stabilizing the situation in the country's international surroundings, provide Russia with a useful arena for discussing common concerns and finding common responses to shared threats and challenges, and even assist the country in coping with a deepening economic crisis by providing what could be termed the know-how for marketizing its economy.

However, the 1993 FPC was a product of what was later seen as a 'romantic Atlanticist' period in Russian foreign policy formulation. It seems that expectations as to how the CSCE could help Russia on its way towards rejoining the West were simply set too high.

In addition, Russia redefined its long-term goals and started reading what was happening on the international scene in a less liberal and more realist way. This change in the first half of the 1990s was due to several factors. Rahr and Krause[62] claim that the most decisive domestic and external factors influencing the evolution of Russian foreign policy in that period were as follows: the West's decision on NATO enlargement; what was seen as a lack of sufficient economic support for Russian reforms; the rejection of what was labelled the Russian CSCE option (transforming the CSCE into a pan-European and trans-Atlantic organization for collective security that could even have a decisive say on the use of NATO's military assets); the high cost of the shock therapy resulting in lack of social security; the syndrome of a lost empire and the Soviet 'mental legacy'. All these factors contributed to changing Russia's approach towards the OSCE. When the West rejected Moscow's proposals on the future role of the OSCE; when it was seen as failing to provide Russia with sufficient assistance, and even warned that it would be enlarging its military alliance, this could only lead to the growth of anti-Western sentiment. Already at that stage there was in Russia a widespread opinion that Russia should not slavishly copy the Western model but base its transformation on its own historical experience and its own political traditions.

This 'soft' anti-Western and realist turn was on the personal plan symbolized by the ascent of Yevgeny Primakov to the post of foreign minister in January 1996. Consequently, the OSCE was no longer seen as an arena of co-operation with the West, but became rather an arena of bargaining and horse-trading with the West, an arena where Russia was to pursue its own goals, which did not always overlap with those of the West. Russia also sometimes indicated the will – but not always the capacity – to challenge the West on various issues, as in the way of handling of separatist conflicts in the post-Soviet space, which was increasingly seen as a zone of Russia's exclusive interests and responsibility. The OSCE was still considered to be a useful institutional tool in Russian foreign policy towards the West – but it was no longer a tool of uncritical co-operation with the West. Now it had become a tool for hammering out Russia's new position in Europe, making Russia more visible in the European security landscape and giving it a stronger say in European matters. It was an institutional tool that was especially useful in a situation when there was still a visible and deep gap between Russia's great-power ambitions and the country's economic and political weakness. At this time, Russia simply lacked the realist power and strong leadership needed to translate its great-power ambitions into a realist great-power policy. The 1998 economic collapse was a clear reminder of this gap between realist ambitions and actual realities.

This painful experience also had a considerable impact on the policy formulation of the early Putin years. When Vladimir Putin came to power in the summer 1999 he inherited a Russia on its knees, and was confronted with a number of challenges stemming mostly from the domestic sphere. This was one reason why he decided to give priority to internal reforms, signalling that Russia could not pursue a very active policy on the international scene without first coping with its domestic problems. This realization of Russia's weakness was probably the main factor influencing Putin's foreign policy and his grand strategy for Russia, which were both depicted as 'pragmatic'. Putin realized that Russia could count only on itself, that most of the problems were of domestic character and that the dream of great-power status would have to wait. Putin's focus on internal issues, on domestic political reforms and on the economic revitalization of the country resulted in his paying less attention to Russia's policy towards the OSCE. The organization was barely mentioned in his major political speeches: and if it was mentioned at all, he presented a rather critical attitude towards its actions.

In Putin's pragmatic view, the OSCE was not central to Russia, as the country could more efficiently tackle the essential issues through other institutional – multilateral and bilateral – tools and fora. Matters pertaining to hard security covered by the first OSCE basket could be dealt with, especially after Putin's pro-American turn in September 2001, either on a bilateral basis directly with the USA and other key Western partners, or multilaterally in the newly established Russia–NATO Council (RNC). Also Russia's strong position in the UN Security Council provided leverage in global and regional hard-security matters.

When it came to issues related to second – economic – basket, Russia did not need OSCE either, especially after development of mutually beneficial trade relations with Russia's main trade partner, the EU, and the economic boom caused by devaluation of the rouble in 1998, followed by boosting domestic production and skyrocketing prices for Russian energy commodities. Russia was no longer a state on the verge of bankruptcy, as the situation had been in 1991 and again in 1998; the country now had important economic leverage in its relations with the outside world – indeed, it was even invited to join that exclusive club of economic giants, the G8 group.

The third basket of the OSCE, the one within which humanitarian issues are to be dealt with, has become the main 'basket of contention' in relations between

Russia and the West. After a decade of decay, Russia began to regain its clout and decided to embark on the policy of becoming a normal great power.[63] It could even seem that the Kremlin leadership, disappointed with the West and its tutorial approach to Russia and other post-Soviet states, thought of transforming Russia into an alternative pole of power, around which those who rejected what was sometimes presented as the Western democratic diktat, could rally. In the words of Dmitrii Trenin, Russia decided to leave the Western solar system and build its own.[64] In this new grand design, the OSCE – initially seen by Russia as an organization that could become a cornerstone of a new security architecture in the post-Cold War Europe – has been increasingly 'read' as an inefficient and biased organization dominated by the enlarged West, and is therefore perceived more as a burden than as an opportunity.

Although Moscow still pays lip service to multilateralism, the evolution of its policy towards the most inclusive of European multilateral organizations, the OSCE, reveals that Russia seems to prefer other ways of doing political business. A good answer as to what could be the international setting preferred by Russia reasserting its international position has been given by Sergei Karaganov, a leading Russian expert in the field, whose voice seems to be music to the Kremlin's ears. In many articles published recently in Russia and in the West, he has called repeatedly for the reintroduction of a modern version of the European – or global – concert of powers.[65] As one Finnish commentator put it in 2001 when commenting on a proposal from Karaganov and others for turning the G8 into a new version of the global concert of powers – a Global Alliance for Security: 'a concert of great powers is not a perfect way to run the world, but it is certainly better than anarchy. If we cannot revamp the UN Security Council, and there is no indication that we could, then a concert of great powers is our best bet. It is not pretty but it works.[66]

This pragmatic logic is evident in Russia's policy towards the most important European multilateral body, the OSCE. A more exclusive multilateral setting, guaranteeing Russia a place with a strong voice at a table where the fate of Europe is to be decided, would seem to suit Moscow's ambitions far better than the OSCE in which Russia is only one of 55 equal members, and not even a *primus inter pares* at that.

9 Russian regional multilateralism

The case of the Arctic Council

Elana Wilson Rowe

Introduction

Since the end of the Cold War, the governments and peoples of the Arctic have increasingly engaged in a range of co-operative activities designed to address issues of shared concern and to raise the profile of the Arctic as a political and geographical region. The subsequent proliferation of activities aimed at promoting stable and ongoing co-operation in the far North has to do with the Arctic being a relatively secure source of non-renewable resources (oil, gas and minerals), awareness of the heightened impact of global environmental problems (such as global warming and trans-boundary pollutants) on the Arctic environment, and the increasing politicization of the Arctic indigenous peoples.[1]

In the process of building regional institutions, 'smaller' states – like Canada and Finland rather than the US or Russian Cold War superpowers – have led the way. However, the involvement of major powers, particularly the USA and Russia, has been essential to the legitimacy and mandate of these new institutions, as these countries are in a position to both facilitate and hinder the Council's work.

Russia has a key role to play in the international politics of the North: it is the largest 'Arctic' state in territory, and an important regional and global actor in an energy market that is increasingly looking northwards. This chapter examines Russia's engagement in the Arctic Council and identifies key features of Russian multilateralism as demonstrated in this regional forum. The structure of the Arctic Council and cross-cutting interests shaping Russia's engagement in the North are presented first, followed by a review and analysis of the country's Arctic Council participation. Key characteristics of Russia's engagement are then covered in detail. Firstly, its variable capacity for agenda setting in this regional context is examined, and ways in which it exerts an almost 'automatic' institutional influence as an important Arctic state are flagged. Secondly, a tendency towards working primarily on 'low political' issues is described and three ways in which the dichotomy between low and high politics is evident in Council activities are highlighted: (1) the seemingly limited mandates of Russian representatives to the Council; (2) the changing definitions of what constitutes an issue of 'low' or 'high' politics; and (3) the tendency to use strategic documents to pursue a basis for even rather technical co-operation. The extent to which an increasingly 'geopoliticized'

North and a more assertive Russian foreign policy stance influence Moscow's engagement in the Arctic Council is explored in the conclusion. This chapter is based on analysis of previously publicly available minutes[2] and summaries of Arctic Council events from 1996 to 2006, and on ten informational interviews with US (September 2007), Norwegian (October–November 2007) and Russian (December 2007) individuals involved in the Arctic Council.

The Arctic Council

Immediate post-Cold War region-building efforts led to the establishment of the eight-country Arctic Council in 1996. The Council brings together governmental and indigenous representatives from Canada, Finland, Greenland (Denmark), Iceland, Norway, Russia, Sweden and the United States and operates on several levels. Senior Arctic Officials representing their respective countries meet once a year, while higher-level 'ministerial meetings' occur every second year. The Council's six working groups, focusing on different aspects of the Arctic environment and involving both civil servants and expert contributors, meet several times a year. Decision-making within the Council is contingent upon full consensus.

The Arctic Council has thus far concentrated on producing and disseminating large-scale environmental assessments of the North (climate, pollution, wildlife). Although the scientific information produced under Arctic Council efforts is often given political application elsewhere in other forums,[3] the policy ambitions of the Council itself remain quite modest. In fact, 'few efforts are made to create rules that are more ambitious or more specific than those already embraced in broader international fora'.[4] Assessment documents produced by Arctic Council working groups do not identify environmental offenders or non-compliance. Such monitoring has lent itself well to co-operation, partly because it does not raise controversial questions about regulation, but also because there are substantial benefits to be reaped from the harmonization of data and joint analysis on the Arctic region.[5]

While the Arctic Council seems set to remain focused primarily on monitoring rather than policy-making, some signs of change are also evident. These changes have likely come in response to increasing geopolitical pressures on the North, particularly the partly intertwined forces of climate change and growing energy demand.[6] Norway has presented an agenda for its Arctic Council chairmanship (2007–2009) that includes an emphasis on more controversial economic and social issues, like natural resource management, that had been originally defined out of the Council's remit.[7] Russia has, interestingly, indicated a willingness to follow Norway's lead on such an expanded focus for the Arctic Council. In his October 2006 address to the Salekhard Ministerial, Minister of Foreign Affairs Sergei Lavrov voiced his ministry's support, stating: 'as an undertaking for the future, we have agreed to launch a new, energy dimension of the Council. The aim is to ensure sustainable oil and gas production in the Arctic zone.'[8] At the same time, it is important to note that the approach to potentially controversial issues remains firmly embedded in the Council's monitoring tradition. The primary manifestation of the new focus on natural resource management is an assessment exercise being carried out by the Sustainable Development Working Group (SDWG), which focuses on summarizing best practices relating to integrated management in the North.

The Russian North

Russia inherited from the Soviet Union an overpopulated North ill-suited to the demands and logic of the market economy. Russian northern policy during the transitional 1990s could be described as haphazard, and focused primarily on emergency measures to alleviate acute fuel and supply shortages, attempting to respond to economic and social crisis in the region. Some areas (Chukotka, for example) experienced conditions of humanitarian crisis, necessitating the involvement of organizations like the Red Cross. Although both the federal and regional governments continue to struggle with the chronic shortages that characterized the Yeltsin era,[9] the contours of a more clearly discernible Russian policy on the North emerged under Putin. As Helge Blakkisrud argues in his comprehensive study of Russia's northern policy, this approach was initially based on principles of market economics with an eye towards ensuring that the North becomes a profitable part of the Russian state.[10] A distinction is now drawn between the 'profitable North' and the 'unprofitable North'. The 'profitable North' – the areas rich in oil and gas and minerals[11] – should be further developed. The 'unprofitable' North – areas dependent on federal support and without prospects for viable economic activity – is slated to be scaled down, and the non-indigenous population encouraged to resettle. Despite gradually improving living conditions in the North, the region continues to face environmental and social challenges.

At the same time, the importance of the North as a natural resource province has increased. From being on the brink of bankruptcy in 1998, Russia's economic recovery has been driven primarily by high oil and gas prices. As the Russian North stands for approximately 95 per cent of the nation's gas and 75 per cent of its oil production, it has again become a crucial factor in Russian economic development. A feature of Putin's second term as president was an increasingly politically and economically assertive foreign policy supported by rising revenues from oil and gas, at times articulated directly via the notion of being an 'energy superpower'. Since 2005, there has been growing attention paid to the question of how to promote private investment (both Russian and foreign), while maintaining control over Russian natural resource assets defined as 'strategic'. The legislation on sub-soil resources that has long been held up in the Duma contains the notion of 'strategic energy fields', which would limit certain investments to companies with a minimum of 51 per cent Russian ownership, with the Russian side ideally represented by the state-controlled companies Gazprom and Rosneft.[12]

The dominant thread that can be construed in Russia's evolving relationship to the North today is a tension between the securitization of northern space and nationalization of northern resources and more international and market-driven orientations. While the social and environmental challenges inherited from the Soviet Union have necessitated the involvement of foreign actors and financial contributions, the strategic significance of natural resources and the increasingly assertive foreign policy built upon these energy resources seems to be pulling in the direction of an increasingly closed North.

One vivid example of this 'closing' of the Russian North comes from the Arctic Military Environmental Co-operation (AMEC), established by the military authorities of Norway, Russia and the USA in 1996. Although not an Arctic Council project, the co-operation involves some of the same actors and agencies connected to the Council. AMEC focuses on spent nuclear fuel containment and remediation of radioactive pollution in the North, with particular attention to the Northern Fleet in Northwest Russia and enhancing Russian capacities for handling radioactive waste. In February 2007, a key Norwegian representative within the AMEC project, Ingjerd Kroken, was denied entry to Russia on a routine work visit. The Russian Ministry of Foreign Affairs later stated that Kroken had been engaged in illegal information gathering, even though all AMEC work had been carried out either on request or agreement from the Russian Northern Fleet and other relevant authorities. This rejection of the AMEC representative sends a signal of changing attitudes in Russian political and security circles towards both being a recipient of 'aid' via capacity-building and the extent to which the Russian North (the military North in particular) is to be open to other actors and multilateral activities.[13] The extent to which Arctic Council co-operation has been affected by this tension is a question to which I return in the conclusion.

Russia and the Arctic Council

Key cross-cutting features shaping Russia's involvement in the North are an increasingly economically and politically assertive Russia and the above-mentioned tension between an 'opened' and 'closed' North. How Russia engages in the Arctic Council against this backdrop, and the extent to which these trends affect regional multilateralism in the North, are questions to be explored in this remainder of this chapter. Russia's involvement in the Arctic Council from a chronological perspective is covered first, followed by a brief look at central actors/governmental bodies. Key characteristics of Russia's regional multilateralism are then discussed in detail.

Except for some interventions from the Russian indigenous peoples' organization RAIPON (which received financial support from the Canadian government), Russia is almost entirely absent from the official record of the Arctic Council's first three years of operation (1996–1999).[14] Despite the low level of actual participation, Russia's status as a 'client' of Arctic Council projects was established early on. Russia began engaging more actively at all levels of the Arctic Council in 1999, but its representatives have rarely proposed or, by extension, funded new projects. Its financial contribution remains largely in the realm of in-kind contributions of administrative and expert services. Indeed, there may seem to be evidence of a mismatch between declared commitment to multilateralism and actual financial commitment, as Zagorski argues elsewhere in this volume. In some instances, it still remains necessary for other member countries to cover the travel costs of Russian experts/scientists and even (although increasingly rarely) representatives from Moscow's Ministries of Foreign Affairs and Natural Resources. One might expect, given the more assertive political and economic stances that Russia has been taking at the international level, that this kind of 'aid' would be out of step with the country's new image. However, as two Norwegian interviewees indicated, the problem in today's financial relationship is primarily one of donor fatigue on the part of other Arctic states.

Many Arctic Council projects still focus on identifying and (to the extent possible) ameliorating environmental problems in the Russian North. The first proposal that seems to have been actively championed by the Russian side was the *National Plan of Action for the Protection of the Marine Environment from Anthropogenic Pollution in the Arctic Region of the Russian Federation* (NPA-Arctic). This proposal, concentrating on the elimination of land-based sources of marine pollution, was included in the sphere of the Protection of the Arctic Marine Environment (PAME) working group and officially welcomed by the Arctic Council in the Inari Declaration, which played an important role in attracting financing.[15] Although Russian Arctic Council representatives promoted the project extensively at Council meetings, the NPA-Arctic was never accepted as an official Arctic Council project, due to its exclusive focus on the Russian North. Thus it seems that the first project proposed by Russia failed to find a home within the multilateral approach practised by the Arctic Council.

In 2001, Russia began making its first proposals outside of the NPA-Arctic, although very few of them came to fruition as projects. These years also saw some off-beat suggestions – such as Russia proposing that the Arctic Council be promoted via a regular magazine comparable to the US *National Geographic.*[16] The 2004–2006 chairmanship was given to Russia in hopes of involving the country to a greater extent (a similar motivation had been behind an earlier chairmanship for the USA). All non-Russian interviewees describe the results of the chairmanship as mixed, arguing that although meetings were well-organized there was little substance to or progress on the Russian chairmanship agenda. More recently, Russia proposed a project on remediation of contaminated areas of Franz Joseph Land under the Arctic Marine Assessment Programme (AMAP) working group that was well-received by other states. Another project currently being followed up is a study on pollutants, food security and indigenous peoples in the Russian North, for which Russia, via its Ministry of Health, has produced new funding.[17]

A broad range of Russian institutions – both governmental bodies and academic institutes – are involved in the Arctic Council. Following a period of what non-Russian interviewees perceived as problematic due to post-2000 turnover and administrative reform (including the disbandment of the State Committee on the North), patterns of co-operation and responsibility seem relatively well-established today. The Ministry of Natural Resources, Roshydromet (Federal Service for

Hydrometeorology and Environmental Monitoring), the Regional Development Ministry, EMERCOM and the Ministry of Economic Development and Trade all send representatives to one or more of the six working groups of the Arctic Council. The Ministry of Foreign Affairs supplies both the ministerial representative and the Russian Senior Arctic Official (SAO).[18] The Russian Academy of Sciences, the Institute for Arctic and Antarctic Research and other regional institutes participate at the working group level as well. A Russian interviewee explained that this network of governmental representatives and experts is co-ordinated via a central, strategic document outlining key responsibilities, and that the 'Russian' position on key Arctic Council issues is discussed at cross-agency meetings preceding the ministerial meetings.

Setting the Agenda?

Capacity is clearly an issue when it comes to Russian efforts to set the Arctic Council agenda. The earliest recorded interventions at the Council by Russian representatives suggest a struggle to provide enough relevant actors for the various working groups and other meetings. Russian representatives repeatedly requested a greater streamlining of Arctic Council activities and meetings, and clarification of working group mandates to avoid overlap and ensure effectiveness.[19] While there is now more involvement overall in terms of representation, Russia still proposes relatively few projects and at times must struggle to provide the necessary data for Council assessment activities.[20] Capacity may also be related to a tendency to prefer or default to more 'straightforward' bilateral solutions, as both Light and Zagorsky argue in this volume. The Arctic Council requires only that each project involve at least two partners, ideally substantively. Several interviewees mentioned the difficulty Russia had in proposing projects that were truly multilateral in nature (e.g. more than two partners) and reported that most Russian projects focus solely on Russia (rather than trans-boundary issues).

When it comes to deliberately shaping the multilateral agenda, Russian actors at the Arctic Council have both succeeded and failed. Two recent examples from the Russian chairmanship – Russia's focus on the 'peopled North', and the efforts to systematize Arctic Council projects – illustrate how this institutional power is exercised in the Arctic Council.

In describing the accomplishments of the Russian chairmanship (2004–2006), Minister of Foreign Affairs Sergei Lavrov emphasized:

> While actively promoting the traditional priority environmental programs, we have sought to build up efforts in the social and economic fields. The aim was to see to it that the people in the North lived comfortably, in a clean natural environment and had a full-fledged access to education, social services and medical assistance…[21]

This focus on 'people' of the North certainly relates to the fact that Russia has the most populous North and represents a contrast to the Council's established focus on environmental problems.[22] This differing emphasis has been a consistent feature of Russian interventions since 1999. At a November 1999 SAO meeting in Washington DC, the then chairman of Goskomsever (the State Committee on the North), Vladimir Goman, stated that he 'would like to see projects expanded to focus on people of the North, including indigenous'.[23] At the June 2001 meeting, this focus on people was reiterated, as Russia mentioned the sustainability of life of the indigenous peoples as important and emphasized health and housing issues. At later meetings, the focus on livelihoods (especially reindeer herding) and anything involving the 'human aspect' was stressed.[24] This was reiterated in the objectives of the Russian chairmanship, with the Russian-authored October 2005 SAO report summarizing that a major focus of the Russian chairmanship had been to establish a 'more balanced approach to sustainable development in the Arctic', particularly through greater focus on the Arctic peoples and the challenges facing them.[25]

On the one hand, Russia's focus on people and on the specificities of the country's own northern problems resulted in project proposals poorly suited to the Arctic Council. The Russian chairmanship was keen to have the Arctic Council link up with the UN Urban Housing Program, which focuses on industrial housing and needier countries and is consequently not relevant to the other less populous and more developed Arctic states. Although the Russian Chair brought it up repeatedly, according to non-Russian interviewees, the issue was eventually dropped due to the other states' lack of interest. On the other hand, Russia's emphasis on people was substantively realized in a project on indigenous peoples and contaminants, involving the Ministry of Health, Roshydromet, the Ministry of Natural Resources and some regional governments. This, the Persistent Toxic Substances Project, was carried out under AMAP auspices and investigated the significance of aquatic food chains as pathways of pollution exposure for indigenous peoples. The project was partially funded by the Russian Ministry of Health, which has now produced fresh funding to enable continuation of the project.

A second emphasis of the Russian chairmanship perhaps relates quite closely to the concerns about working group overlap and a wish for more systematized and streamlined work in light of limited capacity. As early as 2001, the Russian SAO indicated an interest in drafting a proposal for the Sustainable Development Working Group (SDWG) that would co-ordinate the work of the working groups.[26] The Russian chairmanship, which entailed chairmanship of the SDWG, devoted considerable resources to this Sustainable Development Action Plan (SDAP), which was – as noted even in the official minutes – a 'subject for longer discussions and controversies'.[27] Essentially, the Russian chairmanship wanted the SDAP to be a compiled database of all projects and argued that such a database would result in greater co-ordination and perhaps improved results. The proposal suggested that all working groups should submit their activities to the SDWG in a certain format on an annual basis. However, most working groups and other member countries involved in the generally decentralized Arctic Council structure were against adding yet another layer of paperwork and reporting, arguing that it would involve too much of the limited Arctic Council resources in list-making. As one Norwegian interviewee noted, the proposal seemed out of touch with how the

Arctic Council works, since in practice most projects are carried out nationally under national supervision, even if the projects are designed to bring about added value through a measure of international co-operation. While the SDAP was passed as a deliverable of the Russian chairmanship, this was done on the understanding that its later impact would be minimized.

That the SDAP was accepted at all seems to indicate that Russia exerts a certain amount of institutional influence simply due to its importance as the largest Arctic state and a former superpower – it has become essential to propose projects that resonate, at least to some extent, with Russian interests and involve Russian actors. Thus, in regional forums like the Arctic Council, Russia may have greater ability to set the agenda than it does in important global forums like the G8 (see Baev's chapter in this volume).

'Low politics' by default

The studies of EU–Russia relations and NATO–Russia relations covered in this volume reveal a similar characteristic of Russian participation in multilateral settings – the tendency to operate with a clear distinction between high and low politics, and to end up working primarily on issues of low politics in multilateral co-operation. In this dichotomy, 'high politics' often involves questions of war and peace, foreign affairs, defence and domestic security; while 'low politics' concerns social and financial issues.[28] The Arctic Council, almost by definition, should fall into the 'low politics' category, given its focus on environmental and social problems, and the lack of emphasis on policy-making and implementation.

One example of the often rather successful 'low politics' co-operation that can be achieved with Russian partners on non-strategic issues is that of access to the Russian Arctic under the auspices of the International Polar Year (IPY). At an October 2005 Senior Arctic Official meeting, Sweden expressed concern over the high tariffs charged by Russia for icebreaker services in the Northern Sea Route, even for endeavours involving scientific research for the IPY.[29] By the closing ministerial in October 2006, Russian explorer Artur Chilingarov could report in his statement that icebreaker fees would be reduced by 50 per cent for IPY research activities.[30]

Despite the overall 'low politics' nature of the Arctic Council, the low/high dichotomy still manifests itself problematically in three ways. Firstly, individual Russian representatives to the Council may have limited mandates even as regards matters of technical co-operation, and their mandates may decrease further if an issue area borders on questions of a potentially 'high politics' nature. Secondly, problems crop up when what other states treat as a low politics issue of scant significance to security or foreign policy is otherwise defined within Russia. Finally, Russian approaches to what could be established as low political co-operation is often tinged with overtones of the 'high political', with a desire for strategic documents, treaties and international legislation in which other states are reluctant to invest resources and time.

The dichotomy may be compounded by today's highly centralized political system and the primacy of the Russian presidential administration, as less powerful actors assigned to multilateral work may not feel mandated to pursue co-operation that touches on what are seen as areas of high politics and may struggle to reach decision-makers higher up on the ladder of authority. One US working group interviewee noted that although Russia now consistently sends a scientific expert as a representative, that expert seems to struggle to pass relevant information up to the *political* level where permission could be gained for particular activities.

The 2007 Oil and Gas Assessment, which surveyed existing and best practices for High Arctic petroleum extraction and initially enjoyed Russian political support, exemplifies how the distinction between low and high politics can become a problematic matter of definition. Russian inability to deliver promised data for this assessment delayed the project for a year (its release had been scheduled for October 2006). While a Russian interviewee described the delay as caused by the difficulty of obtaining information from the private sector (oil and gas companies), other interviewees suggested that this information was considered secret, in that it related to the economy. One Norwegian interviewee noted that, on the whole, environmental problems in Russia are now treated more strategically and are notably less open for cross-border co-operation than during the 1990s, which may have also influenced the spirit and practice of such an assessment exercise. Thus, the dichotomy between low and high politics, in which the 'low politics' level is seen as encompassing only the most basic and technical of projects, clearly poses a challenge to Arctic Council co-operation.

Although the final point to be made here is difficult to pin down, differences in the culture of political co-operation remain worth exploring. I would argue that in Russia's multilateral engagement there is a tendency towards initiating and sustaining co-operation via treaties and strategic documents rather than through ongoing activity in the form of smaller, practical projects. The Arctic Council minutes report several instances where Russian actors pointed to a need to fill 'legislative gaps and problems' at both the international and national level to underpin the various initiatives being undertaken in the Arctic region.[31] No other countries involved in the Council seem to place such emphasis on legislation and documents. This suggests either that in other states the multilateralism taking place at the Arctic Council does not require such high levels of approval/documentation, or that the overarching structure for multilateralism is more firmly settled. It also indicates that there may be a specifically Russian approach to tackling co-operation within the Arctic Council when such co-operation touches on the potentially 'high political'.

This tendency to introduce new concepts and documents is evident in two examples from the Arctic Council minutes. An ongoing interest of Russian representatives, at the behest of the EMERCOM, had been building 'international co-operation in the field of prevention and elimination of emergency situations in the Arctic'. This proposal entailed establishing a network of international base points through an agreement amongst Arctic states.[32] By 2004, the initiative became known as 'Arctic Rescue'. In April 2006, Russia organized a special workshop on environmental safety, for discussions of the 'Arctic Rescue' concept. In the end, however, participants came to the conclusion that existing treaties and conventions already provide an adequate frame for the work of Emergency Prevention, Preparedness and Response working group and that instead the partners should continue to develop co-operation and exchange of experience in relationship to emergency response in the Arctic.[33] A US interviewee stated that what the Russians were proposing would entail a treaty process, something which other countries were reluctant to go through.

A second example of the tendency to underpin co-operation with strategic documents comes from the Arctic Contaminants Action Programme working group (ACAP). ACAP has faced various challenges within Russia due to its implementation-oriented mandate of remediation of sources of Arctic pollution, many of which are in northern Russia. As a way forward, Russian actors involved in the working group have been developing an integrated hazardous waste management strategy, including terms of reference and proposals as to pilot projects in the region. Getting it all down on paper with the references clearly established in one document was seen as an essential step for moving ahead.

Conclusion

Russia's engagement in the Arctic Council, as outlined above, has played out against the background of an increasingly 'geopoliticized' North and a more assertive foreign policy stance on the part of Moscow. However, the extent to which these trends are shaping Russian multilateral involvement in the Arctic Council as such is debatable, and the relative consistency of this involvement suggests that some of the key characteristics to emerge are signs of institutionalized practices and attitudes. Outside the arc of increasing participation and perhaps gradually increasing financial contribution since 1999, the involvement of Russia in the Arctic Council – marked by variable agenda-setting capacity and a tendency towards low politics – has remained relatively regular over time.

Since 1996, the strategic significance assigned to the North in a number of circumpolar states has once again grown, in part because the region is argued to hold 25 per cent of the world's undiscovered petroleum reserves, and because climate change is rendering the northern 'ice-scape' less predictable in the short term and more open in the long term. Such changes in sea ice are bringing unresolved questions of sovereignty to the fore. However, against this background, the Arctic Council has changed relatively little. Most member states remain committed to a relatively limited mandate for the Arctic Council, maintaining the focus on monitoring and assessment. Russia can probably be included in this group, given that its overall vision of multilateralism remains one of co-ordination of interests and activities, primarily on the level of low politics (see Wilson Rowe and Torjesen, this volume). Nor is there any evidence from primary documents or interviews that Russia has been pushing to expand the Council's mandate, attempting to tackle circumpolar political or legal issues within it, or complicating the work of the Council in an attempt to achieve gains outside of it. That the Arctic Council strictly avoids some of the important security and legal questions arising in the North – most prominently questions of sovereignty and economic zones[34] – seems to protect it from any potential consequences of this northern 'geopoliticization'.

At the same time, with the transition from the Yeltsin to the Putin presidency there came several important changes within Russia in terms of both domestic and foreign policy. These changing policies are well-covered elsewhere in this volume: suffice it to note here that key features of this transition have included re-centralization of power from the regions to Moscow and within Moscow to the Presidential Administration, as well as a more assertive foreign policy underpinned by high energy prices. While this transition and Putin's politics have certainly resulted in the tension between the 'open' and 'closed' North as detailed with the AMEC example above, this tension has not transformed Arctic Council co-operation in a correspondingly dramatic way. Rather, this study has found only two clear signs of the impact of a shift from a Yeltsin to a Putin regime. First, the centralization of power in the presidential administration at the expense of other branches of government may have reduced the mandate of some Arctic Council representatives. Secondly, issues that previously fell comfortably within the realm of 'low politics', such as environmental co-operation, may now be assigned some strategic significance.

It has become a truism that Russia is a political system with a nearly inexhaustible propensity for political change, particularly when a change of leadership is involved. However, given the relative consistency with which the country has engaged in the Arctic Council since 1999, it seems logical to argue that a good deal of Russia's foreign policy traditions and practices may be well-established, perhaps even institutionalized, when it comes to low-profile regional co-operation. This is in part because international co-operation – complex and cross-cutting – is not and cannot be completely centralized. Many ministries, governmental bodies and, importantly, individual civil servants within these bodies represent Russia in various different forums and may even play the decisive role in shaping lower-profile multilateral co-operation. The broad network of Russian actors engaged in the Arctic Council illustrates this well. While high-profile multilateral settings – such as the UN, the G8 or the OSCE – experience significant changes due to changing presidential regimes in Russia, this study of the Arctic Council would indicate that overarching changes in Moscow's foreign policy do not have automatic repercussions on regional co-operation.

10 Russia, the CIS and the EEC
Finally getting it right?

Stina Torjesen

Introduction

Russia's multilateralism in the 'near abroad' is not the same as in the far abroad. This is to a large extent structurally determined. On the global arena, Russia is but one of many larger states, whereas in the Eurasian setting it is massively superior to the other post-Soviet states in terms of territory, military power and economic strength. Nevertheless, Russia after 1991 did not succeeded in building a viable multilateral structure to entrench and institutionalize this predominance. The conventional verdict on multilateralism in the near abroad was that Russia was 'getting it wrong'.[1]

This chapter argues that Russian-led multilateralism in the post-Soviet area is becoming increasingly substantial, although there is still a gap between the ambitious rhetoric of co-operation and actual state of multilateral interactions in the post-Soviet space. The importance of formal and informal bilateral ties between Russia and the former Soviet states also continues to be considerable and still far outweighs multilateral forums. Nevertheless, as noted by Robert Legvold in Chapter 2, the international relations of the former Soviet space are increasingly defined by a consolidation and solidification of Russian-dominated multilateral structures. This may eventually yield considerable long-term advantages for Russia.

The aim of this chapter is to briefly review Russian multilateralism in the former Soviet Union, pointing out the growth of revitalized and more substantial, regional multilateral organizations today. The chapter discusses the CIS and the Eurasian Economic Community (EEC), in order to highlight the serious shortcomings as well as the recent advances of Russian-led multilateral co-operation in the near abroad.

A history of failure

The establishment of the CIS was one of Russia's major multilateral initiatives for the near abroad in the 1990s. Central strategy documents from the time show that entrenching the CIS as the central multilateral structure for organizing inter-state affairs in the near abroad was touted as a top policy priority.[2] The first draft Military Doctrine of 1992 embodied the assumption that the CIS would become a cohesive military mechanism, while a main goal of the 1993 Foreign Policy Concept was to create a belt of security and good neighbourliness around Russia's borders through multilateral co-operation.[3] In the National Security Concept of 2000, the weakening of the integration process in the CIS was defined as a threat. The Foreign Policy Concept of 28 June 2000 gave top priority to the CIS area and associated multilateral structures. Like the earlier concepts, it sought to grapple with the loss of great-power status, looking for ways in which Russia could continue as a central player in world affairs.

Russia may have proclaimed the vital importance of turning the CIS into a viable structure, but all the same, the organization failed in fulfilling the tasks it had set for itself in the early 1990s. The responsibilities the CIS had taken on included the creation of a common economic space, a common market, co-ordinated customs policies, co-operation in the environmental protection, developing communication and transport systems and combating organized crime.[4] An impressive organizational machinery was established.[5] This structure was, nevertheless, unable to ensure effective implementation of signed CIS agreements – fewer than one-tenth of these were implemented.

Under Putin, the dismal CIS track-record was finally acknowledged officially. From 2001 onwards the Russian leadership further elevated the importance of working through bilateral relations in the near abroad, as well as strengthening multilateral co-operation with states that were ready for it.[6] In 2005, President Putin gave a sombre analysis of the CIS and its failure, while also indicating the continued, albeit moderate, relevance of the organization:

> The disappointment with the CIS is due to excessive expectations. If anyone expected the CIS to achieve any particular objectives in the fields of economic, political or military co-operation, etc. naturally this was not accomplished because it could not have been. Declared objectives were one thing, but in reality the CIS was created to make the disintegration of the Union as civilised as possible…The CIS was never supposed to achieve major economic tasks or specific objectives in the field of economic integration. It is a very useful club for mutual exchange of information and for clarification of general, political, humanitarian and administrative issues.'[7]

In what seems to be a *post hoc* justification of failure ('declared objectives were one thing') Putin relegated the CIS to a 'club' that was useful for 'clarification', but not charged with 'achieving any particular objective'. The failure of the CIS to materialize into an effective and relevant structure has been debated extensively.[8] Various challenges beyond Russia's control worked to undermine meaningful multilateral co-operation through the CIS;[9] but aside from external aspects, might part of the reason for the CIS failure be limited capacity on the part of the lead state to develop and sustain a complex regional architecture for multilateral co-operation?

Key features of Russia's politics in the 1990s constrained its multilateral policies in the near abroad. First, regional polices were not fully co-ordinated. The presidential administration, the foreign ministry, the defence ministry and large state companies, such as Gazprom, at times enacted contradictory policies that, together, came to constitute Moscow's foreign policy. This lack of co-ordination or joint strategizing undermined Russia's abilities to ensure consolidation of the CIS as the central arena for multilateral co-operation. Second, a main difficulty riddling the CIS lay in the low rates of implementation for agreements signed. Rather than serving as a key promoter in ensuring implementation, Russia was among the worst offenders when it came to putting policy into practice. Agreements signed by the CIS heads of state would often face difficulties when sent to the Russian State Duma, where deputies refused or postponed ratifying many agreements. Third and related to this, those agreements that were ratified by Russia and other parliaments still encountered problems of implementation due to the limited financial and organizational resources available in Russia and other CIS member states. Fourth, Russia seldom displayed diplomatic skills in carefully crafting consensus or creating win–win solutions to pressing inter-state issues. This precluded the CIS from developing into an arena where complex multilateral bargains could be easily and regularly forged. Fifth and finally, even if Russia as the largest state carried the main burden of financing CIS institutions, Russia did not in the 1990s have the financial power to channel substantial sums through the CIS structures in order to strengthen the allegiance and interest in the organization for other member states.

Towards more effective multilateralism in the near abroad?

The introductory chapter of this volume signalled that under the Putin presidency Russia's engagement in the near abroad has become both more goal-oriented and pragmatic. Cooper, in a subsequent chapter, highlights how Russia has been striving to introduce market principles in its relations with the former Soviet states. Other features include pragmatically allowing for multi-speed integration and focusing on smaller clusters of states for which dense co-operation mechanisms are created. The development of the EEC, with a more moderate organizational yet also more ambitious agenda than the CIS, offers significant insights into these aspects. With the difficulties facing the Unified Economic Space (UES) initiative and hitches in Russian-Belarusian integration as backdrop, the Russian leadership has put considerable emphasis on the EEC. Moreover, alongside the CSTO, the EEC is one of the central multilateral frameworks in the region. These factors warrant the special focus on the EEC in this chapter.

As early as in 1995, Belarus, Kazakhstan, Kyrgyzstan and Russia committed themselves to creating a customs union aimed at deepening economic integration. Tajikistan joined in 1999. The initiative led to the formulation of policy aims and strategies for free trade, as well as pledges to construct common external trade barriers.[10] This prompted member countries to abolish formal import tariffs on goods from other member countries – a key achievement.[11] This ambition was reiterated later with the 'Agreement on observance of principles of free transit'.[12]

In 2000 the five countries initiated a more ambitious project, which was to become the EEC. As explained by the Deputy Secretary of EEC,

> the need for real integration, the pressure from globalization processes, concern for the stabilization of the post-Soviet economy – all this enabled a new look at the potential for integration and facilitated a search for functioning mechanisms for interaction. This is why in 2000 (...) the decision was taken to convert the customs union into (...) EEC.[13]

Kazakhstani EEC expert Gulnur Rakhmatullina has similarly stressed that the major tasks of the new organization were to 'increase the competitiveness of the economies of the EEC states, ensure their security and oppose the dangers of globalization'.[14]

The new organization merged the legal base of the Customs Union and adopted a more extensive institutional framework, with new mechanisms for decision-making. Most decisions required support from only 2/3 of all votes; and the proportion of votes was distributed as follows: Russia 40 per cent, Belarus and Kazakhstan 20 per cent each, Kyrgyzstan and Tajikistan 10 per cent each. The new organization also allowed for multi-speed integration processes: even if not all member countries were able to undertake the required domestic policy changes at the same time, integration would still move forward among those that had completed the necessary procedures. The newly formed EEC may have had a less elaborate organizational machinery than the CIS, but, notably, it had a more ambitious structure, which included elements of integration and not merely multilateral co-operation. Decision-making power is weighted according to financial contribution rather than based on the one state–one vote principle of the CIS. This differential voting mechanism clearly favoured Russia, in effect enshrining its great-power dominance in the organization.

A key achievement of the EEC was the creation of a list of commodities for which the members were to agree on common external tariffs. This was closely linked up with the WTO, and the timing of Russia's push for harmonization corresponded notably with WTO membership negotiations. WTO membership would, as is discussed below, put restrictions on the kinds of common tariffs agreed on after membership. Clearly, then, Russia was in a hurry to get other member states to sign up to its tariff system before WTO entrance. Russia's efforts were, in other words, a *reaction* to challenges coming from global actors and institutions.

The EEC harmonization plan envisioned that 11,086 commodities would form part of a harmonized system. In September 2003, member states reached agreement on a Basic List covering 6178 tariff lines, for which Russia, Kazakhstan and Belarus set common tariffs. In addition, they created three other lists, including one for commodities for which tariff differences were less than 5 per cent

(4.2 per cent of the total commodities) and one for commodities for which differences in tariff rates among the members were over 5 per cent (25 per cent of total).[15]

It bears stressing that whereas this has been the main achievement of the EEC to date, the key aims of the organization go far beyond merely co-ordinating external customs tariffs. In 2006 President Putin left little doubt as to the intended scope of the organization '[the EEC] envisages free movement of capital, goods and people. This is the basis of the integration process.'[16]

Problems

What can we say of the EEC's progress? Has the EEC done better than the CIS in forging tangible multilateral co-operation, or even integration, among its member states? Legvold in Chapter 2 gave a mixed assessment of the EEC's prospects for becoming an influential and relevant institution in Eurasia. In the subsequent chapter, Cooper voices concern at the limited trade interdependencies that underpin the EEC. The relevance and importance of the organization can usefully be assessed by examining its performance on three specific issues: free trade, WTO negotiations and migration.

Free trade regime

The underlying objective and rationale for the EEC was facilitation of inter-member trade. There are signs, however, that the framework provided was not sufficiently comprehensive to constitute a true free trade regime. Kazakhstan and Russia, two of the main proponents of the EEC, devoted a large part of their bilateral relations to negotiations on a range of fairly minor bilateral trade issues. For example, in 2000 Kazakhstan's embassy in Russia reported that the two countries were working out an agreement 'On the principles of levying indirect taxes on inter-trade'.[17] In the same year, the Russian customs committee temporarily halted shipments of Kazakhstani sulphuric acid and cyanic natrium through Russian border regions to a final destination in Kazakhstan (the road network in northern Kazakhstan transits Russia). This decision led the two sides to initiate work on a separate protocol 'On the order of transfer of goods moving from Kazakhstani territory to Kazakhstani territory through Russia, and also transfer of goods from Russian territory to Russian territory through Kazakhstan'.[18]

A similar situation existed with regard to Kazakhstan–Kyrgyzstan bilateral relations. Between 1995 and 2004, accords signed by the two countries included agreements on such matters as the transit of Kyrgyzstani goods through Kazakhstan (26 March 2004);[19] the exchange of information related to breaches of the tax code (March 2001);[20] the ease of licensing procedures for cement exported from Kyrgyzstan to Kazakhstan (July 1999);[21] the determination of Value Added Tax *(NDS)* on imported goods (February 1997);[22] and the regulation of the imposition of licenses on specific goods (alcohol products) (June 1997).[23] The two also signed a transit agreement in 2004.[24] Here, the parties noted in the introductory paragraphs their wish 'to implement provisions of the Protocol on Customs Control of Goods and Means of Transport Transferred Between the Customs Bodies of the Customs Union Member States as of 17 February 2000'.[25] The agreement then listed the specific measures meant to guide the transit regime of Kyrgyzstani goods through Kazakhstani territory. A Ministry of Trade representative from Kyrgyzstan stressed in an interview that the country had pressed for such a free transit regime for several years, but that it was only during bilateral trade negotiations with Kyrgyzstan on Kazakhstan's WTO entry that Kazakhstan had agreed.[26]

External customs barriers and WTO negotiations

Russia initially proposed that all EEC members except Kyrgyzstan should negotiate jointly and enter as a unified bloc, a suggestion that would probably have improved co-ordination but also enabled Russia to better entrench its position as regional leader and ensure that its national interests were defended in negotiations – both typical of Russia's 'great-power' and 'instrumental' multilateral approach noted in the introduction to this book.[27]

The goal of joint negotiations proved too difficult, however. The countries opted to negotiate individually, but to share information with other EEC members on the status of their negotiations. This created a sequencing dilemma: either the EEC members would first have to raise their common external tariffs to EEC levels and then apply for WTO membership, or first apply for WTO membership and then deal with the challenge of creating common external tariffs that could be in line with their individual obligations towards the WTO. At the EEC summits in 2003 and 2004, members voiced support for the former approach, but in practice both Kazakhstan and Tajikistan followed the latter strategy.[28]

Above it was mentioned that Belarus and Kazakhstan established tariff levels similar to those of Russia on most import items. Russia generally had higher tariffs than the other members. In the case of Kyrgyzstan, which joined the WTO in 1998, this was soon identified as a problem: should EEC fully implement the agreements on common external customs barriers, then Kyrgyzstan would be unable to move to meet those levels if they proved higher than the ones set through its WTO membership.[29] The WTO is compatible with regional trade organizations and, provided certain criteria are met, it supports the emergence of new regional organizations. In this way, it should in principle be possible for the WTO and the EEC to function in parallel. Article XXIV of the General Agreement on Tariffs and Trade (GATT) permits regional free trade organizations on the following conditions: external trade barriers after integration into the regional organization do not rise on average (point 5); all tariffs and other regulations of commerce are removed on intra-regional exchanges (point 8); and the WTO is notified. For assessing Eurasian trade, the crucial WTO parameter is the first criterion: trade barriers after integration must not increase.

In 2005 the International Monetary Fund reported that Tajikistan had increased its average tariff level from 5 to 7.7 per cent. The national authorities had justified this move, according to the IMF, with reference to both 'the need to harmonise Tajikistan's tariff with the [EEC] in accordance with the commitments undertaken under the Agreement on Establishment of the Customs Union of February 17, 2000' and 'the intention to preserve some leverage on tariff reduction in the upcoming negotiations on WTO accession'.[30] In fact, these two aims were incompatible. Tajikistan needed to raise its tariff levels further if it wanted to harmonize fully with EEC standards and be part of a future customs union, but in the WTO negotiations, it was likely to face pressure to reduce its tariff levels further.

Would Tajikistan, Kyrgyzstan and Kazakhstan accept higher import tariffs in sectors where Russia, and not themselves, needed to protect domestic producers, thereby enabling a tangible customs union to materialize? Or would they continue to keep a high proportion of their external tariffs lower, in accordance with WTO commitments? WTO negotiations continued into 2007, but by autumn no firm entry date for Russia, Kazakhstan or Tajikistan had yet been set. Sequencing of WTO entry by the EEC states and the establishment of a customs union has remained a difficult issue. Russian Minister of Economic Development and Trade German Gref noted on 5 April 2006 that the customs union of the EEC would be created after Russia and Kazakhstan joined the WTO: 'First Russia and Kazakhstan will join WTO and then we will create a customs union'.[31]

The muddled trade polices in relation to EEC and the WTO revealed two important shortcomings on the part of Russia. It had attempted to manage jointly the WTO entry of several former Soviet states. This proved to be a process beyond its control, and WTO negotiations were left to each individual state. Moreover, by the time Tajikistan and Kazakhstan embarked on serious WTO negotiations, Moscow had not managed to secure a full and final commitment from all EEC states to the type of external tariffs it was seeking. This failure placed EEC tariff co-operation in potential jeopardy, making its future contingent on the outcomes of the various individual WTO negotiation rounds.

Migration

The case of migration offers a further illustration of the EEC's limits. Above it was noted that President Putin saw the 'free movement of people' as a fundamental objective of the organization. Specific initiatives in the sphere of migration were slow to develop. An EEC representative explained that the difficulties with developing viable and common measures in the sphere of migration were linked to the divergence of interests between the receiving countries, namely Russia and Kazakhstan, and the sending countries, Kyrgyzstan and Tajikistan.[32] Moreover, Russia acted unilaterally and bilaterally on migration issues. It brought migration regulations into the 2004/05 negotiations with Tajikistan over agreement on a Russian military base in the country. Russia also adopted a migration law that entered into force 1 April 2007, imposing new restrictions and more cumbersome procedures for labour migrants in Central Asia. This represented a *de facto* diversion from a potential path towards free movement of people in the EEC space.

Assessment

The EEC has certainly given the *appearance* of having a more effective, co-ordinated and goal-oriented approach to inter-state challenges than did the CIS. Nevertheless, the difficulties involved in translating declared intentions of co-operation into action have riddled the EEC as they had the CIS, albeit on a smaller scale. The presence of a multitude of agreements and initiatives on a range of highly specific trade issues between member states indicates that neither the Customs Union nor the EEC has been able to provide an overall and comprehensive framework for enabling free trade.

The decision taken by Kazakhstan and Belarus to co-ordinate most their external customs barriers prior to the former's WTO negotiations marked a significant step forward: two EEC members altered and proactively aligned key national policies (customs barriers) in order to lay the grounds for common external customs policies. Importantly, however, not *all* tariffs were aligned. This introduced considerable uncertainty and could potentially put a future full-scale customs union in jeopardy. A future customs union will need to incorporate the tariffs set through Kazakhstan's WTO negotiations.

In the sphere of migration, old practices of rhetoric over substance have continued, much in keeping with the pattern set in the CIS structure. While President Putin envisaged free movement of people, his government threatened Tajikistan with restrictions on labour migration to Russia and initiated its own migration legislation that ran counter to the long-term aim of 'free movement'. As before, Russia declared its intention to create and support multilateral mechanisms, but at the domestic level it enacted policies that meant quite the opposite.

Thus, several of the problems that plagued the CIS have continued to riddle the EEC. Implementation has been challenged by a variety of domestic policies by the member states and there remains a significant discrepancy between proclaimed intentions of co-operation and actual practice. On the other hand, it can be argued that Russia has performed better in the case of EEC as a lead state seeking to create viable institutions than it had with the CIS.

Russian foreign policy in relation to enhancing the EEC has been more coherent than in the CIS context, and there has no longer been the danger of EEC decisions later becoming stalled at the ratification process by the Russian State Duma. This reflects both how foreign policy making has been more consolidated under Putin than it was under Yeltsin, and the lack of Duma opposition due to the strengthening of the executive vertical in Russia. The making of foreign policy may have become less democratic, but Russia has performed better as an actor in multilateralism.

The partial success in relation to common external customs barriers indicates that Russia has been better able to craft consensus regionally. Moreover, thanks not least to the rise in oil revenues, Russia has been in a better position to underwrite EEC initiatives financially.[33] This demonstrates an increase, albeit moderate, in capacity: Russia has become more able to design and sustain international institutions.

Advantageous multilateral reconfigurations: Uzbekistan–Russia relations

While the EEC is still experiencing some difficulties in realizing its key objectives, like creating a fully functional free trade zone, the organization seems nevertheless increasingly able to deliver broader and more long-term advantages, and to shape outcomes in Russia's favour. This is illustrated well by Russia–Uzbekistan relations, and regional realignments and multilateral reconfigurations in Central Asia during the period 2004 to 2007.

Relations between the once-close allies Uzbekistan and the USA had become strained after the USA began to realize that Uzbekistan was failing to implement the domestic reforms it had pledged under the strategic partnership agreement of 2002.[34] Uzbekistan's leadership was also seriously concerned by the political changes in Georgia and Ukraine, and observed a causal link between significant US assistance to civil society and subsequent 'revolutions'.

Following the upheaval in Andijan in spring 2005, in July 2005 Uzbekistan demanded that the US withdraw the troops stationed in the country.[35] Uzbekistan also supported a statement issued jointly by the SCO members in Astana on 6 July that Washington set a deadline for removing troops from Central Asia.[36] In parallel Uzbekistan stepped up its contact with Russia. Uzbekistan then joined EEC on 25 January and the CSTO on 17 August 2006,[37] It also signed several large-scale agreements with Gazprom on 20 January 2006.[38] Kyrgyzstan, unlike Georgia and Ukraine, did not alter its foreign-policy course after changes in the political leadership after the 'tulip revolution', but opted to maintain close relations with Russia and Kazakhstan.

The changing configurations in regional inter-state relations resulted in some remarkable alterations in the landscape of multilateral institutions. Russia entered the Central Asian Co-operation Organization (CACO) as an observer in 1996 and then as a full-fledged member at the 29 May 2005 CACO meeting in Astana.[39] Uzbekistan joined the EEC in January 2006. This change meant that (save for the additional presence of Belarus in the EEC) CACO and the EEC overlapped in terms of membership. At the CACO summit in St. Petersburg 7 October 2005, the member countries surprisingly declared that TAS would merge with the EEC – thereby abolishing the entire CACO framework overnight.[40] The announcement was made at a joint news conference to which all the four Central Asian leaders arrived in the same vehicle – driven by President Putin.

Uzbekistan shifted from being fiercely critical of the EEC to posing as a strong supporter. Russia welcomed this shift, and praised Uzbekistan's engagement and commitment to Russian-favoured multilateral frameworks for the region. Nevertheless, it is important to stress that any deep commitment to the EEC agenda of free movement of goods, capital and people is highly unlikely under the Karimov regime. Uzbekistan's economic tradition of heavy state interference in the key economic sectors and anti-free-trade policies do not resonate well with the goals that Putin has proclaimed for the EEC. Moscow's enthusiasm for Uzbekistan's membership is primarily based on the fact that Uzbek leadership has thereby signalled a pro-Russian stance, rather than any hopes that the actual activities of the EEC will be invigorated through Uzbekistani membership.

Uzbekistan is also one of the states which have started to champion the idea of merging the CSTO and EEC into one solid structure in which security and economic issues could be tackled together.[41] The bolstered multilateral set-up was also strengthened by the formation of a Russian-Kazakhstani Eurasian Development Bank intended to invest in major projects in EEC membership countries. In parallel with developments in the EEC, as discussed in chapter 12, the functioning and scope of the SCO increased considerably after 2004. Indeed, SCO Secretary General Zhang Deguang noted in 2006 that the preceding five years had been a 'sowing season' and that the next five years would be a 'harvest season'.[42]

Prospects

In sum, nowadays Russia seems to be getting it more right than wrong with regard to multilateralism in its near abroad. The multilateral landscape in parts of Eurasia has consolidated substantially. By merging the EEC and CACO, Russia managed to eliminate specifically Central Asian organizations. More importantly, by ensuring that Uzbekistan became a member of the CSTO and the EEC, considerable coherence was brought upon the Eurasian region, improving the EEC's prospects of becoming a more important platform for Eurasian co-operation and co-ordination. Uzbekistan's balancing behaviours with foreign powers against Russia in the region had represented a main strategic challenge for Moscow in the near abroad. Now Uzbekistan has become locked into the EEC and CSTO structures. Moreover, there has been increasing co-ordination and positive interplay between the SCO and EEC and the SCO and CSTO. With SCO co-operation forming a vital part of Uzbekistani economic strategies, Russia's grip on Uzbekistan has become further strengthened.

This consolidation of the multilateral architecture is likely to provide Russia with considerable long-term advantages. The new multilateral set-up with a consolidated EEC working in close co-ordination with the SCO offers both Russia and China favourable inroads into the Eurasian region. Through 'great-power multilateralism', it enables them not only to back up their bilateral ventures in the area, but also co-ordinate their efforts to keep other great powers out of the region.

11 Russia's trade relations within the Commonwealth of Independent States

Julian Cooper

Introduction

It is now over fifteen years since the USSR collapsed and Russia and the other fourteen republics became independent countries. For as many years, the Russian Federation and the non-Baltic successor countries have been members of the Commonwealth of Independent States (CIS), within which, over time, various trading communities have been formed or are in process of formation. Since the summer of 1993 Russia has been attempting to join the World Trade Organization (WTO). At the time of writing, early 2007, the goal is at last in sight with a genuine possibility of accession in the first half of 2008 – one of the most protracted accessions in the organization's history. President Putin's second term of office has seen a turn to more market-based economic relations with CIS neighbours, leading to the development of new tensions and raising questions about the future development of trading relations in the ex-Soviet economic space. Russia is by far the strongest economic power within the CIS, but formally it is a commonwealth of equals. Do Russia's relations with its partners accord with the principles of multilateralism, or are these relations governed by other rules, perhaps shaped to some extent by the Soviet past?

The chapter opens with a brief consideration of overall trends in Russia's foreign trade and the significance within it of trade with other CIS member countries. The trends identified are such that the significance of the CIS for Russia is increasingly called into question. The chapter then explores Russia's protracted process of accession to the WTO, leading to a review of CIS trading relations. This includes examination of the evolution of the Eurasian Economic Community (EEC), the Union of Russia and Belarus, and prospects for the creation of a new trading community, the Unified Economic Space (UES). The role of energy within these relations is then considered, together with some future challenges. Key characteristics of Russia's multilateral engagement in the CIS illustrated in the chapter include Moscow's newer focus on market-based economic relations – a type of competitive regional multilateralism in which expansion of the EU and the WTO provide an impetus for invigorated attempts to establish free trade arrangements in the region, and a continued reliance upon bilateral relations, even within a multilateral framework. The chapter concludes with some reflections on the extent to which Russia's economic relations with CIS partners can be considered to represent multilateral engagement.

Russia's foreign trade

In order to establish the context of Russia's trade relations within the CIS it is helpful to consider the evolution of the country's foreign trade in general. Do the CIS trade partners account for a significant share of this trade, and are there trends which may influence the extent to which maintaining co-operative multilateral relations within the CIS figures as a policy priority for Moscow?

In recent years the volume of Russia's foreign trade has expanded to a substantial degree. Exports have grown rapidly, but have been focused to an increasing extent on hydrocarbons and other minerals (see Figure 11.1).

Between 1999 and 2005 the growth of exports was fuelled by the rising price of oil (Figure 11.2).

Imports at first grew at a more moderate pace, but gradually their rate of growth began to outstrip that of exports, with a diminishing trade balance now in prospect. The structure of Russian merchandise trade is shown in Table 11.1, which indicates the rising share of mineral products (especially hydrocarbons) in total exports and the declining share of machinery and other manufactured goods. In the structure of imports, we see that machinery, equipment and other manufactured goods predominate, with a declining share of food and agricultural products.

The structure of Russia's foreign trade cannot be divorced from the competitiveness of the country's industry. Detailed analysis undertaken by the author of Russia's 2004 exports in terms of revealed comparative advantage (RCA) shows that the most competitive products are minerals, including hydrocarbons, and other natural resources, often with a low level of processing (see Table 11.2).

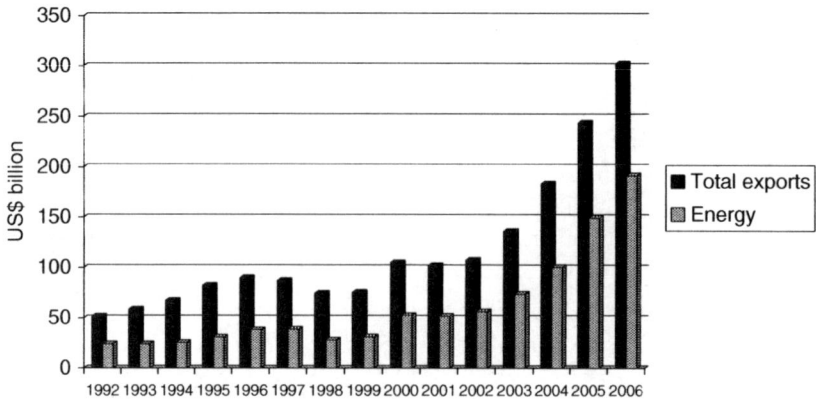

Figure 11.1 Volume of Russian exports, 1992–2006, total and fuel-energy (US$ billion).

Source: Central Bank of Russia data (http//www.cbr.ru/statistics).

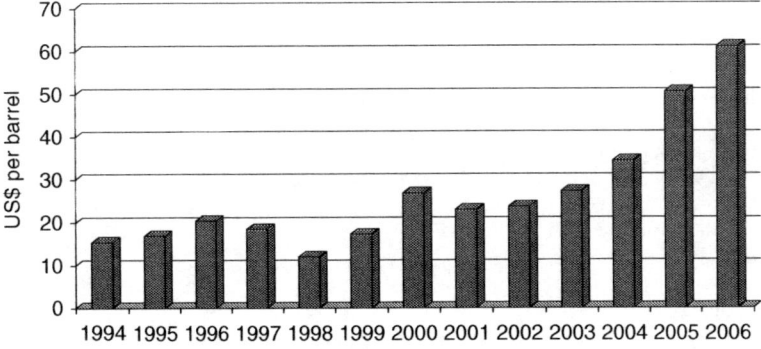

Figure 11.2 Annual average price of oil (Urals) (US$ per barrel).

Source: Ministry of Economic Development and Trade, various monitoring reports on economy (http://www.economy.gov.ru).

Table 11.1 Structure of Russian foreign trade, 1995–2005 (total exports and imports, %)

	Exports			Imports		
	1995	*2000*	*2005*	*1995*	*2000*	*2005*
Food, agricultural goods	1.8	1.6	1.9	28.1	21.8	17.7
Mineral products[a]	42.5	53.8	64.6	6.4	6.3	3.1
Chemicals, rubber	10.0	7.2	5.9	10.9	18.0	16.5
Timber, pulp, paper	5.6	4.3	3.4	2.4	3.8	3.3
Metals, gem stones	26.7	21.7	17.0	8.5	8.3	7.7
Machinery, equipment	10.2	8.8	5.6	33.6	31.4	44.0
Textiles, footwear, leather	1.9	1.1	0.5	6.0	6.3	4.0
Other	1.3	1.5	1.1	4.1	4.1	3.7
Total	100.0	100.0	100.0	100.0	100.0	100.0

Source: 1995, 2000: Goskomstat RF, *Statisticheskii ezhegodnik 2005*, sections 23.10–23.15 2005: http://www.gks.ru, accessed 20 January 2007.

[a] Including crude oil and natural gas.

The largest RCA was found to be in rough timber. Among the 70 product groups found to have a positive RCA, only four were end-product manufactured goods: rail freight wagons (wide gauge, for use on Soviet-built rail systems), and equipment for Soviet-built, or now being built by Russia, nuclear power stations – nuclear fuel elements, condensers and steam turbines. Published trade statistics do not permit an analysis of exports of armaments, but it is likely that Russia has positive RCA in relation to combat aircraft, helicopters and some types of naval equipment. In information technology and other civilian high and medium technology, Russian goods show only relative comparative disadvantages. Relatively poor CIS partner-countries provide Russia with markets for goods of

Table 11.2 Competitiveness of Russian exports: Top 30 product groups with greatest revealed comparative advantage (RCA), 2004

Product group	RCA	Product group	RCA
1. Coniferous wood, rough worked	18.1	17. Silicon electrical steel, flat-rolled	5.8
2. Pig iron in primary form	17.9	18. Other ferrous scrap metals	5.5
3. Nickel, Ni alloys, unwrought	16.4	19. Condensers for boilers[b]	5.3
4. Nuclear reactor fuel elements	12.8	20. Calcium phosphates (fertilizers)	5.1
5. Semi-finished iron and steel	12.0		
6. Chemical wood pulp	11.3	21. Iron and steel cold-formed rods, bars	4.9
7. Asbestos	10.6		
8. Anthracite	9.8	22. Sulphur	4.7
9. Fertilizers n.e.s.	9.4	23. Titanium, zirconium etc (unwrought)	4.6
10. Crude oil	9.3		
11. Natural gas	8.7	24. Heavy petroleum products	4.2
12. Potassium chemical fertilizers	7.7	25. Wooden railway sleepers	4.1
		26. Flat-rolled iron	4.0
13. Titanium semi-manufactures	7.1	27. Other coal, not agglomerated	4.0
14. 'Special transactions'[a]	6.7	28. Other inorganic bases, metal oxides	3.9
15. Nitrogenous chemical fertilizers	6.6		
		29. Synthetic rubber	3.7
16. Aluminium and Al alloys	6.4	30. Carbon	3.4

Source: J. Cooper, 'Can Russia compete in the global economy?' *Eurasian Geography and Economics,* vol. 47, 2006, 410–11.

[a] Includes gold, silver, gem stones, uranium, ammunition and, probably, some types of armaments.

[b] Mainly for nuclear power stations under construction.

somewhat backward technology, goods that would be very difficult to sell to more demanding customers. The fact that such goods can still find export markets to some extent limits the competitive pressure on Russian manufacturing industry to modernize production.

In terms of the geography of Russia's foreign trade, a significant trend has been the declining share of ex-Soviet countries now members of the Commonwealth of Independent States (CIS). The share of imports from CIS countries has fallen to a greater extent than the share of exports to the same countries, reflecting above all the dependence of many of them on Russian oil and natural gas. The overall trends are shown in Table 11.3, which also shows the shares of the two principal CIS trading communities, the Eurasian Economic Community (EEC) and the embryo Unified Economic Space (UES), which, if formed, will encompass the four largest ex-Soviet economies.

Another significant feature of Russia's foreign trade since the mid-1990s has been the steady build-up of trade with China, in particular the rapid growth of imports. It is generally acknowledged that statistics of the Federal Customs Service fail to capture informal cross-border trading with China, so the data shown in Table 11.4 illustrate the overall trends but understate the extent of the increased Chinese import share.[1] In terms of the scale of imports, China is now a more

Table 11.3 Russia's trade with CIS member countries, 1995–2006 (total exports and imports, %)

	1995	2000	2001	2002	2003	2004	2005	2006
Exports	18.5	13.4	14.6	14.7	15.3	16.2	13.5	14.0
– incl. EEC	7.4	7.8	8.2	8.0	8.4	9.0	7.2	7.6[a]
UES	16.2	12.5	13.5	13.3	13.8	14.7	12.0	12.3
Imports	29.1	34.2	26.7	22.1	22.9	23.4	19.2	16.2
– incl. EEC	10.9	18.3	14.8	13.2	13.1	13.4	9.3	8.0[a]
UES	24.6	28.2	23.5	19.8	21.4	21.7	16.9	14.5

Sources: 1995–2005: calculated from: http://www.gks.ru/free_doc/2006/b06_11/25-03.htm; 2006, calculated from http://www.customs.ru/stats/stats/popup.php?id286=239 (in both cases data of Russian Federal Customs Service).

[a] For comparability, excluding Uzbekistan, which joined the EEC in 2006. With Uzbekistan, 8.0 and 8.9 per cent respectively.
EEC: Eurasian Economic Community (Russia, Belarus, Kazakhstan, Kyrgyzstan, Tajikistan).
UES: Unified Economic Space (Russia, Belarus, Kazakhstan, Ukraine).

Table 11.4 Trade with China, 1995–2006 (total exports and imports, %)

	1995	2000	2001	2002	2003	2004	2005	2006
Exports	4.3	5.1	5.6	6.4	6.3	5.6	5.4	5.2
Imports	2.0	2.8	3.9	5.2	5.7	6.3	7.4	9.4

Source: as Table 11.1.

significant trade partner than the EEC. These overall trends in Russia's foreign trade suggest that the importance of the CIS is diminishing and thus the economic grounds for maintaining good relations with ex-Soviet partners may now be less compelling than in the 1990s.

CIS foreign trade

The share of CIS member countries in world trade is extremely modest, especially if Russia is excluded, although with higher energy prices there was a slight increase after the year 2000. Without Russia, the CIS accounts for less than 1 per cent of world trade (Table 11.5).

For most CIS member countries, trade with other CIS economies has gradually become of diminishing importance. As a result, by 2005 only for Belarus did trade with CIS partners represent more than half the country's total trade turnover. For six of the twelve countries the share was under 40 per cent, with Russia showing the lowest level of CIS trade dependence, less than 15 per cent of turnover (Table 11.6).

Notwithstanding the decline in intra-CIS trade dependence over time, the data presented in Table 11.6 show that the CIS remains a rather 'introverted' trading

Table 11.5 Share of CIS member countries in world exports and imports, 1990–2005 (%)

	1990[a]	1993	1996	2000	2003	2005
Total CIS exports	11.9	2.4	2.3	2.3	2.6	3.3
– excluding Russia	5.8	0.8	0.7	0.7	0.8	0.9
Total CIS import	11.8	2.0	1.6	1.1	1.5	2.1
– excluding Russia	6.2	0.9	0.7	0.5	0.7	0.9

Sources: 1990–2003: Broadman, *From disintegration to reintegration*, p. 66; 2005: WTO statistical database (http://stat.wto.org).

[a] Countries later joining the CIS.

Table 11.6 CIS trade dependency, 2005 (CIS trade as percentage of total trade)

	Exports (%)	Imports (%)	Trade turnover (%)	GDP per capita (PPP$) 2005
Armenia	19.2	29.0	25.5	5060
Azerbaijan	11.3	30.5	22.5	4890
Belarus	44.2	66.7	55.7	7890
Georgia	47.9	40.1	42.1	3270
Kazakhstan	19.6	42.7	31.2	7730
Kyrgyzstan	39.7	36.8	37.5	1870
Moldova	52.3	39.5	43.5	2150
Russian Federation	9.5	18.3	14.4	10,640
Tajikistan	19.6	65.0	46.6	1260
Turkmensitan	53.9	36.8	48.4	n.d.
Ukraine	31.5	46.7	39.3	6720
Uzbekistan	46.1	48.7	47.3	2020

Calculated from IMF, Directions of Trade database, November 2006 GNI per capita (PPP$): World Bank, http://www.worldbank.org (no equivalent World Bank data available for Turkmenistan).

community; but this requires qualification: there is a close inverse correlation between the share of CIS trade and per capita GDP as measured in purchasing power parity terms: the poorer the CIS member country, the greater the trade dependence on other CIS countries.[2] The exception is Belarus, which in its trading relations behaves as if it were poorer than would be expected from the level of per capita income.

It is of some interest to examine trends over time to determine which CIS countries have been most active in diversifying their trade away from ex-Soviet partners, in particular Russia, and to which other markets they have been turning. Table 11.7 shows the shares of the CIS, Russia, the European Union and Asia in trade turnover for the years 1995, 2000 and 2005. We find a consistent pattern: in all cases, the CIS share has fallen, but to varying degrees, and in all but one case – Tajikistan – there has been a decline in the Russian share, sometimes of substantial magnitude, leaving the Russian share at under 20 per cent for the three

Table 11.7 Shares of major trading partners in total trade turnover of CIS countries, 1995–2005 (%)

		Percentage of total turnover			
		CIS	*RF*	*EU*	*Asia*
Armenia	2005	25.5	13.0	34.6	5.3
	2000	20.7	15.3	36.1	1.1
	1995	47.8	18.8	18.3	0.1
Azerbaijan	2005	22.5	8.3	40.0	6.1
	2000	15.5	9.0	53.9	1.1
	1995	44.3	18.8	17.5	0.3
Belarus	2005	55.7	48.4	32.5	4.2
	2000	65.5	62.6	24.3	3.1
	1995	66.2	50.8	26.0	1.9
Georgia	2005	42.1	16.1	25.0	2.6
	2000	35.1	16.0	25.3	1.4
	1995	46.6	17.5	15.5	0.5
Kazakhstan	2005	31.2	25.0	37.7	19.7
	2000	34.3	28.1	23.2	8.1
	1995	61.2	47.1	22.2	7.1
Kyrgyzstan	2005	37.5	19.5	5.8	40.4
	2000	47.8	18.7	24.9	10.2
	1995	71.2	25.0	9.8	11.5
Moldova	2005	43.5	18.4	31.1	3.7
	2000	42.9	26.4	32.4	1.6
	1995	64.5	39.7	15.8	0.3
Russia	2005	14.4		52.6	11.1
	2000	19.1		50.8	8.8
	1995	22.4		46.4	8.8
Tajikistan	2005	46.6	15.1	28.6	5.9
	2000	65.5	25.3	18.7	2.3
	1995	46.8	14.8	40.0	1.3
Turkmenistan	2005	48.4	3.8	15.8	3.5
	2000	46.4	29.9	18.0	1.9
	1995	51.6	5.0	23.7	4.2
Ukraine	2005	39.3	29.0	30.1	9.5
	2000	43.4	32.7	27.9	7.5
	1995	47.0	38.7	22.7	4.3
Uzbekistan	2005	47.3	26.6	18.6	22.8
	2000	45.3	21.3	27.7	12.2
	1995	53.7	29.8	26.1	8.8

Calculated from IMF, Directions of Trade database, November 2006.

Caucasian countries, plus Moldova, Tajikistan and Turkmenistan. Data for eleven months of 2006 show that Kazakhstan is about to join this group.[3] In this respect Belarus stands out as an exception: Russia still accounts for almost half its total trade turnover, although the trend is one of a gradual decline. However, Belarus' overall trade turnover data conceal a significant trend: imports from Russia remain at a high level, but Russia's share of Belarus' exports has been declining quite rapidly – from 50.6 per cent of total exports in 2000 to 35.8 per cent in 2005. For the more European CIS member countries, trade has been diverted to the European Union, but in the case of some Central Asian countries it has been diverted to Asia: this is notably the case for Kyrgyzstan, Uzbekistan and Kazakhstan, with a rapid growth of trade with China. An expansion of trade with the Middle East has been important for Turkmenistan (18.5 per cent of 2005 turnover) and to a lesser extent Kyrgyzstan.

In considering these overall trends, allowance must be made for the fact that Russia's share of the trade turnover of some CIS partners has been inflated over the past five years by exceptionally high energy prices, above all for oil. Gas prices have also been rising, but Russia has encountered difficulties in getting its CIS neighbours to pay higher tariffs – as exemplified by the conflict with Ukraine at the start of 2005 and the tense last-minute deal concluded with Belarus at the end of 2006. If oil prices were to fall back to the 2003–2004 level of some $30–40 per barrel, there would be a further decline in Russia's share of the trade of several CIS countries, and the share of the CIS in Russia's own trade turnover could quickly fall below 10 per cent. These trends raise questions as to whether the CIS, and sub-regional trade groupings within the Commonwealth, now have real significance for Russia. There is perhaps a growing asymmetry: the future of the CIS as an economic community may be of more importance to certain individual, poorer, member countries than it is to its dominant power.

Russia, CIS and the WTO

Four CIS countries – Armenia, Georgia, Kyrgyzstan and Moldova – were accepted as members of the World Trade Organization (WTO) during the years 1998 to 2003, with Kyrgyzstan as the pioneer, joining in December 1998. Next to accede will probably be Ukraine and Russia, both of which now have realistic chances of membership before the end of 2007 or early 2008. Azerbaijan and Kazakhstan have also been making steady progress; however, for Belarus, Tajikistan and Uzbekistan the accession process is likely to be more protracted. Turkmenistan is alone in not having made an application to join, although this may change under the post-Niyazov regime. The current situation is summarized in Table 11.8.

Chapter 9 of this volume briefly highlighted key dilemmas that WTO member-ship poses for Russia and its favoured trading regimes. Here we explore in greater detail some issues connected to relations within the CIS. Today Russia is by far the largest economy outside the WTO, and the country's leadership is well aware that this 'outsider' status is anomalous, given its G8 membership and the aspiration to play a more prominent role on the world stage. However, the pursuit of WTO membership and the need to adapt trading practices to its rules have not always been compatible with the pursuit of deeper economic integration within the CIS. In recent years, as discussed below, it has been WTO accession that has been granted first priority.

Table 11.8 WTO accession and CIS countries, status as of September 2007

	Applied	First WP mtg[a]	No. of WP mtgs	Most recent WP mtg	Draft WP report	Accession
Members						
Kyrgyzstan	1/96	3/97				12/98
Georgia	7/96	3/98				6/00
Moldova	11/93	6/97				7/01
Armenia	11/93	1/96				2/03
Applicants						
Azerbaijan	6/97	6/02	4	3/06	—	
Belarus	9/93	6/97	8	10/05	—	
Kazakhstan	1/96	3/97	9	11/06	5/05	
Russian Federation	6/93	7/95	30	3/06	3/02	
Tajikistan	5/01	3/04	2	4/05	—	
Ukraine	11/93	2/95	16	6/06	3/04	
Uzbekistan	12/94	7/02	3	10/05	—	
Non-applicant						
Turkmenistan						

Sources: compiled from http://www.wto.org; http://www.wto.ru; http://www.wto.kz.

[a] WP mtg: Working Party meeting.

Russia applied for membership in 1993, but the accession process proved exceptionally difficult. A major breakthrough was achieved in the autumn of 2006 when a bilateral protocol was agreed with the United States. At the time of writing, early 2007, almost all bilateral agreements have been concluded and signed, the only exceptions being Cambodia, a new WTO member which has decided to open bilateral negotiations, and Guatemala, with which an agreement has been concluded but not signed. However, the agreement with Georgia, concluded in 2004, has been opened up to new negotiations, as Georgia maintains that Russia has not implemented agreed measures concerning customs posts on the Russian borders of the breakaway regions Abkhazia and Northern Ossetia. Russia maintains that this is not an issue relevant to WTO accession negotiations. This unresolved bilateral dispute may complicate the final stage of multilateral negotiations in Geneva. According to Maksim Medvedkov, chief Russian negotiator, speaking in January 2007, up to 15 issues remained to be resolved in the final multilateral negotiations, including some problems of intellectual property rights and the administration of customs. In his view, all could be decided by mid-2007, giving a possibility of accession before the end of the year.[4] Moscow appears satisfied with the terms agreed for both goods and services, in particular with the fact that the USA, after tough opposition, finally agreed to a Russian demand that foreign banks will not be able to establish branches on Russian territory but only subsidiary companies registered locally, and that some limitations on the participation of foreign insurance companies will be retained during a transitional period. When the WTO eventually agrees to accept Russia as a member, a final hurdle will have to be cleared: accession will have to be ratified by the Federal Assembly within one month. Putin's backing of accession should ensure a successful outcome, but many deputies still have reservations about the desirability of WTO membership, so ratification cannot be taken for granted.

In the case of Ukraine, all necessary legislation has been adopted and there are confident predictions that membership can be secured by the end of 2007.[5] There has been concern in Moscow that Ukraine may join the WTO before Russia, and then insist on joining the Working Party for Russian accession, which would oblige Russia to embark on potentially difficult bilateral negotiations. However, in circumstances of somewhat improved relations from the summer of 2006, Kiev and Moscow appear to be agreed that both will gain from early accession, suggesting that Ukraine will take no action to obstruct Russia's progress. As of the end of 2006, Kazakhstan had still to complete bilateral negotiations with seven partners, including the European Union and USA. In these circumstances, accession before 2008 seems unlikely.

It is evident that Russia has not found relations with the WTO easy to handle. As noted in the introduction, in June 2007 Putin criticized 'archaic, undemocratic and inflexible' international economic institutions, citing the WTO as an example. The WTO is a multilateral agency in which all members, however small, in principle possess equal rights. At an earlier stage of the accession process, Moscow apparently expected rapid progress once agreement had been reached with the great powers, above all the USA, EU and Japan, and that other countries would then quickly resolve any outstanding issues; but Russia has since found that such countries as Costa Rica, Guatemala and Georgia can exercise their rights and create difficulties for accession. There is an additional frustration for Moscow: WTO membership has to be secured before Russia can join the OECD. This multilateral agency is viewed as prestigious and there is clearly a conviction in Moscow that Russia, as a 'great power' with a dynamic economy, now has a natural right to join, with a minimum of delay.

CIS trading arrangements

Trading arrangements within the CIS are complex and to a considerable extent non-transparent.[6] There have been agreements at the CIS level, but implementation has been uneven and not all agreements have been ratified by the parties concerned. Of the numerous bilateral agreements between pairs of member countries, many have remained on paper or have been implemented for a period and then lapsed. The lack of success in developing viable arrangements at the CIS level has prompted efforts to create more limited, but meaningful, regional trading regimes. The most significant have been the Eurasian Economic Community (EEC), the Central Asian Co-operation Organization, which has now merged with the EEC, the Union of Russia and Belarus, and the Unified Economic Space.

As early as March 1992 there was a CIS agreement on customs policy which envisaged the development of a common external tariff. However, not all member countries signed, and it was ratified by only Belarus, Tajikistan and Uzbekistan. Russia signed, but did not ratify. A September 1993 Treaty on Economic Union was signed and ratified by all members except Ukraine. In 1994 all CIS members signed an agreement on a free trade area, but Russia and Turkmenistan again failed to ratify. From the outset, the multilateral agreements of the CIS have had limited practical impact: it has been estimated that 90 per cent of all multilateral documents that create the legal basis of the CIS are ineffective.[7]

With inadequate multilateral agreements, Russia and other members have resorted to multiple bilateral agreements, many of which have remained unimplemented. Russia began to promote more limited agreements with a view to the eventual creation of a customs union, first with Belarus and Kazakhstan in 1995, followed by Kyrgyzstan in 1997 and Tajikistan in the following year. These developments laid the foundations for the EEC, which was established in October 2000. By that time, Russia had clearly decided that CIS-level agreements were unlikely to produce meaningful results. In 1999 the CIS members, except Turkmenistan, agreed a protocol amending the 1994 free trade initiative in a manner that clarified the treatment of exemptions from the free trade area. Again, Russia did not ratify.

By the time the EEC was established, three other sub-regional groupings had already been formed. In 1994 Kazakhstan, Kyrgyzstan and Uzbekistan established a Central Asian Economic Community. In 1998 this was joined by Tajikistan, and in 2002 it became the Central Asian Co-operation Organization, with Russia becoming a member two years later.[8] In 1997 Georgia, Ukraine, Azerbaijan and Moldova formed GUAM, which became GUUAM when Uzbekistan joined in April 1999. While there is a multilateral agreement to establish a free trade zone, in practice this organization has been more of a political grouping than an economic community, and from the outset has been regarded with suspicion by Russia. Uzbekistan left in May 2005. Also in 2005, after the 'Orange Revolution' in Ukraine, at a summit meeting in Kiev the organization was renamed the Organization for Democracy and Economic Development – GUAM.[9]

The third sub-regional organization, the Union State of Belarus and Russia, has its origins in a decision of 1996 to develop co-operation, with an agreement the following year to form a Union. In December 1999, presidents Boris Yeltsin of Russia and Aleksandr Lukashenka of Belarus signed an agreement on the creation of a Union State.[10] As a result of these agreements Belarus and Russia already consider themselves to be a 'single customs territory' and, as such, according to WTO rules, should join the WTO together. However, reality is different, and as a result there has been no problem for accession, Russia accepting in the negotiation process, implicitly at least, that a single customs territory does not exist. Since 1999 it has not proved possible to reach agreement on a constitution for the Union State, and relations between the two countries have come under strain. Over time it has become increasingly apparent that the two parties hold opposed views of the future Union: for Russia, it must be founded on common economic principles, which have to be established before a Union can be formed; for Belarus, the Union is above all a matter of politics, the economic dimension being regarded as secondary.

These different approaches became manifest in late 2006 and early 2007 in disputes over prices and transit of gas and oil.

One country of the CIS has shown no interest in joining sub-regional economic groupings. Turkmenistan has chosen to pursue its own path and has played little part in CIS activities. This is in line with Turkmenistan's 1995 decision to adopt a status of permanent neutrality, according to which it cannot participate in supra-state bodies. The late president, Supamurat Niyazov, very rarely participated in official CIS meetings, preferring to send a deputy of the cabinet of ministers. At the Kazan meeting of CIS leaders in August 2005, Turkmenistan made an official declaration of associate membership.[11]

As outlined in Chapter 9 and briefly reviewed here, the Eurasian Economic Community (EEC) was formed in October 2000 by Russia, Belarus, Kazakhstan, Kyrgyzstan and Tajikistan. Since May 2002, Moldova and Ukraine have had observer status, followed by Armenia in 2003; in 2006 Uzbekistan became a member. With the accession of Uzbekistan, the EEC merged with the Central Asian Co-operation Organization. This development has led to a growing convergence between the EEC and the Collective Security Treaty Organization of the CIS, the formation of which dates back to 1992, which now has a similar membership except that it includes Armenia. There has been some consideration of the possibility of Armenia becoming a full member of the EEC, but its relevance is limited to some extent by the fact that there are no common borders with the existing members. The supreme organization of the EEC is the interstate council of heads of states and governments. At the level of heads of states, decisions are taken by consensus, but in working organs of the Community by a two-thirds vote, members have voting rights weighted by the share of each country in the organization's budget.[12] There is a secretariat, with offices in Almaty and Moscow. Grigorii Rapota was appointed as general secretary of the EEC in October 2001. EEC has an inter-parliamentary assembly, with a number of deputies from the parliaments of each member country. By August 2006 the Community had signed 93 agreements, 75 of which were in operation.[13]

Until recently, the EEC has focused on establishing a regime of free trade as a preliminary to a second stage of integration, the formation of a customs union. The formation of a customs union is now regarded as a priority task, but its development cannot be divorced from an alternative, or perhaps complementary, project, the creation of a Economic Space (*edinoe ekonomicheskoe prostranstvo*) (hereafter, UES).[14] In February 2003 the presidents of Russia, Belarus, Kazakhstan and Ukraine (at the time, Leonid Kuchma) decided to create a Unified Economic Space, with the eventual goal of securing the free movement of goods, capital and labour. An agreement to proceed was formally signed at a meeting in Yalta in September, and was formally ratified by the parliaments of the four countries in April 2003. However, the four partners lacked a common understanding of what the UES would be. Some in Russia had the hope that it would oblige the members to co-ordinate the terms and schedules of WTO accession, but Gref, who has shown little public enthusiasm for the UES, has favoured entry of each country into the WTO one by one and then the pursuit of measures for further integration.[15] Ukraine, even before the 'Orange Revolution', made it quite clear that WTO entry would be pursued with determination regardless of the UES.[16] As of April 2006, Ukraine indicated willingness to sign only 11 of the 38 agreements prepared to establish the UES – those concerning the establishment of a free trade zone. According to Anatoly Kinakh, then secretary of the Ukrainian National Security and Defence Council, measures for further integration would be considered only after all UES members had become WTO members.[17] The leaders of Russia, Belarus and Kazakhstan appear to have accepted that the formation of the UES will have to be delayed.[18] This has been acknowledged by Russian economics minister German Gref, who declared, in November 2006, that the creation of the UES would only be possible after all four member countries had joined the WTO. Its creation, he emphasized, would be a lengthy process.[19] In effect, the development of the UES has been frozen.[20]

It was this realization that prompted the leaders of Russia, Kazakhstan and Belarus to focus on the EEC. At its Minsk summit in June 2006 it was decided to proceed with the formation of a customs union within the framework of the EEC, but using some of the groundwork already undertaken for the creation of the UES. Furthermore, it was agreed that the organizational structures established for the formation of the UES would be absorbed into the secretariat of the EEC.[21] The first stage will be the development of a customs union of Russia, Kazakhstan and Belarus. This decision to develop the customs union was taken at a time when Russia was failing to secure agreement with the United States on terms for WTO accession. In Chapter 9 it was noted that the Russian position, as voiced by Gref, had previously been that a customs union would be created only after Russia and Kazakhstan had joined the WTO. This condition, however, is no longer referred to, and it can be speculated that Russia may now consider an EEC customs union as an alternative option, at least in the interim, in the event that WTO accession is not secured during the next year or more.

Thus, a two-tier EEC has been emerging *de facto*. The goal was to have all legislation for the customs union drafted and agreed by early 2007, then ratified by the parliaments of the three countries so that the union can go into operation from the beginning of 2008.[22] This means in practice that Belarus and Kazakhstan will in the main accept the same binding tariffs on WTO accession as agreed by Russia. It has been claimed that as of July/August 2006 the tariffs of the three countries had been unified to 62 per cent. For Tajikistan, the corresponding figure was 80 per cent, but for Kyrgyzstan and Uzbekistan only 30 per cent.[23] It is envisaged that in time the three Central Asian members of the EEC will join the customs union as conditions permit, Tajikistan being the best prepared.

Whether this will be to the advantage of all EEC members is debatable. As Michalopoulos and Tarr have argued,[24] a customs union may be unfavourable for small CIS countries and more generally may serve to orient trade towards traditional Soviet Union partners, with costs in terms of the maintenance of traditional production structures and technologies. In their view, a major driving force for the creation of an EEC customs union has been traditional exporters of Russia, keeping alive trading relations established during Soviet times. This conclusion is also echoed by the analysis of Tumbarello, who questions the wisdom of CIS countries becoming members of a sub-regional customs union in advance of accession to the WTO.[25]

At one time it appeared that the complexity and lack of transparency of Russia's trading relations within the CIS could threaten the country's process of accession to the WTO. In principle, WTO rules allow the creation and retention of customs unions and free trade zones. However, for this, Russia should have ratified the basic agreements establishing the free trade zone (those of April 1994 and April 1999) – which it has not done – and most of the additional 60 or so agreements in this field developed by the CIS remain unimplemented. Thus trade within the CIS is conducted according to largely *ad hoc* tariff preferences, special prices and barter agreements.[26] The WTO had asked Medvedkov, the chief Russian negotiator, to provide a list of the privileges Russia provides to CIS partners, but in an interview in January 2003 he declared that this was 'technically impossible'.[27] This admission probably reflects the reality that the privileges are often of an informal character, temporary, and nowhere systematically codified. The Working Party for Russia's accession decided that there was no point in pursuing the matter further, and from about 2003 the issue of CIS trading relations ceased to figure in public discussion of Russia's accession prospects.

The energy factor and the future of the CIS

During Putin's second term of office as president there has been a change in policy towards CIS partner countries. It was the 'coloured' revolutions in Georgia and Ukraine that hardened attitudes. In March 2005 at a press conference in Erevan, President Putin, echoing a long-held view in the West, declared that the CIS was only 'a form of civilized divorce' and that it did not have any special achievements to its credit – nor would it have any. This led to a new policy of 'realism', focusing above all on energy.[28] In the words of three journalists writing in December 2006, Russia had previously, in exchange for political loyalty, granted CIS countries economic preferences, selling energy at low prices; now, 'the policy of "carrots" has exhausted itself'.[29] The new policy is one of putting trade relations on to a normal commercial basis, eliminating subsidies to partner economies, and accepting that during a transition period political relations may become strained.

Until recently the new policy has focused on gas supply. The major actors have been Gazprom, responsible for over 85 per cent of Russia's gas output and possessing monopoly rights with respect to export pipelines; the presidential administration, which appears to have consistently backed the new policy and Gazprom's actions; and the Ministry of Economic Development and Trade, clearly concerned to put the country's trade on to a commercial footing. It is apparent that Moscow is determined to oblige CIS partners to pay for gas at prices comparable to those charged European customers, with long-term supply agreements.[30] At the same time Gazprom has been seeking a large measure of control over pipelines, in particular those vital to the transit of gas to Europe. The position of Moscow was made clear in the dispute with Ukraine in late 2005/early 2006: Russia is intent on freeing as much gas as possible for sale to Europe. If its CIS partners are not willing, or able, to pay European prices, then Moscow will seek to secure alternative sources of supply, at least during a transition period. So, in the case of Ukraine, the major supplier of gas is now Turkmenistan, which has been willing to accept lower prices than Gazprom is prepared to. However, this solution may prove to not very stable, as Turkmenistan has been seeking alternative markets and pipeline routes, to Iran, China and other countries, bypassing the Russian controlled pipeline system. Moscow's leverage is limited, partly because there is now only a small Russian community in Turkmenistan and no significant Russia-oriented political forces. If the current plans are fulfilled, Ashgabad will cease to be dependent on access to Gazprom controlled pipelines.

Tensions over energy came to a head during late 2006 and early 2007 in the dispute with Belarus over the terms of supply of both gas and oil. This is not the place to analyse in detail this clash between the two members of the 'Union State': suffice it to say that this indicated a new resolve in Moscow to enforce different rules of the game in economic relations with the 'Union' partner. The Russian side did not manage to secure all that it was demanding, having to accept compromises in the interests of achieving a solution that Minsk would accept, but the overall outcome was a significant reduction in the subsidy provided to the Belarus economy. This episode brought into the open several divisions in the Russian political establishment. To the fore in applying pressure for higher gas prices and duties on oil exports to, and from, Belarus were the Ministry of Economic Development and Trade, under German Gref, Gazprom, and another company close to the Kremlin, Transneft; but their pressure on Belarus met opposition. There is no doubt that military and security interests were extremely concerned that the close security relationship with Belarus was being threatened, and in left-leaning and nationalist political circles there was clearly expressed support for Lukashenka.[31] Beyond these circles, there was openly voiced concern that Russia's longer-term national interests had been sacrificed to the short-term commercial interests of Gazprom.[32] There is general agreement that the future of the Union State is now in doubt, although this may well not be of great concern to Gref and other economic 'liberals'.

However, it is not only Russia's pressure on Ukraine and Belarus for higher gas prices that has caused problems for intra-CIS relations. Similar demands have added to the difficulties of relations with Georgia. In the case of Azerbaijan, a demand that Gazprom be paid a price of $230 per thousand cubic metres led President Aliev, usually well-disposed to Moscow, to express the view that participation of his country in the CIS was 'without value'.[33] Disputes over gas prices are likely to continue. According to Dmitrii Medvedev, first deputy premier and chair of the board of Gazprom, the aim is to go over to 'market' prices for gas with all CIS members by 2008.[34] It remains to be seen how much further strain will be placed on Russia's relations with its CIS partners and how far some will go in seeking alternative sources of supply.

Russia's energy interests in the CIS are not restricted to natural gas and oil. The electric power interest (in particular RAO 'UES Rossii' led by Anatolii Chubais, one-time advocate of a policy of 'liberal imperialism' in relation to CIS partners), and the nuclear industry (led by former prime minister Sergei Kirienko) both favour CIS-wide co-operation, the latter apparently seeking to restore a single nuclear industry under Russian control within the ex-Soviet space. The electricity industry has been at the fore in pursuit of an active investment policy in neighbouring countries.

For Russia, another important factor in CIS economic relations is the main-tenance of supply links relating to the production of armaments and other military hardware. Russian arms producers still depend to a quite substantial extent on inputs of materials and components from ex-Soviet partners, especially enterprises in Belarus, Ukraine, Kazakhstan and, to a lesser extent, Uzbekistan, Armenia and Moldova. These extensive supply networks date from Soviet times, as do most of the end-product weapon systems built today by Russian companies, albeit in modernized versions. Rather than create new domestic capacity to produce components and materials for these weapons, Russian defence industry producers have preferred to import from traditional suppliers, partly because in some cases no payment is involved, components being simply exchanged on a barter basis.[35] It may also be the case that the maintenance of these supply links has inclined CIS partners to procure Russian-built weapons on preferential terms within the framework of the Collective Security Treaty Organization. However, in recent years, Russia has been pursuing a policy of import substitution designed to reduce dependence on suppliers considered potentially unreliable. Since the 'Orange Revolution' this has applied in particular to Ukraine, a major supplier of engines for aircraft and helicopters, power units and other equipment for naval ships, radar systems and other electronic goods.[36]

For some time Russia has been interested in a reform of the CIS to improve its effectiveness. Little progress has been made because of failure to agree on the basic principles of reform. Two rival approaches are in play. President Nazarbaev of Kazakhstan backs the idea of multi-speed integration, permitting those member countries willing to move ahead with further economic and security integration to advance, leaving the others to follow later if they so decide. Belarus takes a contrary view. In the opinion of Lukashenka, all CIS member countries should move ahead together, without differentiation between an advance guard and laggards. In his view, CIS integration is above all a political process, with the economic dimension being secondary. Russia has clearly supported the Kazakh stance, taking the view that economic integration, focused first on those countries willing and ready to proceed, should take precedence over political integration, the later being seen as an eventual outcome of the former.[37] Given the deterioration of relations with Belarus as a result of the gas/oil conflict, it is possible that Moscow will now ignore the stance of Lukashenka and seek to gain agreement for a CIS reform on the principles advocated by Kazakhstan.

Future challenges

The only CIS countries with which Russia now enjoys reasonably smooth and co-operative economic relations are Kazakhstan, Armenia and Tajikistan, and to lesser extent Kyrgyzstan, plus, at the moment, Uzbekistan; with all the rest there are problems of varying degrees of severity. The general trend is towards more pragmatic, 'market-based' relations, with a phasing-out of subsidies and privileges. Furthermore, Russia sees the neighbouring countries as targets for investment, with growing property stakes as means of exerting influence now that the more emotional political appeals of a common Soviet past have begun to fade. Russia is becoming increasingly pragmatic and seems to care less and less whether the CIS partners are well-disposed to Moscow or not: 'normal' economic relations are replacing sentiment.

In the longer term, what value do the CIS partner countries have for Russia – apart from being elements of policies for energy and security? As noted above, the CIS now represents an increasingly modest share of Russian foreign trade. Ukraine, Moldova and Georgia have a clearly expressed European orientation. The future evolution of Belarus is now uncertain, and a turn to Europe by Lukashenka (or, more likely, his successor) cannot be ruled out. Russia has been showing growing interest in relations with China, and to this end the Shanghai Co-operation Organization (Russia, China and the Central Asian countries excluding Turkmenistan) has gained a more prominent role, partly as a bridge to China, but also as a means of trying to maintain overall strategic influence and balance in Central Asia. Thus, in time, Russia's engagement with what is left of the CIS could become merely one component of its overall Asian policy. Eurasec (EEC) could in effect become 'Rusasec'.

Notwithstanding rhetorical recognition of the independence of CIS partner countries and their right to choose their own destinies, many of the Moscow political, security and economic elite still appear to regard Russia as the dominant partner, the hegemon of the former Soviet space. In reality, economic relations within the CIS have not been conducted on the basis of the principles of multilateralism, respecting the equality of the partner countries. Instead, Moscow has sought to maintain influence and shape trade relations above all through the active pursuit of bilateral relations. Gatherings of heads of states of the CIS and the EEC have tended to endorse positions already agreed in principle through discussions with the countries that Moscow considers most significant for the pursuit of Russia's interests – Kazakhstan and Belarus and, when agreement can be reached, Ukraine.

The Kremlin's policy could be characterized as one, not of multilateralism, even in its 'great-power' form, but of extended, hegemonic bilateralism. In fact, this approach to economic relations with ex-communist neighbours is not new: it is highly reminiscent of Soviet attitudes and behaviour in relation to partners in the former Council for Mutual Economic Assistance. As such there are potential problems for Moscow, perhaps already becoming a reality. Heavy-handed actions foster resentment against Russia and serve to promote a desire for less dependent relations. The steadily falling shares of trade with Russia now apparent for almost all CIS partner countries may, at least in part, be an expression of this. Moscow's determination to enforce 'market' terms for energy supplies is likely to reinforce these processes. Looking to the future, we must ask how much longer the CIS, and sub-regional trading groups within it, will retain any meaningful existence.

12 Russia as a military great power

The uses of the CSTO and the SCO in Central Asia

*Stina Torjesen**

Introduction

Multilateral security co-operation provides an interesting starting point for assessing the multilateral dimension of Russian foreign policy. Security relations constitute an arena where Russia has performed relatively forcefully and, at times, successfully. Even if due more to Russia's nuclear arsenal and less to fighting capacity, it is Russia's military might that primarily underpins its bid for great power status. Alliances and multilateral security co-operation constitute a cornerstone of this military prowess. This chapter outlines the development of the Collective Security Treaty Organization (CSTO) and the Shanghai Co-operation Organization (SCO), from Russia's perspective. It assesses the achievements and shortcomings of these two multilateral frameworks and also offers insights into Russia's multilateral activities within these organizations.

Three major aspects underpin Russia's multilateral diplomacy in the security field in Central Asia. First, the military structures that Russia and the other Soviet successor states inherited from the Soviet Union were deployed across the entire post-Soviet space. When the Soviet Union collapsed, Russia sought, as far as possible, to keep this integrated defence system intact so as to best protect its own national security. However, since Russia was dealing with new independent states, it was forced to develop complex inter-state co-operation, in order to preserve these integrated defence structures. In this way Russia's immediate security concerns spurred Russia's regional multilateral diplomacy. Second, Moscow also identified a range of security threats in neighbouring regions, which were defined as potentially threatening to Russia itself – such as drug trafficking, Islamic terrorism and ethnic conflict. This provided an additional incentive to enhance the defence capabilities of neighbouring countries through regional multilateral co-operation.

Third, a degree of 'instrumentalism' has also featured prominently in Russia's security-related multilateralism. A key purpose of Russia's multilateral efforts

* The author would like to thank Domitilla Sagramoso for her input and guidance in writing this chapter.

seems also to have been its desire to secure the military allegiance of its neighbouring states. The aim was to create a 'security belt' around the Russian Federation and in this way, maintain Moscow's hegemonic presence on the Eurasian continent.[1] There has, at times, also been a 'reactive' aspect to Russia's to these multilateral security initiatives. The increase in multilateral efforts after 2001 also as a reaction to the engagement of other outside powers in Eurasia, primarily the US and China. As will be highlight later in this chapter, some of the activities in the region were intended to signal a Russian presence in the area as much as to provide effective solutions to the many pressing security challenges of the region.

The CSTO and the SCO were set up in the 1990s in order to address emerging regional security needs. The Collective Security Treaty (CST) was established in May 1992 shortly after the collapse of the Soviet Union, within the framework of the Commonwealth of Independent States (CIS). The initial aim was to preserve a united security space involving all the former Soviet states and to prevent, as far as possible, the total disintegration of what had been the Soviet military complex. In 2002 the bulk of the original signatory states (Armenia, Belarus, Kazakhstan, Kyrgyzstan, Russia and Tajikistan) transformed the Collective Security Treaty into the Collective Treaty Organization (CSTO).

The Shanghai Forum (later the Shanghai Co-operation Organization, or SCO) emerged in 1996 to address border disputes and reduce tensions involving China, the new countries of Central Asia and Russia. During the 1990s and early 2000s, the mandate and remit of both organizations expanded significantly to encompass newly emerging threats related primarily to terrorism and religious extremism. The SCO is a particularly relevant organisation when assessing Russia's multilateral diplomacy in view of Moscow's highly positive views of it. The SCO, and the particular kind of multilateral behaviour associated with it, was promoted by President Putin as the country's preferred model of multilateral co-operation.[2]

This chapter first gives an outline of the post-Soviet security challenges faced by the post-Soviet states in Central Asia, and then discusses the collective responses given to these challenges by Russia and the Central Asian states within the CST/O framework. The chapter then assesses the emergence of the SCO and Russia's role in the development and functioning of this organization. It concludes by highlighting how the CSTO and SCO have helped to underpin Russia's bid for great-power status in the global arena.

Post-Soviet security challenges

When the Soviet Union collapsed, the new sovereign states inherited a unified military structure, while also finding themselves compelled to fill an emerging security vacuum. This involved taking control over the existing Soviet military formations and equipment based in the area, as well as curbing the potential proliferation of weapons of mass destruction, and creating new security structures capable of addressing the new threats. The Central Asian states were faced with a whole new array of security threats related to their new socio-economic and political situation, as well as ethnic tensions, internal disturbances and violence carried out by terrorist groups, and the trafficking in drugs through porous borders. In addition, countries in Central Asia were forced to address the challenges of state- and nation-building, which implied the strengthening of national identities and state institutions, the securing of external borders, and the prevention of conflicts over disputed territories. Finally, states in Central Asia were confronted with the instabilities emanating from the civil wars in Tajikistan and neighbouring Afghanistan.

Many of the initial challenges related to the disintegration of the Soviet Union were dealt with quite successfully by Central Asian states, often in co-operation with Russia, through the CST and then the Shanghai Forum. However, some of the threats which emerged at a later stage failed to be properly addressed. In the late 1990s and early 2000s, the Central Asian states witnessed an increase in drugs trafficking, as well as an upsurge of Islamic extremism and political violence. The threat posed by radical movements ready to employ violence increased considerably in the late 1990s, partly in response to declining socio-economic conditions and the strengthening of authoritarian and repressive regimes in most Central Asian states.[3] The CST and the Shanghai Forum tried to address some of these challenges in a multilateral fashion, but failed to provide a fully adequate response.

The collective security treaty and the collective security treaty organization

The CIS was born out of the collapse of the Soviet Union to manage the transition from a unified state to a group of newly independent countries, and to preserve, as far as possible, a united economic and military space. In order to preserve the existing military-security structures, and to ensure collective action against external threats, the Collective Security Treaty (CST) was signed in May 1992 by Russia, Armenia and all the states of Central Asia, with the exception of Turkmenistan.[4] However, the preservation of a unified military structure failed to materialize, as all signatory states went ahead with setting up their own national armed forces.[5] Still, CST member states were able to prevent the random and violent appropriation of military equipment belonging to the armed forces of the defunct Soviet Union. They also managed to create an embryonic collective security structure through the establishment of various military co-ordination organs within the CST framework. They also succeeded in creating a mechanism for dialogue and communication within the CST. Moreover, the CST provided a multilateral framework or umbrella for the creation of the various national armies, all of which were expected to work in concert when addressing a common threat.[6]

In the mid-1990s, a debate ensued as to the type of organizational structure the CST military should adopt. Most Central Asian states favoured a NATO-type collective decision-making structure, whereas Russia and Uzbekistan supported the establishment of a hierarchical structure along the lines of the former Warsaw Pact model. None of these models was eventually adopted. Instead, a hybrid mechanism emerged, whereby each country had its say in the decision-making process, but Russia retained a predominant voice.[6] Moreover, as lack of agreement over the military structure of the CST persisted throughout the 1990s, the Kremlin decided to support the Central Asian states' efforts to create national armies, through a series of bilateral military co-operation agreements. It also provided assistance with border protection on a bilateral basis, and reached agreement on the presence of Russian forces in some countries of the region. All these activities, although conducted on a bilateral basis, were cloaked under a thin layer of CST multilateralism. Interestingly, at the same time most states in the region, with the exception of Tajikistan, joined NATO's Partnership for Peace programme – an issue which caused great concern in the Russian military leadership.

In the mid-1990s, the CST managed to address the various challenges related to the disintegration of the Soviet Union quite successfully. Russia played a relevant role in that respect, by assisting the Central Asian states in setting up their national armies and protecting their external borders.[6] However, the CST failed to develop into an effective collective security organization with a multilateral character, because of the existence of highly divergent views regarding the nature and objectives of the organization. It also failed to gain a supranational identity, primarily due to the inability of its member states to identify common adversaries outside the CIS area – with the exception of the Taliban. The CST also proved unable to develop a functioning mandate to address the new threats that were primarily of an internal nature. When the Tajik civil war broke out in 1992, CST member states failed to act collectively. Instead, Russia and Uzbekistan provided bilateral military assistance to the government of Tajikistan. The deployment of CIS/CST peacekeeping forces in 1993, involving contingents from Russia, Kazakhstan, Kyrgyzstan and Uzbekistan, may have indicated a willingness on the part of the member states to operate collectively within the CST framework, but the modalities of the peacekeeping operation distorted the very idea of collective action. Russian forces assumed a predominant role and often engaged in conventional military operations in support of the incumbent regime. In this way, the Russian experience and its method of peacekeeping both precluded the emergence of CIS/CST peacekeeping as a model for future military multilateral co-operation.[7]

The advance of the Taliban in Afghanistan in the mid- to late 1990s, and the potential spread of Islamic fundamentalism into Central Asia, were perceived as new significant threats to the region. Although efforts to address the Taliban advance were not conducted within the CST framework, concern over the spread of Islamic radicalism did create an incentive for growing co-operation in the sphere of security. In the summers of 1999 and 2000, the Islamic Movement of Uzbekistan (IMU) conducted a series of military incursions from its bases in Tajikistan and Afghanistan into Uzbekistan and Kyrgyzstan. The immediate response of countries in the region was un-co-ordinated and ineffective. The Uzbek military operations resulted in accidental bombings on Kyrgyz territory, which in turn led to mutual recriminations and a significant deterioration in relations between the two countries.[8] Russia failed to provide adequate military support to repulse the incursion, and Kyrgyzstan proved incapable of effectively countering the IMU attack. The various responses brought to light the shortcomings of the CST, and the inability of its member states to act in concert when facing a serious challenge. The response also indicated the complete lack of preparedness of the Central Asian militaries to effectively undertake counter-insurgency operations.

To address these shortcomings, Central Asian states, led by Russia, decided to enhance their military co-operation within the CST framework. A series of joint military exercises involving Russia, Kyrgyzstan, Kazakhstan, Tajikistan and Uzbekistan were held in 1999 and 2000, under Russian leadership (*CIS Southern Shield-99* and *CIS Southern Shield 2000*). The objective was to train military forces to fight jointly against a common terrorist threat. In October 2000, Russia, Kazakhstan, Tajikistan and Kyrgyzstan agreed to establish an anti-terrorist centre in Bishkek to exchange information and conduct joint threat assessments. The centre was headed by a Russian general from the Federal Security Services. In May 2001, agreement was also reached on the creation of a collective Rapid Reaction Force expected to address the new terrorist threats. All these developments indicated a readiness to act multilaterally, albeit under Russian leadership. As the main provider of funding, equipment and expertise, Russia assumed a dominant role.

The attacks of 11 September 2001, the war in Afghanistan and the ensuing US military presence in Central Asia gave an additional boost to regional military co-operation within the CST framework. The US presence in Central Asia created great concern among the Russian policymakers that their country might be displaced from Central Asia. These worries led to an energetic effort by Moscow to revive the CIS collective security system, under the mantra of fighting international terrorism. The enhancement of regional military co-operation also had the support of Central Asian leaders, all of whom were deeply concerned over the potential spread of radical Islam and possible emergence of violent opposition movements to their regimes. Although many Central Asian states developed close ties with NATO and the US at the time, most were still eager to enhance their ties with Russia and the CST. Thus, in May 2002, Russia, Kazakhstan, Kyrgyzstan and Tajikistan, together with Armenia and Belarus, agreed to transform the CST into the Collective Security Treaty Organization (CSTO). The objective was to have a full-fledged organization capable of addressing the new threats and challenges to the region – through a joint military command located in Moscow, a rapid reaction force based in Central Asia (originally agreed upon in May 2001) and a common air defence system. These measures entailed a significant upgrade of the CST, and also indicated the emergence of a 'reactive' form of multilateralism – directed against the American military presence in the region – especially on the part of Russia (see chapters by Legvold and Wilson Rowe and Torjesen in this volume for a further discussion of reactive multilateralism). The upgrade in CST capabilities had been spurred primarily by fears over the deteriorating security situation in Central Asia after the IMU incursions in 1999 and 2001. However, the intensity in Russia's multilateral push in Central Asia also increased after the establishment of US bases in Central Asia. Ironically this was a time when the threat posed by the IMU, the initial trigger of the Russian-led security upgrade in Central Asia, had been largely eliminated by the US-led 'Operation Enduring Freedom' in Afghanistan.

With the establishment of the CSTO the member countries also pledged to better co-ordinate their foreign, security and defence policies within the organization's framework. To this end, a political co-operation directorate was set up. A military co-operation directorate to manage military operations, and a directorate to tackle common challenges and threats were also established. In 2003, CSTO member states agreed to assign two reinforced battalions each (three in the case of Tajikistan), in permanent combat readiness, to a standing rapid-reaction force. Despite the notional equality of contributions, Russia became the dominant military and financial sponsor of the force, which was expected to operate under a Russian commander when deployed. In addition, Russia opened a new air base in Kant (Kyrgyzstan) to provide support for the CSTO forces, and agreement was reached on the establishment of a permanent military base for the Russian 201st Motor Rifle division based in Tajikistan. Various military exercises involving the collective rapid reaction forces were conducted to enhance military co-operation.[9] Efforts were also made in 2006 and 2007 to increase inter-operability between the CSTO and the SCO.

All these developments led to a significant improvement of the CSTO's institutional structures and defence capabilities. Central Asian states are showing growing participation within the organisation, but Russia remains the main driving force behind the CSTO's military enhancement. Although Moscow has proven ready to work within a multilateral framework it has retained a position of predominance within the organization. It has managed to set the agenda, drive the integration process and keep a leading position within all structures of the organization. It has also used the existing structures to become the leading security manager of the Central Asian region, and in this way, obtain recognition of the CSTO as a security actor co-equal to, or above, NATO in the Central Asia (see also Adomeit in this volume for a discussion of Russia–NATO relations).[10] However, the ability of the CSTO to work effectively when faced with serious threats is questionable, given its past history and doubtful military capabilities. Moreover, many Central Asian states, especially Kazakhstan and Kyrgyzstan, have begun to develop close ties with Western military establishments. Although Uzbekistan joined the CSTO in 2006, Turkmenistan has stayed outside the system. Finally, doubts remain as to the effectiveness of the Russian military to address counter-terrorist threats effectively, despite its apparent and relative successes in Chechnya.

The Shanghai Co-operation Organization

The SCO has its origins in the negotiations that began in 1989 between the Soviet Union and China to reduce tensions along their mutual border through the introduction of confidence-building measures and the implementation of progressive demilitarization. The aim was also to resolve existing border disputes along the extended frontier between the two countries. Starting in 1992, and following on these negotiations, regular meetings were held between Russia, China, Kazakhstan, Kyrgyzstan and Tajikistan to discuss joint disarmament proposals and the introduction of confidence-building measures along the borders. These talks also involved negotiations on the delimitation of mutual borders.

Initial meetings were held on a bilateral basis, until the first joint summit was held in Shanghai in April 1996. At this summit, an *Agreement on Confidence Building Measures in the Military Sphere in the Border Areas* was reached, and one year later, an *Agreement on the Mutual Reduction of Military Forces in Border Areas* was signed in Moscow. With these two agreements, the five states pledged to take specific steps to reduce tensions and increase trust along their border areas. Progress was also made on the delimitation of borders. By 1999, Russia and China had delimited 97 percent of their mutual boundaries. Similar agreements were reached by China and Kazakhstan in 1998, and by China and Kyrgyzstan in 1999. Agreement on the border between China and Tajikistan was reached in 2002. The Shanghai Forum thus became a successful framework where Russia, China and the Central Asian states managed to address issues of regional border security in a multilateral fashion.

In July 1998, at the Almaty summit, the remit of the Forum was expanded. The Shanghai Five agreed to discuss broader regional security questions and strengthen regional economic co-operation. Such developments reflected recognition of the need for a more coherent and collective response to both regional security threats and emerging economic challenges.[11] Concerned about the increasing threat posed by radical Islamic groups, separatist movements, and criminal organizations, the Shanghai Five agreed, at their summit in Bishkek in 1999, to set up an anti-terrorist centre in Tashkent. The objective was to ensure the exchange of data on terrorism and effective co-operation in addressing common terrorist threats.

In 2000, at the SCO summit in Dushanbe, member states agreed to transform the Shanghai Forum into a more formal regional institution. The Shanghai summit a year later marked the official transformation of the Shanghai Five into an international organization, the *Shanghai Co-operation Organization*. The goals of the organization were made clear – strengthening of mutual confidence and friendship among members; encouraging effective co-operation in the political, economic and social spheres; promoting joint efforts to maintain regional peace and security; and helping the build-up of a new democratic and just political and international order. The SCO developed a focus on trans-border as well as intra-state security, which was properly spelled out at the SCO 2001 Shanghai summit. At the meeting SCO member states proclaimed the 'Shanghai Covenant on the Suppression of Terrorism, Separatism and Religious Extremism', which clearly expressed their desire jointly to address the 'three evils' of terrorism, separatism and extremism. The SCO claimed not to be an organization directed against any other state or region, although member states pledged to both consult each other and co-ordinate their responses when addressing issues of regional and international security.

Initially, the organizational structure of the SCO remained relatively loose, and was largely built around a mechanism of regular multilateral consultations at various government levels. No serious efforts were made to develop multilateral co-operation on traditional defence issues. Although meetings of defence ministers took place on a regular basis, and China began providing security and defence assistance to Central Asian states on a bilateral basis, the organization remained focused on addressing counter-terrorism and border security issues. More recently, however, there have been efforts to develop a more effective political and military structure. SCO permanent representatives have been sent to all member states, and a secretariat has been established in Beijing to co-ordinate activities and provide technical support.[12]

Moreover, a Regional Anti-Terrorist Structure (RATS) has been set up in Tashkent to co-ordinate anti-terrorist activity and exchange relevant information.[13] Although progress towards the development of a military capability has been slow, various military training exercises have been conducted since 2002, indicating a willingness to enhance military operability and jointly address common threats. In October 2002, China and Kyrgyzstan held bilateral military counter-terrorism manoeuvres along their border zones, and in August 2003, *Co-operation 2003*, a SCO joint-command-post exercise combined with field manoeuvres, and involving several SCO states was held in several SCO states.[14] In August 2005, Russia and China conducted joint bilateral military exercises, *Peace Mission 2005,* on China's Shandong peninsula, and near Vladivostok in Russia, within the SCO framework.[15]

The economic dimension of the SCO also gained salience after a permanent secretariat was set up and this is primarily a result of Chinese insistence. Initially, China viewed the organization mainly as a mechanism for addressing common threats faced by the region, and for obtaining Central Asian support in its fight against Uighur separatism in northwestern China. Recently, however, the economic potential of Central Asia has been receiving growing attention. China increasingly sees the SCO as a mechanism for closer regional economic co-operation (it is pushing for trade liberalization and is funding many infrastructure projects in the region) and as a way of tapping into the region's hydrocarbon and hydro-electric resources. Development of the economic potential of the SCO has also received the support of Kazakhstan and of India, a SCO observer state. Russia and other Central Asian states, especially Uzbekistan, have been more reluctant to liberalize trade and open up their markets to Chinese products. There is little doubt, nevertheless, that the economic dimension of the SCO will become more significant in the future. However, the potential growth of economic exchanges within the SCO could pose a dilemma for Russia. The Moscow sponsored economic multilateral organization, the Eurasian Economic Community (EEC), is attempting to set up a free trade zone in Central Asia. If trade liberalisation under SCO auspices also goes ahead, EEC trade mechanisms could potentially be diluted within the larger SCO area, forcing Russia to relinquish its dominant economic position in the region to China (see Torjesen in this volume for a discussion of EEC). Indeed, Russia is not keen to develop the full economic potential inherent within the SCO framework. As noted by *Moscow News* in September 2006,

> fears of China's extraordinary economic expansion…[have] prompted Russian government officials to stress…[that] The Shanghai Cooperation Organization does not envision the formation of a single economic space, as [EEC] does.[16]

Instead it was stressed that the SCO's primary goal was to carry out infrastructure projects.[17]

Although doubts persist as to its military effectiveness, the SCO remains one of the few regional organizations where Russia has tended to operate in a multilateral fashion. This is partly explained by the fact that its influence is counter-balanced by that of another major regional power – China – even though its weight within the organization is stronger than that of the Central Asian states. Russia's multilateral behaviour within the SCO has permitted the Central Asian states to operate in a regional multilateral security organization on a more equal footing with other larger regional powers. In this way, the SCO has become a channel through which Central Asian states can engage with China, and Russia, on a common security agenda in order jointly to address common threats.

Russia has been very supportive of this arrangement, appreciating the opportunities both to engage constructively with China, a potential rival in the region, and to form a broader alliance with the Central Asian states. More significantly, through the SCO, Russia also manages to uphold the principle of 'multipolarity' in the international system – an important concept and aim for Russia's foreign policy-makers. Although addressing Central Asia's security challenges remains the key rationale behind the creation of the SCO, Russia also views the organization as an important counter-weight to US presence in the region. Moscow attaches considerable value to the SCO as a platform for the adoption of common positions among its member states on questions of international security. This was clearly illustrated in 2005, when the SCO members issued a joint statement in their summit in Astana, asking Washington to set a deadline for the removal of its troops from Central Asia.[18] Moscow's engagement in the SCO is also determined by its desire to work together with China at the regional level. Still, Russian and Chinese interests in the SCO go beyond the desire to address common threats collectively. As highlighted recently by Bailes *et al.*, in their work on the SCO, Russia and China also obtain 'normative' as well as strategic gains at the global level, through their participation in the SCO.[19] Strategically, the SCO balances Chinese and Russian weight vis-à-vis US global might, and normatively, it allows Russia and China to promote norms of international conduct that are more preferable to them. The SCO emphasizes the principles state sovereignty, territorial integrity and non-interferences in the internal affairs of states, and also challenges the claim that Western-style democracy and human rights should serve as universal parameters for the internal conduct of states. In this way, the SCO challenges the tendency towards normative and strategic unipolarity that emerged after the end of the Cold War in the international system.

The 2007 SCO annual summit in Bishkek (Kyrgyzstan) was significant in that it displayed the strategic importance that both countries have attached to the organization. In wake of the summit, Russia put forward a conceptual document proposing that military co-operation within the SCO be significantly expanded. This raised the prospect of the SCO becoming a regional security organization, along the lines of NATO, with mutually-binding security obligations among its member states. Such initiatives were compounded with a series of large-scale military exercises (*Peace Mission 2007*) which took place in August 2007, and which involved the participation of over 80 warplanes backed up 6500 troops from all member states. Military forces conducted a series of manoeuvres that began in China and continued in Russia's Chelyabinsk oblast. The event was labelled an 'anti-terrorist exercise', although some analysts saw it as having been aimed at countering a large-scale military threat, such as the collapse of a state or an American invasion of the region.[20] The exercises clearly indicated a growing trend towards deeper security co-operation among SCO member states. However, the limits to these initiatives soon became evident. The exercises involved mostly Russian and Chinese troops, and the security threats they sought to address (state failure or foreign attack) did not correspond to the most pressing security challenges faced by the region – terrorism and drugs trafficking. In light of this, the event could be interpreted as an attempt by China and Russia to signal their independent military strength to the US, rather than view it as an effort by SCO states jointly to address common threats.[21] More generally, the prospects of the SCO becoming a defence alliance similar to NATO remain remote, given the lack of a coherent threat perception among its member states, beyond the existing concerns over the spread of 'terrorism, extremism and separatism'.

Moreover, the operational ability of the organization to address common threats still needs to be put to test. There is some scepticism regarding the ability of the SCO to become an effective security provider. Even if the SCO becomes more institutionalized in the near future, its potential for the co-ordination of regional security might still be limited. This is due primarily to the reluctance of both Russia and China to address real security challenges entirely on a multilateral basis. However, as pointed out by Ruslan Maksutov, the Regional Anti-Terrorism Structure is alleged to have managed to thwart over 263 acts of terrorism and cross border crime in 2006.[22]

Concluding thoughts

The CSTO seems to have dealt relatively successfully with the challenges posed by a disintegrating Soviet military structure. However, it was proven quite ineffective when dealing with specific military threats emerging from the region, especially during the 1999 and 2000 IMU military incursions into Kyrgyzstan and Uzbekistan. It was only after these events, and especially after the US troop deployments in 2001, that substantial improvements to the CSTO's regional organization and practice finally occurred. However, despite its weaknesses, the CSTO has served to underpin Russia's position as a great power in the Central Asian region, by tying many Central Asian states into a Russian-led security alliance. For the time being at least, the CSTO seems to have succeeded in preserving Russia's influence in the region. It has also managed to limit quite significantly any serious external engagement in the region, even though this has been achieved mostly through symbolic and organisational advances rather than through a fully convincing performance of Russia as regional security guarantor.

Within the SCO, Russia has also strongly supported the development of security co-operation among its member states. Security relations constitute an arena where Russia can operate rather effectively and quite comfortably, and as a result it can assert itself as a relevant and leading player. The SCO's ability to meet the region's security challenges remains, however, mixed. Although border disputes have been resolved and agreement has been reached on issues of common concern, co-operation among member states at a practical and operational level remains limited. Nevertheless, initiatives like the large-scale Russia–Chinese military exercise *Peace Mission 2007* have clearly been to the benefit of Russia, as they have further bolstered the latter's image as a major global player.

Conversely and interestingly, Russia's positive experiences within the SCO have strengthened its belief in multilateralism – albeit multilateralism of a distinct kind. The successes of the SCO have demonstrated the benefits of co-operating with a potential competitor like China. They have also indicated the possibility of developing multilateral diplomacy according to Moscow's preferences. The SCO experience proved to Russia that multilateralism of a different kind – in the form of limited inter-governmental co-operation, devoid of the principles of democracy, liberalism and human rights – can work. Precisely these principles have been highlighted by President Putin as forming part of a 'new model of successful international co-operation'.[23]

The benefits that have been derived thus far from the SCO have served to inform Russia's general outlook on multilateralism. Moscow can now relate more confidently and, if necessary, distance itself from Western institutions, which generally tend to cater to Western values and interests. With a thriving SCO, Russia does not need to fear the prospect of 'going it alone' should it decide to abandon other global multilateral structures because they are considered either too demanding or too compromising of its national interests. In the extreme, this may lead in the future to Russia's possible disengagement from the Western multilateral commitments it entered in to the 1990s and 2000s. At the very least, however, the SCO provides Russia with alternatives – and this strengthens Russia's bargaining position when it comes to dealing with the challenges posed by the more established and Western-centric multilateral frameworks.

Notes

1 Key features of Russian multilateralism

1 R. Legvold, Chapter 2, this volume.
2 E. Haas, *The Uniting of Europe: Political, Economic and Social forces, 1950–1957*, Stanford, CA: Stanford University Press, 2004.
3 B. Lo, *Vladimir Putin and the Evolution of Russian Foreign Policy*, London and Oxford: Royal Institute of International Affairs and Blackwell's, 2003.
4 Stephen Krasner has identified regimes as 'sets of implicit or explicit principles, norms, rules, and decision making procedures around which actors' expectations converge in a given area of international relations'. S.D. Krasner, 'Structural causes and regime consequences: regimes as intervening variables', in S.D. Krasner (ed.) *International Regimes*, Ithaca, NY: Cornell University Press, 1983, p. 2.
5 D. A. Baldwin, *Neorealism and Neoliberalism: The Contemporary Debate*, New York: Columbia University Press, 1993; J. Grieco, 'Anarchy and the limits of cooperation: a realist critique of the newest liberal institutionalism', *International Organization*, vol. 42, no. 3, 1988.
6 While the term 'near abroad' certainly and at times problematically connotes that the former Soviet space is still centred on Moscow, we have chosen to use this term because it encapsulates a key idea, primarily demonstrated in practice rather than in rhetoric under Putin's presidency – namely, that different foreign policy rules apply closer to home.
7 The Soviet and Yeltsin-era approaches are described in detail in Legvold's contribution to this volume.
8 Lo, *Vladimir Putin*, pp. 43–4.
9 D. Trenin and B. Lo, *The Landscape of Russian Foreign Policy Decision-Making*. Moscow: Carnegie Moscow Centre. Online. Available HTTP: <http://www.carnegie.ru> (accessed 1 May 2007); S. Secrieru, *Russia's Quest for Strategic Identity*, *NATO Defence College Occasional Paper*, November 2006.
10 Lo, *Vladimir Putin*, p. 15.
11 A. Tysgankov, *Russia's Foreign Policy: Change and Continuity in National Identity*, Lanham, MD: Rowman and Littlefield, 2006.
12 A. Tysgankov, 'Vladimir Putin's vision of Russia as a normal great power', *Post-Soviet Affairs*, vol. 21, no. 2, 2005, 132–58.
13 R. Sakwa, *Putin: Russia's Choice*, London: Routledge, 2004; Lo, *Vladimir Putin*; Trenin and Lo, *Landscape*.
14 Trenin and Lo, *Landscape*, p. 18.
15 Lo, *Vladimir Putin*, pp. 74–5.
16 Secrieru, *Russia's quest*, p. 46.

17 D. Lynch, 'Misperceptions and divergences', *What Russia Sees/Chaillot Paper 74*, Institute for Security Studies, January 2005.
18 Secrieru, *Russia's quest*, p. 55.
19 H. Balzer, 'Will Putin Go Multinational?' *RFE/RL Newsline*, 15 August 2007.
20 Lo, *Vladimir Putin*, p. 82.
21 Putin interview with newspaper journalists from G8 member countries, *Johnson's Russia List*, 4 June 2007. Online. Available HTTP: <http://www.cdi.org/russia/johnson/2007-127-25.cfm> (accessed 22 June 2007).
22 *Foreign Policy Concept of the Russian Federation 2000*. Online. Available HTTP: <http://www.fas.org/nuke/guide/russia/doctrine/econcept.htm> (accessed 22 June 2007).
23 Secrieru, *Russia's quest for strategic identity*, p. 55.
24 Trenin and Lo, *Landscape*.
25 M. Barnett and R. Duvall, 'Power in global governance', in M. Barnett and R. Duvall (eds) *Power in Global Governance*, Cambridge: Cambridge University Press, 2005, p. 3.
26 Available HTTP: < http://www.securityconference.de/konferenzen/rede.php?sprache=en&id=179> (accessed 8 October 2007).
27 Trenin and Lo, *Landscape*, p. 11.
28 Putin interview with newspaper journalists from G8 member countries, *Johnson's Russia List*, 4 June 2007. Online. Available HTTP: <http://www.cdi.org/russia/johnson/2007-127-25.cfm> (accessed 22 June 2007).
29 This organization is sometimes called the 'Single Economic Space' or the 'Common Economic Space'.
30 V. Khristenko, 'Making headway to integration', *Russia in Global Politics*, no.2, March–April 2004. Online. Available HTTP: <http://eng.globalaffairs.ru/numbers/6/508.html> (accessed 15 June 2007).
31 B. Lo, *Russian Foreign Policy in the Post-Soviet Era: Reality, Illusion and Mythmaking*, Basingstoke: Palgrave, 2002, pp. 6–7, 66–98.
32 Ibid. pp. 6–7
33 BBC World Wide Monitoring, 'Putin outlines Russia's strategy to prevent CIS disintegration', 19 July 2004; see also pages 13-14 of E. Vinokurov, 'Russian approaches to integration on the post-Soviet space in the 2000s (draft manuscript)'. Online. Available HTTP: <http://www.vinokurov.info/downloads/russianapproachestointegration.pdf> (accessed 1 May 2007).
34 Roy Allison, 'Regionalism, regional structures and security management in Central Asia', *International Affairs*, vol. 80, no. 3, 2004, p. 479.
35 Barnett and Duvall, 'Power in global governance', p. 3.
36 I. Kobrinskaya, 'The CIS in Russian foreign policy: causes and effects' in H. Smith (ed.) *Russia and Its Foreign Policy Influences, Interests and Issues*, Helsinki: Aleksanteri Institute, 2005, p. 87
37 *President Vladimir Putin's Speech at the XI St. Petersburg International Economic Forum, 11 June 2007*. Online. Available HTTP: <http://www.russiaprofile.org/page.php?pageid=CDI+Russia+Profile+List&articleid=a1181663766> (accessed 22 June 2007).

2 The role of multilateralism in Russian foreign policy

1 *Joint Declaration of the Russian Federation and the Republic of India, 3 December 2004*. Online. Available HTTP: <http://www.kremlin.ru/interdocs/2004/12/03/1349_type72067_80548.shtml?type=72067 > (accessed 1 February 2007).
2 On the tension between the two, the reader may find helpful: L.M. Reed and C. Kaysen (eds) *Emerging Norms of Justified Intervention*, Cambridge, MA: American Academy of Arts and Sciences, 1998; N. J. Wheeler, *Helping Strangers: Humanitarian*

Intervention in International Society, Oxford: Oxford University Press, 2000; Stephen D. Krasner, 'Sharing sovereignty: New institutions for collapsed and failing states', *International Security*, vol. 29, no. 2, 2004, 85–120; J. Chopra and T. Weiss, 'Sovereignty is no longer sacrosanct: Codifying humanitarian intervention', *Ethics and International Affairs*, vol. 6, 1992, 95–117; and the reports from the four Pugwash conferences on Intervention and Sovereignty (1999–2001). Online. Available HTTP: <http://www.pugwash.org/reports/rc/rclist.htm> (accessed 1 February 2007).

3   A. Dallin, *The Soviet Union at the United Nations*, New York: Praeger, 1962, p. 6.

4   For the disagreement, see M. Beloff, *Foreign policy of Soviet Russia, 1929–1941*, vol. 1, New York: Oxford University Press, 1947–1949; L. Fischer, *The Soviets in World Affairs*, Princeton, NJ: Princeton University Press, 1951; Jonathan Haslam, *The Soviet Union and the Struggle for Collective Security, 1933–39*, Cambridge: St. Martin's Press, 1984; and Jirí Hochman, *The Soviet Union and the Failure of Collective Security, 1934–1938*, Ithaca, NY: Cornell University Press, 1984.

5   Two excellent accounts of the change are: T, Trister Gati, 'The UN rediscovered: Soviet and American policy in the United Nations of the 1990s' in R. Jervis and S. Bialer (eds) *Soviet–American Relations after the Cold War*, Durham, NC: Duke University Press, 1991, 197–223, and E. C. Luck and T. Trister Gati, 'Gorbachev, the United Nations, and US policy', *Washington Quarterly*, 11, Autumn 1988, 19–31.

6   In addition to Gati, 'The UN rediscovered', pp. 202–04, see also D. Bourantonis and R. A. Panagiotou, 'Russia's attitude towards the reform of the United Nations Security Council, 1990–2000', *Journal of Communist Studies and Transition Politics*, vol. 20, December 2004, pp. 83–4.

7   The quotation is from Bourantonis and Panagiotou, 'Russia's attitude', p. 96, which offers a fuller account of the events described here.

8   From Sergei Lavrov's speech to the international conference 'Democracy, International Governance and the World Order', published in *Rossiya v globalnoi politike*, November–December 2004, pp. 8–9.

9   Ibid., p. 14.

10 Putin has argued that China, India, and Brazil need to be included in a dialogue with the G8 on economic and energy issues, and, during his presidency of the G8, ensured that China and India were invited for consultations on the sidelines of the July 2006 St. Petersburg summit. But, when asked point-blank whether he favoured their membership, he responded, 'And if our partners consider it possible to put these issues in practice then of course we would support decisions of this kind.' (Press conference, 16 July 2006. Online. Available HTTP: <http://www.kremlin.ru/appears/2006/07/15/0313_type63380type82634_108795.shtml> (accessed 1 February 2007).

11 J, Kirton, in his 'From collective security to concert: The UN, G8 and global security governance', paper for the conference on 'Security Overspill: Between Economic Integration and Social Exclusion', Centre Études Internationales et Mondialisation, Université de Québec, 27–28 October 2005, makes a rather sweeping claim for how much of a role the G8 has already assumed.

12 Presentation to the World Political Forum, General Assembly, Turin, Italy, 4–6 March 2005.

13 'Vystuplenie Ministra inostrannykh del Rossii S.V. Lavrova na 62-i sessii Generalnoi Assamblei OON, Nyu-Iork', 28 September 2007. Online. Available HTTP: <http://www.mid.ru/brp_4.nsf/0/6A633F27DF51F6B8C32573650027B70A> (accessed 1 October 2007).

14 See, for example, 'Address of Mr. Sergey V. Lavrov, Minister of Foreign Affairs of the Russian Federation, before the 14th Meeting of the OSCE Ministerial'. Online. Available HTTP: <http://www.osce.org/documents/mcs/2006/12/22408_en.pdf> (accessed 1 February 2007).

15 See J. Quigley, 'Perestroika and international law', *American Journal of International Law*, vol. 82, no. 4, October 1988, p. 790.

16 B. Lo, *Russian Foreign Policy in the Post-Soviet Era: Reality, Illusion and Mythmaking*, New York: Palgrave Macmillan, 2003, pp. 87–91.

17 'Multilateralism – a small state perspective', speech by Phil Goff at the Deutsche Gesellschaft für Auswärtige Politik (Berlin), 2 April 2004. Online. Available HTTP: <http://www.dgap.org/dgap/veranstaltungen/archive/view/aaaa9d422d5c11db9720a3 cab53839f239f2.html> (accessed 1 February 2007).

18 N. Bowen, 'Multilateralism, multipolarity, and regionalism: the French foreign policy discourse', *Mediterranean Quarterly*, Winter 2005, p. 108.

19 Sergei Lavrov, 'Statement before the First Committee of the 58th Session of the United Nations General Assembly', 9 October 2003. Online. Available HTTP: <http://www.geneva.mid.ru/speeches/08.html> (accessed 1 February 2007).

20 The list is from Sergei V. Lavrov's 'Statement at the 59th Session of the U.N. General Assembly', 23 September 2004. Online. Available HTTP: <http://www.rusembcanada.mid.ru/pr/240904_e.html> (accessed 1 February 2007).

21 See footnote 13.

22 Y. Primakov, 'OON: Vyzovy vremeni', *Rossiya v Globalnoi Politike*, September–October 2004, p. 76.

23 Ibid.

24 Ibid., p. 75.

25 The literature on the relationship of regionalism to multilateralism is overwhelmingly devoted to issues of international political economy. There is relatively little on the tension between what I am calling regional and global multilateralism in the broader sense – and virtually none that deals with the case of Russia. For a tangential literature that raises relevant aspects of the general problem, see: K. Graham and T. Felício, *Regional Security and Global Governance: A Study of Interactions between Regional Agencies and the UN Security Council with a Proposal for a Regional-Global Security Mechanism*, Brussels: VUB Brussels University Press, 2006; A. Gamble and A. Payne, *Regionalism and World Order*, London: Macmillan, 1996; B. Buzan and O. Wæver, *Regions and Powers: The Structure of International Security*, Cambridge: Cambridge University Press, 2003; A. Hurrell, 'Regionalism in theoretical perspective' in L. Fawcett and A. Hurrell (eds) *Regionalism in World Politics: Regional Organization and International Order*, Oxford: Oxford University Press, 1995; and A. Acharva, *Regionalism and Multilateralism: Essays on Cooperative Security in the Asia-Pacific*, Springer Netherlands, 2007.

26 Yuri V. Fedotov, 'A Russian perspective', in C. U. Bhaskar, U. K. Sinha, K. Santhanam and T. Meenai (eds) *United Nations: Multilateralism and International Security*, New Delhi: Shipra, 2005.

27 Primakov, 'OON: Vyzovy vremeni', p. 76.

28 M.B. Olcott, A. Aslund and S. W. Garnett, *Getting It Wrong: Regional Cooperation and the Commonwealth of Independent States*, Washington, DC: Carnegie Endowment for International Peace, 1999, p. 82.

29 'V Bishkeke proidet zasedanie Komiteta sekretarei sovetov besopasnosti gosudarstv-chlenov ODKB'. Online. Available HTTP: <http://www.dkb.gov.ru/start/index.htm> (accessed 1 November 2007).

30 'Secretary-General hails growing regional role Of Shanghai Cooperation Organization in message to grouping's sixth summit', UN Secretary-General, SG/SM/10510, 12 June 2006. Online. Available HTTP: <http://www.un.org/News/Press/docs/2006/sgsm10510.doc.htm> (accessed 1 February 2007).

31 E. Vinokurov, 'Russian approaches to integration on the post-Soviet space in the 2000s', draft manuscript. Online. Available HTTP: <http://www.vinokurov.info/downloads/russianapproachestointegration.pdf> (accessed 1 February 2007).

32 For a refined argument that the EU sphere represents, along with the post-Soviet space, one of Russia's only two natural trading conglomerations, see V. Ivanenko,

'Rossiya: gravitatsiya i integratsiya', *Rossiya v Globalnoi Politike,* May–June 2007, 175–88.

33 For a more complete discussion of the developing Russian relationship with the EU, see M. Light, 'Russian political engagement with the European Union', in R. Allison, M. Light and S. White, *Putin's Russia and the Enlarged Europe*, London: Blackwell, 2006, pp. 45–71, as well as Light's chapter in this volume. On the central role of bureaucrats in shaping Russia's relations with the EU and the disadvantages this imposes on Russia, see S. Sokolov, 'Russia and the EU to negotiate a new partnership agreement', *Russia in Global Affairs,* vol. 5, no. 3, July–September 2007, 187–88.

34 This from an undated 2007 interview in *Regnum*. Online. Available HTTP: <http://www.mamf.ru/odkb/jubilee/index.htm> (accessed 1 November 2007).

35 V. Baranovsky, 'Humanitarian intervention: Russian perspectives', Pugwash Study Group on Intervention, Sovereignty, and International Security, *Pugwash Occasional Papers*, vol., no. 1, January 2001, p. 2. Online. Available HTTP: <http://www.pugwash.org/publication/op/opv2n1.htm> (accessed 1 February 2007).

36 This is from the joint heads of state declaration signed at the end of Jiang Zemin's visit to Russia in July 2001. Online. Available HTTP: < http://www.shaps.hawaii.edu/fp/russia/r_c_js_20010716.html> (accessed 1 February 2007). They and their spokesmen have made the point often. Putin's earliest foreign policy remarks contain it, as does the 2000 Russian foreign policy concept paper.

37 An excellent and subtle analysis of Russia's position on the Kosovo war is found in Baranovsky, 'Humanitarian intervention', pp. 7–9.

38 *The Foreign Policy Concept of the Russian Federation*, approved by the President of the Russian Federation, V. Putin, 28 June 2000. Online. Available HTTP: <http://www.fas.org/nuke/guide/russia/doctrine/econcept.htm> (accessed 1 February 2007).

39 S. Lavrov, 'Demokratiya, mezhdunarodnoe upravlenie i budushchee miroustroistvo', *Rossiya v Globalnoi Politike,* vol. 3, November–December 2004, p. 14.

40 Baranovksy, 'Humanitarian intervention', p. 11.

41 Primakov, 'OON: Vyzovy vremeni', pp. 71–2.

42 Primakov justified this under what he called the 'criteria for interference' under Chapter VII of the UN Charter – a curiously permissive notion, since Chapter VII applies only to a 'threat to the peace, breach of the peace, or act of aggression'. (Primakov, 'OON: Vyzovy vremeni', p. 72).

43 Quoted by Baranovksy in 'Humanitarian intervention', p. 13.

44 L. Shanglin, 'China, Russia, India hold first trilateral summit', Xinhua, 18 July 2006. Online. Available HTTP: <http://news.xinhuanet.com/english/2006-07/18/content_4846589.htm> (accessed 1 February 2007).

45 S. Blagov, 'Lavrov meets Chinese, Indian counterparts in Vladivostok', *Eurasia Daily Monitor,* vol. 2, no. 108, 3 June 2005.

46 S. Blagov, 'Russia–China–India: an axis of denials', *Asia Times Online,* 3 July 2003. Online. Available HTTP: <http://www.atimes.com/atimes/Central_Asia/EG03Ag03.html> (accessed 1 February 2007).

47 'Vystuplenie Ministra inostrannykh del Rossii S.V. Lavrova v MGIMO(U) po sluchayu nachala novogo uchebnogo goda', 3 September 2007. Online. Available HTTP: <http://www.mid.ru/brp_4.nsf/2fee282eb6df40e643256999005e6e8c/db37503de27befd9c325734b003176dc?OpenDocument> (accessed 1 October 2007).

48 'Putin stands for Russia–China–India strategic cooperation', *People's Daily* (Beijing), 1 October 2000. Online. Available HTTP: <http://english.people.com.cn/english/200010/01/eng20001001_51704.html> (accessed 1 February 2007).

49 K. K. Katyal, 'Beijing–Moscow–New Delhi trialogue', *The Hindu,* 22 September 2003.

50 I have been more explicit on this in the 'Conclusion', in R. Legvold and C.A. Wallander (eds) *Swords and Sustenance: The Economics of Security in Belarus and Ukraine,* Cambridge, MA: MIT Press, 2004, especially pp. 240–59.

3　Multilateralism in Russian foreign policy approaches

1　R. Kagan, 'Multilateralism, American style', *The Washington Post*, 12 September 2002. Online. Available HTTP: <http://www.newamericancentury.org/global-091302.htm> (accessed 1 February 2007).

2　The review was undertaken by the Ministry for Foreign Affairs in 2006 for the first time in the Russian Federation. In fact it was intended neither to provide a properly critical assessment of Russia's foreign-policy objectives, nor to replace the former foreign policy doctrine of 2000. Instead, it provides a consolidated update of where Russian foreign policy stands today, after several initiatives to revise national security and foreign policy doctrines had failed in the past two years. The review was not a product of inter-agency consensus-building, nor was it passed formally through the Security Council, as a new doctrine would have to. It was submitted to the President later in 2006, however, and was released upon receiving the green light from the Kremlin. This means that it does not have the status of an official foreign policy doctrine officially endorsed by the President upon the recommendation of the Security Council. It is perceived, however, as a summary of Russia's current foreign policy guidelines in practice approved by the President.

3　*Vystuplenie i diskussiya na Myunchenskoy konferentsii po voprosam politiki bezopasnosty* (Statement and discussion at the Munich security conference), 10 February 2007. Online. Available HTTP: <http://www.president.kremlin.ru/text/appears/2007/02/118109.shtml> (accessed 1 March 2007).

4　*Obzor vneshney politiki Rossiiskoy Federatsii (Foreign Policy Review of the Russian Federation)*, published by the Press and Information Service of the Russian Foreign Ministry on 27 March 2007. Online. Available HTTP: <http://www.mid.ru/ns-osndoc.nsf/0e9272befa34209743256c630042d1aa/d925d1dd235d3ec7c32573060039aea4?OpenDocument> (accessed 1 April 2007).

5　*The Russian Federation Foreign Policy Review*, Chapter on the multilateral diplomacy, subchapter on the United Nations, para. 1.

6　Ibid. Chapter on the multilateral diplomacy, subchapter on the Russian participation in the G8, para. 3.

7　Andrei Zagorski, 'Global and regional security governance. Security threats and institutional response. Russia survey 2006', revised paper for the EU GARNET workshop 5–8 October 2006. The poll collected 54 returns from 22 members of relevant committees of both chambers of the Russian Federal Assembly, as well as 28 security policy experts and four senior government officials. The survey targeted, in the first instance, two groups of the Russian security community: members of the relevant parliamentary committees (Foreign Relations, Defence, Security, CIS) of the State Duma (Lower Chamber) and the Council of Federation (Upper Chamber), and security policy experts outside the government. Twenty-two valid responses were received from MPs (16 from the State Duma and six from the Council of Federation). In addition, 14 individual interviews were conducted with MPs. Most MP responses (50 per cent) were received from members of the ruling Single Russia party. Two respondents identified themselves as members of the Rodina (Motherland) party (currently the base for the 'Just Russia' party), and one as a member of the Communist Party of the Russian Federation. The group of independent Members of the State Duma was represented with two returns. Six respondents identified themselves as not belonging to any political party. One identified himself as member of 'a liberal party' and one as belonging to the faction of the European Democrats in the Parliamentary Assembly of the Council of Europe. As to committee membership, Foreign Relations dominated, with 14 responses (64 per cent). Returns were also received from members of the Security (one return) and CIS (two returns) Committees of the State Duma, the Defence and Security as well as the CIS Committees of the Council of Federation (two from each). Responses from the two Chambers of Parliament represent 20 per cent of the members of their relevant Committees, and party distribution reflects the majority picture. Twenty-eight returns were received from non-governmental experts: two identified themselves as members of the 'Yabloko', a pan-Russian democratic party not represented in the Parliament since December 2003, and one as belonging to the Rodina party.

8 See *Foreign Policy Review of the Russian Federation*, Chapter on the multilateral diplomacy, subchapter on the United Nations, recommendation in para. 8.

9 Ibid, Chapter on the multilateral diplomacy, subchapter on the United Nations, para. 5.

4 Leading in the concert of great powers: Lessons from Russia's G8 chairmanship

1 After this interview to *Interfax* agency on 19 December 2006 (Online. Available HTTP: <http://www.mid.ru/brp_4.nsf/spsvy?OpenView&Start=1.58> (accessed 1 February 2007)), Lavrov has barely mentioned the G8 chairmanship in his statements and articles in 2007.

2 Mikhail Gorbachev was for the first time invited to the G7 London summit in 1991 in order to discuss the request for Western support for his reforms – which was obviously too late, since the August 1991 coup triggered the collapse of the USSR. Thoughtful reflections on the impact of multilateralism on Russia's new identity can be found in D.Trenin, *Intergratsiya i Identichnost* (Integration and Identity), Moscow: Evropa, 2006, particularly pp. 277–80.

3 Putin insisted on speaking at the conference that had never been a 'presidential' event; the English translation of his 10 February 2007 speech is available at the presidential website. Available HTTP: <http://president.kremlin.ru/eng/speeches/2007/02/10/0138_type82912type82914type82917type84779_118135.shtml> (accessed 1 March 2007). In the ensuing avalanche of commentary, Fedor Lukyanov pointed out that the content of the Munich speech did not differ so markedly from Putin's celebrated speech in the German Bundestag in September 2001, it was the tone that made the difference. See 'From Berlin to Munich', *Gazeta.ru* (in Russian), 15 February 2007. Online. Available HTTP: <http://www.gazeta.ru/column/lukyanov/1377298.shtml> (accessed 1 March 2007).

4 According to research conducted at the G8 Information Center, University of Toronto, and at the Higher School of Economics, Moscow, the statistical assessment of Russia's delivery on its promises shows significant improvement: see J. Kirton, 'The "Big Eight" after St. Petersburg', *Russia in Global Affairs*, January–February 2007; and M. Larionova, 'The score sheet for the "Big Eight"', *Russia in Global Affairs*, November–December 2006.

5 A good overview of this plan can be found in V.A. Orlov and M. Fugfugosh, 'The G8 Strelna summit and Russia's national power', *The Washington Quarterly*, vol. 29, no. 3, Summer 2006, pp. 35–48; for my preview see P. Baev, 'Chairing the G8: Russian energy and great-power aspirations', *PONARS Memo* 382, Washington, DC: CSIS, December 2005.

6 See I. Rubanov, 'Taking a stand against burying ourselves', *Expert*, 5 March 2007. Online. Available HTTP: <http://www.expert.ru/printissues/expert/2007/09/demograficheskaya_situaciya_v_rossii/> (accessed 1 April 2007); on a particularly acute issue, see C.A. Wallander, 'The politics of Russian AIDS policy', *PONARS Memo* 389, Washington, DC: CSIS, December 2005.

7 The idea of expanding G8 to G20 was originally advanced by Canadian Prime Minister Paul Martin; for a concise argument, see J.F. Lynn and C.I. Bradford, 'The irrelevant G8 summit in St. Petersburg', 25 July 2006, *Global Economics* (The Brookings Institution). Online. Available HTTP: http://www.brookings.edu/views/op-ed/200607irg8.htm (accessed 1 March 2007); the activities of the financial G20 are presented on the group's website (http://www.g20.org/).

8 The seven finance ministers agreed to keep the format intact in late 2005; see Y. Petrovskaya, A. Blinov and E. Grigoriev, 'Quasi-Chairmanship', *Nezavisimaya*

gazeta, 2 December 2005. Nevertheless, Kudrin was instructed by the Kremlin to keep trying; see N. Kulikova, 'Russia on the way to G8 financial club', RIA-*Novosti*, 6 July 2006. Online. Available HTTP: <http://en.rian.ru/analysis/20060706/50987811.html> (accessed 1 March 2007).

9 As an editorial in the business-oriented *Vedomosti* succinctly argued, 'for the miracle to happen, investments have to be a few times larger.' See 'A miracle is promised', *Vedomosti*, 29 January 2007.

10 D. Yergin has argued that the 'desire to cut ourselves out of the global energy markets is senseless and unrealistic', but re-conceptualizing energy independence as energy security could turn political rhetoric in a constructive direction; see 'Energy security: independence is impossible', *Vedomosti*, 24 January 2007; also A.F. Alhajji and G. Longmuir, 'The fantasy of energy independence', *Vedomosti*, 12 April 2007.

11 See 'Energy security according to Illarionov', *Lenta.ru*, 8 July 2006. Online. Available HTTP: <http://lenta.ru/articles/2006/06/08/illarionov/> (accessed 1 March 2007). Illarionov also argued that Russia, as neither an economically developed nor a politically free country, did not belong to the G8, so the scandalous summit could only signify readiness in the club 'to compromise over the basic values of the Western civilization'; see Andrei Illarionov, 'The death of the G8', *Vedomosti*, 18 April 2006.

12 This thesis – 'all of us should recognize and admit that "energy egoism" in a modern and highly interdependent world is a road to nowhere' – was advanced by Putin in the article 'The upcoming G8 summit in St. Petersburg: challenges, opportunities and responsibility'. Online. Available HTTP: < http://president.kremlin.ru/eng/speeches/2006/03/01/1152_type104017_102507.shtml> (accessed 1 March 2007).

13 Jacques Sapir offered a positive assessment based on the assumption that 'if stable prices are an integral part of energy security, they should be established by non-market means.' See J. Sapir, 'Energy security as a common good', *Russia in Global Affairs*, November–December 2006.

14 The 15-page document is available on the official Strelna summit website (http://en.g8russia.ru/docs/11.html).As one Russian expert commented, the language was as convoluted as in an ancient manuscript where one line was written in Latin, another in Greek, and third in Hebrew; see L. Grigoryev, 'Everyone has own energy security', *Polit.ru*, 1 September 2006. Online. Available HTTP: <http://polit.ru/lectures/2006/08/04/grigoriev.html> (accessed 1 March 2007).

15 The saga of the dismemberment of the oil company *Yukos* and the persecution of its owner Mikhail Khodorkovsky and his associates cannot be examined here; Andrei Illarionov correctly identified it as the crucial watershed in the evolution of Putin's regime: see 'Dangerous turn', *Rossiiskaya gazeta*, 23 September 2005; for my brief reflections, see P. Baev, 'The destruction of Yukos and Putin's estrangement from the West', *Eurasia Daily Monitor*, 26 October 2004. Online. Available HTTP: <http://jamestown.org/edm/article.php?article_id=2368744> (accessed 1 March 2007).

16 Putin's visit to China in March 2006 was intended to mark a breakthrough in Russia's gas export in the Eastern direction but fell significantly short; see I. Rubanov, 'China is for a long term', *Expert*, 27 March 2006. Substantial criticism of this attempt at diversifying energy export can be found in V. Milov, 'Catching a crane in a dark room', *Russia in Global Affairs*, November–December 2006; for my more elaborate analysis, see P. Baev, 'Russia aspires to the status of "energy super-power"', *Strategic Analysis*, vol. 31, no. 3, May–June 2007, pp. 447–65.

17 Incisive current analysis of that 'offensive' can be found in several articles constituting the 'Russia and the EU' section in *Kommersant*, 15 November 2006; the key contradictions were outlined in A. Monaghan, 'Russia–EU relations: an emerging

energy security dilemma', *Pro et Contra*, vol. 10, no 2–3, March–June 2006; for a more updated analysis see V. Milov, 'The Russia–EU energy dialogue: filling the vacuum', *Russia in Global Affairs*, September/October 2007, pp. 135–46.

18 On the contradiction between Russia's growing ambitions and declining production base, see V. Inozemtsev, 'Mini-great-power', *Bolshaya Politika*, no. 6, June 2006, pp. 40–7; see also V.Milov, 'The economic results of 2006 for the energy sector', presentation of the Institute of Energy Policy report, 18 January 2007. Online. Available HTTP: <http://www.milov.info/speech.php?id=421> (accessed 1 March 2007). And for a short comment see P. Baev, 'Russian politics and economics face an energy crisis', *Eurasia Daily Monitor*, 23 October 2006. Online. Available HTTP: <http://jamestown.org/edm/article.php?article_id=2371566> (accessed 1 March 2007).

19 The FSB insisted that the explosion was not an accident but a carefully executed 'special operation'; for sharp criticism see Y. Latynina, 'The special operation of the Almighty – but not of Patrushev', *Ezhednevny Zhurnal*, 10 July 2006. Online. Available HTTP: <http://www.ej.ru/dayTheme/entry/4262/> (accessed 1 March 2007).

20 For a brief evaluation of this theme at Gleneagles, see P. Baev, 'Putin's agenda prevails at the G8 summit: It is terrorism, comrades!', *Eurasia Daily Monitor*, 11 July 2005. Online. Available HTTP: <http://jamestown.org/edm/article.php?article_id=2369996> (accessed 1 March 2007).

21 Prevailing assessments of the situation in the North Caucasus were grave up until the end of 2006; see, for instance, J. Dunlop and R. Menon, 'Chaos in the North Caucasus and Russia's future', *Survival*, vol. 48, no. 2, Summer 2006, pp. 97–114. For a more recent analysis see P. Baev, 'The targets of terrorism and the aims of counter-terrorism in Moscow, Chechnya and the North Caucasus', paper presented at the International Studies Association annual conference, Chicago, 3 March 2007.

22 See I. Plugatarev, 'The Prishtina march to Lebanon', *Nezavisimoe voennoe obozrenie*, 15 September 2006.

23 A competent evaluation of this manoeuvring is A. Malashenko, 'The Islamic factor in Russian foreign policy', *Russia in Global Affairs*, no. 2, March–April 2007.

24 One example of such assessments is V. Ovchinsky, 'Afghanistan without coalition', *Russia in Global Affairs*, no. 1, January–February 2007; for a short comment see P. Baev, 'Russia ignores the Riga summit and expects NATO to fail in Afghanistan', *Eurasia Daily Monitor*, 4 December 2006. Online. Available HTTP: <http://jamestown.org/edm/article.php?article_id=2371704> (accessed 1 March 2007).

25 See A. Kots, 'Russia returns to Afghanistan', *Komsomolskaya pravda*, 17 and 18 April 2007; G.Esfandiari, 'Afghanistan: New political bloc unites old adversaries', *Eurasia Insight*, 7 April 2007. Online. Available HTTP: <http://eurasianet.org/departments/insight/articles/pp040707a.shtml#> (accessed 1 May 2007).

26 Rose Gottemoeller has insightfully examined this give-and-take, see for instance, 'The Russia card', *New York Times*, 3 May 2006; 'US–Russia: Holding the line against nukes', *International Herald Tribune*, 25 August 2006.

27 My evaluation of that surprise initiative is in P. Baev, 'Putin sails through his last G8 summit', *Eurasia Daily Monitor*, 11 June 2007. Online. Available HTTP: <http://jamestown.org/edm/article.php?article_id=2372220> (accessed 1 July 2007). A British journalist who was allowed inside the Gabala control room described it as 'borrowed from the set of a very old James Bond film'; see R. Galpin, 'Inside Russia's missile defence base', *BBC News*, 2 July 2007. Online. Available HTTP: <http://news.bbc.co.uk/2/hi/europe/6262220.stm> (accessed 1 August 2007).

28 For recent takes on this problem see P. Baev, 'The Iranian test for Putin's new course', *Eurasia Daily Monitor*, 26 February 2007. Online. Available HTTP: <http://jamestown.org/edm/article.php?article_id=2371946> (accessed 1 March 2007) and P. Baev, 'Moscow measures the new Western unity on Iran', *Eurasia Daily*

Monitor, 1 October 2007. Online. Available HTTP: <http://jamestown.org/edm/article. php?article_id=2372465> (accessed 1 November 2007).

29 For an insightful overview of these calculations, see D. Trenin, 'Russia leaves the West', *Foreign Affairs*, July/August 2006.

30 See Gleb Pavlovsky, 'It was a deliberately nasty statement', interview with *Strana.ru*, 4 May 2006. Online. Available HTTP: http://www.strana.ru/stories/01/11/14/ 2017/280734.html (accessed 1 February 2007); Andrei Illarionov, 'Cool war', *Kommersant*, 12 May 2006; also P. Baev, 'After Vilnius, Putin has to reconsider his prospects', *Eurasia Daily Monitor*, 8 May 2006. Online. Available HTTP: <http://jamestown.org/edm/article.php?article_id=2371059> (accessed 1 March 2007).

31 Putin's annual address to the parliament was delivered a few days after Cheney's speech and the famous 'comrade Wolf' remark was certainly meant as a response. For the official English translation, see <http://president.kremlin.ru/eng/ speeches/2006/05/10/1823_type70029type82912_105566.shtml>.

32 Surkov took pains to explain that Russian 'sovereign democracy' was in line with European standards; see 'Vladislav Surkov defined democracy as sovereign or managed', *Kommersant*, 29 June 2006.

33 See 'Criticizing Russia with good reason', *International Herald Tribune*, 3 July 2006.

34 One important contribution to shaping this consensus was the report of the Council on Foreign Relations 'Russia's Wrong Direction' (Available HTTP: <http:// www.cfr.org/publication/9997/> (accessed 1 October 2007)). Michael McFaul clarified that Cheney's speech confirmed that the Bush administration 'no longer has any hopes for Russia as a strategic partner': see 'The end of partnership', *Kommersant*, 11 May 2006. For my assessment of the Strelna talks see P. Baev, 'Bush downplays "sovereign democracy" at Putin's barbecue', *Eurasia Daily Monitor*, 17 July 2006. Online. Available HTTP: <http://jamestown.org/edm/article.php?article_id=2371280> (accessed 1 March 2007) and, on the tête-à-tête a year later, Pavel Baev, 'Arms control as a "safe issue" at Kennebunkport', *Eurasia Daily Monitor*, 3 July 2007. Online. Available HTTP: <http://jamestown.org/edm/article.php?article_id=2372268> (accessed 1 August 2007).

35 For a sober evaluation see C. A. Wallander, 'Suspended animation: The US and Russia after the G8', *Current History*, vol. 105, no. 693, October 2006, pp. 315–20.

36 Many German analysts still prefer the Schröder line of ever-closer rapprochement; see for instance, A. Rahr, 'Germany and Russia : a special relationship', *The Washington Quarterly*, vol. 30, no. 2, Spring 2007, 137–45.

37 One good evaluation of the Polish 'intrigue' is A. Moshes, 'Diplomacy with gas', *Gazeta.ru*, 15 November 2006. Online. Available HTTP: <http://www.gazeta.ru/ comments/2006/11/15_x_1053907.shtml> (accessed 1 March 2007)).

38 As one commentator put it: 'The main non-event of 2006 was the St. Petersburg G8 summit: The main political event of the year did not happen so triumphantly and demonstratively that the debate about what had been the aims is still alive.' See D. Butrin, 'The lost year of the puzzled country', *Gazeta.ru*, 18 December 2006. Online. Available HTTP: <http://www.gazeta.ru/column/butrin/1166048.shtml> (accessed 1 March 2007).

39 For keen analysis of the shortcomings of the new industrial policy see V. Inozemtsev, 'Phantom of competitiveness', *Nezavisimaya gazeta*, 11 April 2007. Putin's address is available in English at (http://president.kremlin.ru/eng/speeches/ 2007/04/26/1209_type70029_125494.shtml).

40 One incisive analysis is A. Arbatov, 'Moscow and Munich: New framework for Russia's domestic and foreign policies', *Working Papers* no. 3, Moscow Carnegie Center, 2007.

41 Thoughtful reflections on the implementation of the 'Munich' guidelines are found in D.Trenin, 'Russia's strategic choice', *Briefing Papers* no.50, Moscow Carnegie Center, May 2007. For my take on the tensions in Russia–EU relations, see

P. Baev, 'Putin compares US missile defence to Cuban crisis', *Eurasia Daily Monitor*, 29 October 2007. Online. Available HTTP: <http://jamestown.org/edm/article.php? article_id=2372541> (accessed 1 November 2007).

42 A competent and representative view is V. Litovkin, 'The CFE history of no-confidence', *Nezavisimoe voennoe obozrenie*, 20 July 2007.

5 Russia's attitude towards nuclear non-proliferation regimes and institutions: An example of multilateralism?

1 Concept of National Security of the Russian Federation. Concept of Foreign Policy of the Russian Federation. Military Doctrine of the Russian Federation. Full Russian text of the documents can be found on the web site of the Russian Ministry of Foreign Affairs. Available HTTP: <www.mid.ru>.

2 Full text of presentation and answers of S. V. Lavrov, Russian Minister of Foreign Affairs, on questions of the media at a press conference devoted to activities of Russian diplomacy in 2006, Moscow, 20 December 2006 (in Russian), Ministry of Foreign Affairs of the Russian Federation, Department of Information and Press, Press Release 2240-20-12-2006.

3 On US–Russian relations regarding Kosovo see, for example: A. Arbatov. 'Conflict in the Balkans: an attempt to establish new world order?' ('Konflikt na Balkanakh: popytka ustanovleniya novogo miroporyadka?'), Chapter 1 in *Russia: Security Environment in the End of XX Century. IMEMO Disarmament and Security Yearbook 1999–2000,(Rossiya: Sreda bezopasnosti v kontse XX veka. Razoruzheniye i bezopasnost'. Ezhegodnik IMEMO 1999 – 2000), Moscow: Nauka, 2001, pp. 15–38 (in Russian).

4 See, e.g. A. Pikayev. 'Russia: a part of the "northern ring" or of the "greater south"?' ('Rossiya: chast' "Severnogo kol'tsa ili" Bol'shogo yuga'?' Chapter 1 in *International Security: IMEMO Disarmament and Security Yearbook 2001–2002(Mezhdunarodnaya bezopasnost': novyye ugrozy novogo tysyacheletiya. Razoruzheniye i bezopasnost'. Ezhegodnik IMEMO 2001–2002*, Moscow: Nauka, 2003, pp. 21–37 (in Russian).

5 See, e.g. V. Mizin, 'Russia and evolution of the international nuclear non-proliferation regime' ('Rossiya i evolyutsiya regima nerasprostraneniya yadernogo oruzhiya'), Chapter 10 in *New Approaches to International Security. IMEMO Disarmament and Security Yearbook 2004–2005 (Novyye podkhody k mezhdunarodnoy bezopasnosti. Razoruzheniye i bezopasnost'. Ezhegodnik IMEMO 2004–2005), Moscow: Nauka, 2007, pp. 186–210 (in Russian)

6 See, e.g. A. Pikayev and E. Stepanova, 'Non-proliferation and nuclear terrorism', ('Nerasprostraneniye i yaderny terrorism'). Chapter 11 in A. Arbatov (ed) *Nuclear Weapons After the Cold War (Yadernoye oruzhiye posle kholodnoy voyny)*, Moscow: Rosspen, 2006, pp. 310–57 (in Russian)

7 V. Novikov, 'Iran: Has the Nuclear Threshold Been Passed?' ('Iran: pereiden li yaderny porog?'), Chapter 2 in A. Arbatov and V. Naumkin (eds) *Threats to the Non-Proliferation Regime in the Middle East (Ugrozy rezhimu nerasprostraneniya na Blizhnem i Srednem Vostoke)*, Moscow: Carnegie Moscow Center, 2005, pp. 16–24 (in Russian).

8 Joint Statement by U.S. President George Bush and Russian Federation President V. V. Putin Announcing the Global Initiative to Combat Nuclear Terrorism, July 15, 2006. Online. Available HTTP: <www.whitehouse.gov/news/releases/2006/07/20060715-2.html> (accessed 1 February 2007).

9 A. Arbatov, 'Problems of the NPT and non-proliferation regime' ('Problemy Dogovora i reghima nerasprostraneniya'), Chapter 4 in *Nuclear Weapons After the Cold War*, pp. 141–55. (in Russian).

10 Author's interview with diplomat from a CIS country, May 2004.

11 This is discussed in further detail below. See also A. Arbatov and V. Naumkin (eds) *Threats to Non-Proliferation Regime in the Middle East (Ugrozy reghimu*

nerasprostraneiya na Blizhnem i Srednem Vostoke), Moscow: Carnegie Moscow Center, 2005.

12 See note 9.

13 Interviews with Russian and US officials, Moscow and Washington, DC, 1999.

14 For more on the Korean case, see A. Arbatov and V. Mikheev (eds) *Nuclear Proliferation in North-East Asia (Yadernoie raqsprostraneniye v Severo-vostochnoi Azii)*, Moscow: Carnegie Moscow Center, 2005 (in Russian).

15 For general reviews of Iran–Russia relations, see note 7.

16 Author's interview with Rosatom official, Moscow, Sept. 2006.

17 Interview of S. V. Lavrov, Minister of Foreign Affairs of Russia, for *Vremya Novostei*, 11 September 2006, text (in Russian) from Ministry of Foreign Affairs, Department for Information and Press, Press Release of 11-09-2006. The group of six, or G6, are the permanent members of the UN Security Council plus Germany

18 Interview with *Interfax* news agency, 19 December 2006 (in Russian). English version available online. Available HTTP: <http://www.interfax.ru/e/B/0/0.html?id_issue=11649423> (accessed 1 March 2007).

6 Russia and Europe and the process of EU enlargement

1 This chapter is based on research for the project 'Inclusion without membership? Bringing Russia, Ukraine and Belarus closer to "Europe"', which is funded by the UK Economic and Social Research Council under grant RES-00-23-0146 to Stephen White, Roy Allison and Margot Light. Fuller details of the project are available at http://ww.lbss.gla.ac.uk/politics/inclusionwithoutmembership/.

2 Joseph Nye has defined 'high politics' as 'symbol-laden, emotive, and based on attitudes characterized by greater intensity and duration than "low" politics'. 'Low politics' is more susceptible to the rational calculation of benefits associated with economic problems.' J.S. Nye, 'Patterns and catalysts in regional integration', *International Organization*, vol. 19, no. 4, 1965, p. 871.

3 V. Likhachev, 'Rossiya i yevropeiskii soyuz', *Mezhdunarodnaya Zhizn'*, no. 12, 2002, p. 30.

4 *Otnosheniya Rossii i Yevropeiskogo Soyuza: Sovremennaya Situatsiya i Perspektivy*, Situatsionnyi analiz pod rukovodstvom S.A. Karaganova. Moscow, 2005, p. 2. Online. Available HTTP: <http://www.globalaffairs.ru/numbers/13/3947.html> (accessed 1 February 2007).

5 Communication from the Commission to the Council and the European Parliament on relations with Russia, COM, 2004, 106, p. 2.

6 *Russia and the European Union: Options for Deepening Strategic Partnership*, Russia in a United Europe Committee (RUE), Moscow, 2002, p. 38.

7 A more detailed account of Russian–EU relations can be found in R. Allison, M. Light and S.White, *Putin's Russia and the Enlarged Europe*, Oxford and London: Blackwell and Royal Institute of International Relations, 2006, on which this chapter is based.

8 EuropeAid Financial Statistics, Tables summarizing the allocation of TACIS resources, 1991–2002, Table 1. Online. Available HTTP: <http://europa.eu.int/comm/europeaid/projects/tacis/financial_en.htm> (accessed 1 February 2006). Russia also participates in TACIS-funded cross-border and regional programmes. For details of TACIS programmes in Russia, see 'The EU–Russia Cooperation Programme/TACIS Russia'. Online.. Available HTTP: <http://www.delrus.cec.eu.int/en/p_260.htm> (accessed 1 February 2006).

9 The EU's Common Strategy on Russia is published in *Official Journal of the European Communities*, L157/1, 24/06/1999.

10 Strategiya razvitiya otnoshenii Rossiiskoi Federatsii s Evropeiskim Soyuzom na srednesrochnuyu perspektivu (2000–2010 gg)', *Diplomaticheskii vestnik*, no. 11, 1999,

pp. 20–8. For an interesting comparison between the two strategies, see M. Menkiszak, *Russia vs. the European Union: A 'Strategic Partnership' Crisis*, Warsaw: Centre for Eastern Studies, January 2006, Appendix III, pp. 67–8.

11 Cologne European Council, Presidency Conclusions, Annexes to the Presidency Conclusions, Annex 3, CAB 150/99, p. 33. Online. Available HTTP: <http://ue.eu. int/ueDocs/cms_Data/docs/pressdata/en/ec/57886.pdf> (accessed 1 February 2006).

12 'Kontseptsiya Natsional'noi Bezopasnosti Rossiiskoi Federatsii' (The Concept of National Security), *Nezavisimoye voennoye obozreniye*, 14 January 2000; 'Voennaya doktrina Rossiiskoi Federatsii' (The Military Doctrine of the Russian Federation), *Nezavisimaya gazeta*, 22 April 2000.

13 For further details about EU–Russia trade, see *European Commission*, Trade Statistics. Online. Available HTTP: <http://trade-info.cec.eu.int/doclib/html/113440. htm> (accessed 3 February 2006).

14 See Helsinki European Council, Presidency Conclusions, Annex 2, 10 and 11 December 1999. Online. Available HTTP: <http://europa.eu.int/council/off/conclu/ dec99/dec99_en.htm#annexII> (accessed 4 February 2006). The sanctions were removed after six months.

15 See, for example, the newspaper article by K. Ugodnikov and A.Chichkin, 'Yevropa grozit zabit' okno v Rossiyu', *Rossiskaya gazeta*, 28 January 2000.

16 His address was published in *Rossiiskaya gazeta*, 4 April 2001.

17 V. Lukin, in 'In 2004, Russian foreign policy moved ahead cementing its achievements and never losing initiative', *International Affairs* (Moscow), vol. 1, 2005, p. 58.

18 *Razshireniya ES: ugroza ili shans dlya Rossii?* RUE, Moscow, 2002, pp. 17–18.

19 *Otnosheniya Rossii i Yevropeiskogo Soyuza: sovremennaya situatsiya i perspektivy*, pp. 21–2.

20 T. Bordachev, 'Toward a strategic alliance', *Russia in Global Affairs*, vol. 4, no. 2, 2006, p. 115.

21 Bordachev, 'Toward a strategic alliance', p. 8.

22 Rolf Shuette, EU–Russia relations: interests and values – a European perspective, *Carnegie Papers*, 54, December 2004, pp. 1–2.

23 Karen Smith, 'Enlargement and European order', in C. Hill and M. Smith (eds), *International Relations and the European Union*, Oxford: Oxford University Press, 2005, p. 286.

24 Armed terrorists took more than 1200 school children and adults hostage on September 1, 2004 in the town of Beslan in North Ossetia. On the third day, gunfire broke out between the hostage-takers and Russian security forces. According to official data, 344 civilians were killed, 186 of them children, and hundreds more wounded.

25 Deputy Foreign Minister Vladimir Chizhov, *Izvestiya*, 25 February 2004, p. 2

26 See the report on Surkov's speech in *Moscow News*, 12 July 2005.

27 S. White, M. Light and I. McAllister, 'Russia and the West: Is there a values gap?' *International Politics*, 42, vol. 3, 2005, pp. 316–19.

28 See: Report with a proposal for a European Parliament recommendation to the Council on EU–Russia relations (2003/2230(INI)). Online. Available HTTP: <http://www. europarl.europa.eu/sides/getDoc.do?pubRef= −//EP//NONSGML+REPORT+A5-2004-0053+0+DOC+PDF+V0//EN&language=EN> (accessed 20 December 2006).

29 EU–Russia Summit, Moscow, 10 May 2005, Conclusions. Online. Available HTTP: <http://europa.eu.int/comm/external_relations/russia/summit_05_05/finalroad maps.pdf#fsj> (accessed 20 July 2005).

30 *Itar-Tass Weekly News*, 3 December 2002; 28 November 2003.

31 His remark is quoted in 'Russia: Beslan hostage tragedy leads to spat with EU', *RFE/RL Newsline*, 6 September 2004. Online. Available HTTP: <http://www.rferl.org/ featuresarticle/2004/09/6ea40e08-57e6-4d7c-98d7-65360c989f8d.html> (accessed 11 July 2007).

32 *Itar-Tass Weekly News*, 4 September 2004.
33 Sergei Lavrov, 'In the face of a common threat', *Diplomatic Yearbook 2004*, see Russian Ministry of Press Release, Russia, European Union Human Rights Consultations in Luxembourg, 397-02-03-2005, 2 March 2005.
34 See Nabi Abdullaev, 'How Russia's NGO law stacks up', *Moscow Times*, 15 February 2006.
35 Commission of the European Communities, Communication from the Commission to the Council and the European Parliament, 'Wider Europe – Neighbourhood: A new framework for relations with our eastern and southern neighbours', COM (2003) 104, Brussels, 11 March 2003, p. 3.
36 *Itar-Tass Weekly News,* 9 November 2004 and V. Chizhov, 'European Union: a partnership strategy', *International Affairs* (Moscow), 6, 2004, p. 85.
37 For details of the European Neighbourhood Policy, see Commission of the European Communities, Communication from the Commission, European Neighbourhood Policy Strategy Paper, COM(2004) 373, Brussels, 12 May 2004.
38 The list is set out in a report produced by the Russian National Investment Council with the support of the Ministry of Foreign Affairs, *The effect of the EU enlargement on Russia's economy,* Moscow, 2004. Online. Available HTTP: <http://www.europe2020. org/en/section_voisin/doc/EU_eng.pdf> (accessed 10 October 2005). Chizhov's statement can be found in Press release 161-30-01-2004, Ministry of Foreign Affairs of the Russian Federation, and the EU response is in 2563rd External Relations Council meeting – Brussels 23.02.2004, Press:49 Nr: 6294/04. Online. Available HTTP: <http:// ue.eu.int/ueDocs/cms_Data/docs/pressData/en/gena/79150.pdf> (accessed 10 October 2005).
39 *Izvestiya*, 26 February 2004 and *Moscow Times*, 25 February 2004.
40 Protocol to the Partnership and Co-operation Agreement, Brussels, 27 April 2004. Online. Available HTTP: <http://www.europa.eu.int/comm/external_relations/russia/ russia_docs/protocol_0404.htm> and Joint Statement on EU Enlargement and EU–Russia Relations, 27 April 2004. Online. Available HTTP: <http://www.europa.eu. int/comm/external_relations/russia/russia_docs/js_elarg_270404.htm> (both accessed 10 October 2005).
41 *EU–Russia Trade Relations*, p. 8. Online. Available HTTP: <http://trade.ec.europa. eu/doclib/docs/2006/may/tradoc_113440.pdf> (accessed 17 May 2006); see also A. Gubaidullin and N. Kampaner, 'Gaz v Yevrope: est' li alternativa', *Rossiya v Global'noi Politike*, vol. 1, 2006.
42 *Itar-Tass Weekly News*, 2 January 2006
43 A. Gubaidullin and N. Kampaner, 'Gaz v Yevrope'. See Prime Minister Fradkov's message to the European Council in *Itar-Tass Weekly News*, 3 January 2006.
44 Novosti Press Agency, 17 September 2006.
45 *Novosti*, 22 June 2007. Online. Available HTTP: <http://en.rian.ru/business/20070622/ 67679920.html> (accessed 11 July 2007).
46 See M. Bradshaw, 'Battle for Sakhalin', *World Today* (November 2006), p. 19. Mitsui and Mitsubishi are partners in the Sakhalin-II project.
47 European Union – Russia energy dialogue. Online. Available HTTP: <http://ec.europa. eu/energy/russia/overview/index_en.htm> (accessed 17 May 2006).
48 Russia–EU Energy Forum. Online. Available HTTP: <http://www.energyforum.co.uk/ index.php?lang=en> (accessed 17 May 2006).
49 *The Energy Charter Treaty and Related Documents*. Online. Available HTTP: <http:// www.encharter.org/upload/9/12052067451575115819204971474353213193519086 0213f2543v3.pdf> (accessed on 17 May 2006).
50 J. Hughes, 'EU relations with Russia: Partnership or asymmetric interdependency?' in N. Casarini and C. Musu (eds) *The EU's Foreign Policy in an Evolving International System: The Road to Convergence*, Basingstoke: Palgrave, 2006.

7 Inside or outside? Russia's policies towards NATO

1 Defence Ministry of the Russian Federation, Aktual'nye zadachi razvitiia Vooruzhennych Sil Rossiiskoi Federatsii, Moscow, October 2003. Online. Available HTTP: <http://www.mil.ru/articles/article5005.shtml> (accessed 1 February 2007). This document is often referred to in Western discussion as the 'military doctrine' or 'defence white book.'

2 Interview with the *Financial Times*, 11 December 1999.

3 President Putin on 13 March 2000, in an interview with the BBC. Online. Available HTTP: <http://www.gazeta.ru/2001/02/28/putin_i_bbc.shtml> (accessed 1 February 2007).

4 According to NATO's home page, the section on 'NATO-Russia relations: building a lasting and inclusive peace in the Euro-Atlantic area'. Available HTTP: <http://www.nato.int/issues/nato-russia/index.html> (accessed 1 February 2007).

5 In a speech at Moscow State University; 'Òåzisy vystupleniia Ministra inostrannykh del Rossii S. V. Lavrova na vstreche so studentami Fakulteta mirovoi politiki MGU im. M. V. Lomonosova', 11 December 2006. Online. Available HTTP: <http://www.mid.ru/brp_4.nsf/sps/C75D6169BC7444D6C3257241005B6517> (accessed 1 February 2007).

6 The treaty on Conventional Forces in Europe (CFE) was adopted in 1990. Several adaptations to new conditions were made thereafter to take into consideration the dissolution of the Warsaw Pact and the Soviet Union, but the main revision of the treaty was adopted at the Istanbul OSCE summit in November 1999. Only Russia, Ukraine, Belarus and Kazakhstan have ratified the adapted treaty. The NATO countries have refused to do so pending Russia's complete fulfilment of its political commitments made in Istanbul to dissolve military bases and withdraw forces and ammunition from Georgia and Moldova. According to a decree (*ukaz*) signed by Putin on 14 July 2007, Russia will 'suspend' its adherence to the 1990 CFE Treaty and its early (1991) adaptations if the NATO countries had by then still not ratified it. See HTTP: <http://www.kremlin.ru/text/docs/2007/07/137830.shtml> (accessed 1 August 2007).

7 The concept was developed by Vladislav Surkov, a deputy chief of staff in Putin's presidential administration, in August 2006; see 'Narod dolzhen' znat' kuda my idem i zachem', *Izvestia*, 31 August 2006.

8 Yeltsin's letter of 20 December 1991, in *Pravda*, 23 December 1991. At the Brussels meeting, the North Atlantic Co-operation Council (NACC) was created, later renamed Euro-Atlantic Partnership Council.

9 Andrei Kozyrev, on Radio Mayak (Moscow), in Russian, on 23 December 1991, *Foreign Broadcast Information Service, Daily Report*, Soviet Union, FBIS-SOV-91-247, 24 December 1991, p. 41.

10 S. A. Karaganov, 'Die Aussenpolitik Russlands nach dem Putsch', Konrad Adenauer-Stiftung (Bonn/Sankt Augustin), *Auslandsinformationen*, no. 11, 1991, p. 14.

11 S. Blagovolin, in an interview conducted by Sergei Guk, 'NATO mozhet byt' garant bezopaznosti Rossii', *Izvestia*, 22 January 1992.

12 A. Arbatov, 'Rossiya i NATO', *Nezavisimaya gazeta*, 11 March 1992. At the time of writing Arbatov was director of the Centre for Disarmament and Strategic Stability at Russia's Foreign Policy Association.

13 Yeltsin in a speech to the collegium of the defence ministry, *Krasnaia zvezda*, 25 November 1992, and in an address to foreign ministry officials, Interfax (Moscow), 28 October 1992.

14 The text (30 pages) of the study was distributed to journalists at a press conference in Moscow and published in full or in excerpts in all major national newspapers; quotes here are from 'Perspektivy rasshireniia NATO i interesy Rossii. Doklad sluzhby vneshnei razvedki', *Izvestia*, 26 November 1993.

15 ITAR-TASS (in Russian), 5 January 1994.
16 On these contradictory statements and attitudes see Interfax (in Russian), 6 April 1994, and J. Lloyd, 'Russian government in state of disarray', *Financial Times*, 8 April 1994.
17 S. Dardykin, 'Serbov, konechno, zhalko, no eto eshche ne povod gotovit'sia k tret'ei mirovoi voine', *Izvestia*, 15 September 1995, p. 1.
18 The Medium-term Strategy for the Development of Relations Between the Russian Federation and the European Union for the period 2000–2010 constitutes the Russian reply to the EU's Common Strategy towards Russia of June 1999. Above quotes are from 'Strategiia razvitiia otnoshenii Rossiiskoi Federatsii s Evropeiskim Soiuzom na srednesrochnuiu perspektivu', *Diplomaticheskii vestnik* (November 1999; italics mine). Although the document was compiled in 1999, it is valid not only technically (until 2010) but also in terms of conceptual approach – with one major exception being the attitude towards NATO.
19 Deputy Foreign Minister Vladimir Chizov at a press conference on 23 June 2004. Online. Available HTTP: <http://www.fednews.ru> (accessed 1 February 2007); see also RIA Novosti (in Russian), 25 June 2004.
20 Deputy Foreign Minister Chizov, 23 June 2004 press conference (see above).
21 Putin at NATO Headquarters, 3 October 2001; S. Daley, 'Putin softens his stance against NATO expansion', *New York Times*, 4 October 2001.
22 Deputy Foreign Minister Chizov, 23 June 2004 press conference.
23 On 6 September 2004, at a meeting in Novo-Ogarovo with foreign participants in the forum 'Russia at the Eve of the New Millennium' as quoted by one of the participants, Nikolai Zlobin, Director of Russian and Asian Programmes at the Centre for Defence Information (CDI); *Izvestia* (online), 10 September 2004. The term Putin used was *khamstvo*.
24 This view has been attributed to Russian Foreign Minister Sergei Lavrov; 'Moscow sends Foreign Minister Lavrov to NATO summit', RIA 'Novosti' Hotline, 25 June 2004.
25 'NATO–Russia relations'. Online. Available HTTP: <http://www.nato.int/issues/nato-russia/index.html> (accessed 1 February 2007).
26 Ibid.
27 R. E. Hunter and S. M. Rogov, *Engaging Russia as Partner and Participant: The Next Stage of NATO–Russia Relations*, Rand National Security Research Division, Conference Proceedings, Santa Monica, CA: Rand, 2004, p. 7.
28 'NATO–Russia relations'. Online. Available HTTP: <http://www.nato.int/issues/nato-russia/index.html> (accessed 1 February 2007).
29 Ibid.
30 Riga Summit Declaration. Online. Available HTTP: <http://www.nato.int/docu/pr/2006/p06-150e.htm> (accessed 1 February 2007)
31 The purpose of the operation is to prevent or to counter terrorism coming from or conducted at sea. It is also to control illegal acts possibly connected with terrorism, such as human trafficking and smuggling of arms and radioactive substances. Operation Active Endeavour has become more intelligence-based by the sharing of intelligence and information gathered at sea with allies and partners, to enhance their security.
32 At a press conference following an informal NRC meeting at foreign-minister level in Sofia 27–28 April 2006. Online. Available HTTP: <http://www.nato.int/docu/comm/2006/0604-sofia/060427-sofia.htm> (accessed 1 February 2007).
33 Officially, however, practically no information on Russia's participation is available; see HTTP: <http://www.afsouth.nato.int/JFCN_Operations/ActiveEndeavour/Endeavour.htm> (accessed 1 February 2007).
34 See <http://www.securityconference.de/konferenzen/rede.php?menu_2006=&menu_konferenzen=&sprache=de&id=171&>.

35 At the informal NRC meeting at foreign-minister level in Sofia (see note 33).
36 'Rossiisko-amerikansiee voennye ucheniia v sentiabre ne sostoiatsia', RBK.ru, 5 September 2006. Online. Available HTTP: <http://top.rbc.ru/index.shtml?/news/daythemes/2006/09/05/05195101_bod.shtml> (accessed 1 February 2007).
37 Ibid.
38 'Lugar: Attack on allies' energy supplies is attack on NATO alliance. Senator invokes Article V in opening speech of Riga Conference'. Online. Available HTTP: <http://www.rigasummit.lv/en/id/newsin/nid/239/> (accessed 1 February 2007).
39 Personal impressions of the author at the conference.
40 These clarifications are expressly stated in Russia's Medium-term Strategy on relations with the EU (see note 19).
41 Putin's speech to a conference of Russian ambassadors on 12 July 2004, in Moscow. Online. Available HTTP: <http://www.kremlin.ru/texht/appears/2004/07/74399.shtml> (accessed 1 February 2007).
42 'Putin schitaet raspad SSSR obshchenatsional'noi tragediei', *Nasledie oteèestva,* 12 February 2004; 'Khotel uspokoit' liudeji', *Gazeta*, 13 February 2004; and 'Poslanie Federal'nomu Sobraniiu Rossiiskoi Federatsii', 25 April 2005. Online. Available HTTP: <www.kremlin.ru/sdocs/appears.shtml.> (1 February 2007).
43 Thus, in his annual addresses to the federal assembly in April 2005, see HTTP: <www.kremlin.ru/sdocs/appears.shtml> (accessed 1 February 2007). In his annual address in April 2006 Putin said: 'The relations with our closest neighbours were and are the most important part of Russia's foreign policy.'
44 The 'Eurasian NATO' label is that of Belarus's president Lukashenka; see I. Safronov, 'Presidenty prevratili dogovor w organizatsiiu', *Kommersant* (online), 15 May 2002.
45 'Common Vision for a Common European Neighbourhood' was the title of the conference held in Vilnius in May 2006, at which not only the presidents of Central, Eastern and Southeast European countries spoke but also, notoriously and odiously from the Russian perspective, US Vice-President Richard Cheney.
46 All these issues were mentioned earlier by Foreign Minister Lavrov; see above, note 5.
47 Putin on 10 February 2007, at the 43rd Munich International Security Conference. Online. Available HTTP: < http://www.securityconference.de/konferenzen/rede.php?sprache=en&id=179&> (italics mine) (accessed 1 March 2007).
48 When asked what steps if any Russia would take if Ukraine and the Baltic states were invited to join NATO, Yeltsin said he hoped the West would be 'realistic' enough not to embark on such a step. 'In NATO expansion, there is a red line for Russia which should not be crossed', *Guardian* (Manchester), 1 May 1998.
49 Deputy Foreign Minister Vladimir Chizov, press conference 24 June 2004. Online. Available HTTP: <http://www.fednews.ru> (accessed 1 February 2007); see also RIA Novosti (in Russian), 25 June 2004.
50 Thus, for instance, the then special advisor to the president on foreign policy, Sergei Iastrzhembskii, in March 2004 in an interview with the *Financial Times* during a visit at NATO HQ; see J. Dempsey, 'Moscow warns Nato away from the Baltics,' *Financial Times,* 1 March 2004, p. 2.
51 'Russia warns US on Baltic deployment', *IHT,* 19 March 2004, p. 3.
52 'Russische Raketen Richtung Westen', *Frankfurter Allgemeine Zeitung*, 3 March 2004, p. 12.
53 Thus, for instance, Defence Minister Ivanov at the 42nd Munich International Security Conference, 5 February 2006.
54 As one of the many signs of NATO's attempt at isolating Belarus, in November 2002 Czech authorities refused to issue a visa to Lukashenka to attend the Prague NATO summit because of the country's human rights record. Lukashenka apparently assumed that he had a right to attend since Belarus is a member of the Euro-Atlantic Partnership Council (EAPC).

55 V. Zubkov, 'Russia-Moldova: Kremlin wants deeds, not words', *RIA Novosti*, 28 August 2006 (italics mine). Zubkov is RIA Novosti's economic editor.

56 The results of opinion polls were reported in *Den'* (Kiev), no. 48 (24 March 2006), p. 3. The failure of the 'orange' camp to campaign openly for membership did not stop individuals of this camp, among them former foreign minister Boris Tarasyuk, from advocating membership.

57 At a press conference on 9 October 2006. Online. Available HTTP: <http://www.nato.int/docu/speech/2006/s061009a.htm> (accessed 1 February 2007).

58 Riga Summit Declaration, 29 November 2006. Online. Available HTTP: <http://www.nato.int/docu/pr/2006/p06-150e.htm> (accessed 1 February 2007).

59 Thus the portrayal by Russian Defence Minister Sergei Ivanov in an interview with *La Stampa*, posted on the Defence Ministry website on 9 February 2006; see also Interfax (in Russian), 9 February 2006. The view that Western values may be 'a serious destabilizing factor' can be derived from Russian policies after the Orange Revolution, but high-ranking officials rarely admit so frankly to that fact.

60 'NATO to Offer Intensified Dialogue to Georgia,' NATO Update, September 29, 2006 . Online. Available HTTP: <http://www.nato.int/docu/update/2006/09-september/e0921c.htm> (accessed 1 February 2007). The formula of Intensified Dialogue has its roots in the 1997 Madrid summit, at which NATO heads of state and government decided 'to continue the alliance's intensified dialogues with those nations that aspire to NATO membership or that otherwise with to pursue a dialogue with NATO on membership questions'. The dialogues 'cover the full range of political, military, financial and security issues relating to possible NATO membership, without prejudice to any eventual Alliance decision'.

61 I. Plugatar, 'Atlantisty proigryvaiut v Kieve, no torzhestvuiut v Tbilisi,' *Nezavisimoe voennoe obozrenie*, 29 September 2006.

62 'Rossiia trebuet osvobozhdeniia voennykh v Gruzii i vvodit otvetnye mery,' *Agentstvo Natsionalnykh Novostei*, September 28, 2006.

63 'Moskva i Tbilisi na poroge kholodnoi voiny,' Pervyi kanal – novosti, 1 October 2006. Putin's charge of 'state terrorism' was carried by the First Channel of Russian TV but deleted on the Kremlin's website.

64 At a session of the Russian national security council on 1 October 2006. Online. Available HTTP: <http://www.kremlin.ru/appears/2006/10/01/0000_type63378_111833.shtml> (accessed 1 February 2007).

65 Quoted by Y. Simonian *et al.*, 'Tbilisi proshel tochku vozvrata,' *Nezavisimaia gazeta*, 29–30 September 2006. The Kodori Gorge separates Georgia from Abkhazia. Earlier in the summer, Tblisi had successfully dislodged a local militia leader who dominated the gorge, and installed an Abkhaz government in exile there. Georgian President Saakashvili said that the gorge would henceforth be known as Upper Abkhazia and that the restoration of central power there would lead to the return of Abkhazia proper to Georgian control.

66 In an interview the Defence Ministry newspaper, *Krasnaia zvezda* (online), 12 December 2006.

67 'NATO transformation in focus at Portorož meeting,' NATO Update, 29 September 2006. Online. Available HTTP: <http://www.nato.int/docu/update/2006/09-september/e0927a.htm> (italics mine) (accessed 1 February 2007).

68 Lavrov interview, *Krasnaia zvezda* (online), 12 December 2006.

69 Neither Russia's political nor the military leadership is doing much to dispel such negative notions. Thus, NATO attempted to do something about them: In the period from 11 to 26 May 2006, there took place what NATO Secretary General de Hoop Scheffer called a 'NATO–Russia Rally,' a series of public events in Russia from Vladivostok to Kaliningrad intended to 'increase awareness about the new reality of partnership and co-operation'. (At the informal NRC meeting at the foreign ministers' level in Sofia on 27–28 April 2006 (see note 33 above). This was predicated

on public opinion polls indicating that up to 80–85 per cent of Russians were negatively disposed towards the Atlantic alliance (Plugatar, 'Atlantisty proigryvaiut v Kieve, no torzhestvuiut v Tbilisi'; see note 63 above). Given the ambiguous statements about NATO that continue to emanate from the Russian security and defence establishment, it is doubtful that the 'rally events' changed much of that sentiment.

8 Russia and the OSCE: From high expectations to denial?

1 For more on Russian views on the OSCE's role see M. Shelepin, 'Equal security for the OSCE countries', *International Affairs* (Moscow), vol. 46, 2000, 170–82; A. Kvashnin, 'Main security challenges: a military response', *International Affairs* (Moscow), vol. 46, 2000, 48–60, and Y. Gusarov, 'Gelsinskiy process vo vneshney politike Rossii', Lecture at the MFA Diplomatic Academy, 15 June 2000. Online. Available HTTP: <http://www.ln.mid.ru/website/ns-dos.nsf/dososce? OpenView&Start=1&Count=50&Expand=1#1> (accessed 1 June 2007). An overview of official Russian views on the OSCE can be found on the MFA site: http://www.ln.mid.ru/. For a Western discussion on new security architecture see S. Croft. 'The EU, NATO and Europeanisation: the return of architectural debate', *European Security*, vol. 9, 2000, 1–20.
2 B. Buzan and O. Wæver, *Regions and Powers: The Structure of International Security*, Cambridge: Cambridge University Press, 2003.
3 All quotes are from the official version of the Charter of Paris for a New Europe. Online. Available HTTP: <http://www.osce.org/documents/html/ pdftohtml/4045_en.pdf.html> (accessed 1 June 2007).
4 Overview is based on the official version of the Final Act. Online. Available HTTP: <http://www.osce.org/documents/mcs/1975/08/4044_en.pdf> (accessed 1 June 2007).
5 Sergei Karaganov, press conference, *RIA Novosti*, 14 December 2006, reproduced in Johnson Russia List, 2006 #282.
6 Ibid.
7 T.Shakleina and A. Torkunov (eds) *Vneshniaia Politika i Bezopasnost' Sovremennoi Rossii 1991–2002: Khrestomatiia*, Moscow: MGIMO, 2002.
8 *Foreign Policy Concept of the Russian Federation.* The Russian text of the doctrine was published in *Diplomaticheskiy Vestnik* , vypusk spetsialnyy, January 1993. English translation published by *FBIS-USR-93-037,* 25 March 1993, here from p. 4.
9 Ibid., p. 5.
10 Ibid.,p. 7.
11 Ibid., p. 11.
12 Ibid., p. 12.
13 English text of the doctrine was published in *Jane's Intelligence Report,* January 1994. An in-depth analysis of the document can be found in C. Dick, 'The military doctrine of the Russian Federation', *Journal of Slavic Military Studies,* vol. 7, no. 3, September 1994, 481–506.
14 Russian Military Doctrine 1993. Online. Available HTTP: <http://www.fas.org/nuke/ guide/russia/doctrine/russia-mil-doc.html> (accessed 1 June 2007).
15 Published in Russian in *Rossiyskie Vesti* on 25 December 1997; endorsed by Presidential Decree 1300 on 17 December 1997.
16 Endorsed by Presidential Decree 24 on 10 January 2000. Online. Available HTTP: <http://www.mid.ru/ns-osndoc.nsf/0e9272befa34209743256c630042d1aa/a54f9 caa5e68075e432569fb004872a6?OpenDocument> (accessed 1 June 2007).
17 Signed by President Putin on 21 April 2000. Online. Available HTTP: <http:// www.mid.ru/ns-osndoc.nsf/0e9272befa34209743256c630042d1aa/2a959a74cd7ed01 f432569fb004872a3?OpenDocument> (accessed 1 June 2007).

18 Signed by President Vladimir Putin on 28 June 2000. Online (in Russian). Available HTTP: <http://www.mid.ru/ns-osndoc.nsf/0e9272befa34209743256c630042d1aa/fd 86620b371b0cf7432569fb004872a7?OpenDocument> (accessed 1 June 2007).

19 A. Kortunov, SBSE i perspektivy sozdaniya sistemy kollektivnoi bezopasnosti v Yevrazii, in Shakleina and Torkunov 2002, vol. II, pp. 201–15.

20 K. Benediktov, 'Rossia i OBSE: realnyye i mnimyye vozmozhnosti sotrudnichestva' ('Russia and the OSCE: Real and perceived possibilities for co-operation') in Shakleina and Torkunov 2002, vol. II, pp. 216–42, originally published in D.Trenin (ed) *Rossiya i osnovnyye instituty bezopasnosti v Yevrope: vstupaya v 21 vek,* Moscow: Carnegie, 2000.

21 Ibid., p. 225.

22 Online. Available HTTP: <http://www.osce.org/documents/mcs/1992/07/4046_en. pdf> (accessed 1 June 2007).

23 Benediktov, p. 226.

24 Online. Available HTTP: <http://www.osce.org/documents/mcs/1995/12/4166_en. pdf> (accessed 1 June 2007).

25 Yeltsin's address quoted in Benediktov, p. 228.

26 Benediktov, p. 228.

27 Online. Available HTTP: <http://www.osce.org/documents/mcs/1997/12/4167_en. pdf> (accessed 1 June 2007).

28 Quoted in Benediktov, p. 229.

29 Benediktov, pp. 229–230.

30 Text of the Copenhagen Sixth Ministerial Council. Online. Available HTTP: <http://www.osce.org/documents/mcs/1997/12/4167_en.pdf> (accessed 1 June 2007).

31 Online. Available HTTP: <http://www1.osce.org/documents/mcs/1998/12/4168_en. pdf> (accessed 1 June 2007).

32 Yeltsin was especially critical of 'humanitarian intervention', the label used by NATO in order to describe its action in Kosovo. He worded his critique in the following way: 'I have in mind the calls for "humanitarian intervention" – a new idea – in the internal affairs of another state, even when they are made under the pretext of defending human rights and freedoms. We all know what disproportionate consequences such intervention can have. It is sufficient to recall NATO's aggression, spearheaded by the United States of America, against Yugoslavia.'

33 For more on that issue see G. Flikke and J. M. Godzimirski, *Words and Deeds: Russian Foreign Policy and Post-Soviet Secessionist Conflicts*, NUPI Report, Oslo: NUPI, 2007.

34 Online. Available HTTP: <http://www.osce.org/documents/mm/1999/07/458_en.pdf> (accessed 1 June 2007).

35 Ibid.

36 Online. Available HTTP: <http://www.osce.org/documents/mcs/1999/11/4050_en.pdf> (accessed 1 June 2007).

37 Ibid.

38 Ibid.

39 Z. Lachowski. 'Building military stability in Europe: adaptation of the CFE Treaty', *Polish Quarterly of International Affairs*, vol. 8, 2000, pp. 33–63, at p. 53.

40 See R.Huber, 'NATO enlargement and CFE ceilings: a preliminary analysis in anticipation of a Russian proposal', *European Security*, vol. 5, 1996, pp. 396–403. On Russian views, see V. Chernov 'Notes on CFE Treaty', *International Affairs* (Moscow), vol. 48, 2002, 46–52.

41 See for example V. Chizhov. 'The Istanbul Summit', *International Affairs* (Moscow), vol. 46, 2000, 68–73 and D. Gornostayev, 'Rossiya vyigrala u zapada stambulskuyu partiyu', *Nezavisimaya Gazeta,* 20 November 1999.

42 Gornostayev 'Rossiya vyigrala u zapada stambulskuyu partiyu', *Nezavisimaya Gazeta,* 20 November 1999.

43 Online. Available HTTP: <http://www.rferl.org/newsline/2000/04/140400.asp> (accessed 1 June 2007).
44 Online. Available HTTP: <http://www.kremlin.ru/eng/text/speeches/2004/12/23/1806_type82915_81700.shtml> (accessed 1 June 2007).
45 Online. Available HTTP: <http://www.kremlin.ru/eng/text/speeches/2007/04/26/1209_type70029_125494.shtml> (accessed 1 June 2007).
46 Online. Available HTTP: <http://www.ln.mid.ru/ns-dos.nsf/4b8edd3adb064e9f432 569e70041fc52/432569d800223f344325699c003b5ed0?OpenDocument> (accessed 1 June 2007). A similar list of concerns can be found in an interview with the head of the Russian delegation to the OSCE, Alexander Alexeyev, in M. Evstafiev, 'Russian Federation is a strong advocate of the OSCE cause' – interview with Alexander Alexeyev, *OSCE Magazine*, May 2004, 17–21.
47 Online. Available HTTP: <http://www.osce.org/austria2000/documents/concl_statements/cio_closing_statement.pdf> (accessed 1 June 2007)
48 In a statement by the US Secretary of State M. Albright. Online. Available HTTP: <www.usemb.gov.do/IRC/speeches/albrig11.htm> (accessed 1 June 2007).
49 The head of the Russian delegation, Yevgenii Gusarov, was quoted by Russian news agencies as saying: 'We have been warning our Western partners that we oppose the use of the OSCE for interference in the internal affairs of countries situated to the east of Vienna. This time, we are sending a clear signal: we won't allow that to happen.'
50 Online. Available HTTP: <http://www.osce.org/docs/english/1990-1999/mcs/8vienna00e.htm> (accessed 1 June 2007).
51 For Russian reactions to the outcome of the Vienna meeting see D. Gornostayev and Y. Grigoriyev 'OBSE vsyo yeshcho khochet v Checheniyu', *Nezavisimaya Gazeta*, 30 November 2000.
52 The texts are quoted from the final document of the Eleventh Meeting of the Ministerial Council 1 and 2 December 2003 in Maastricht. Online. Available HTTP: <http://www.osce.org/documents/mcs/2003/12/4175_en.pdf> (accessed 1 June 2007).
53 Online. Available HTTP: <http://www.osce.org/documents/mcs/2005/02/4324_en.pdf> (accessed 1 June 2007).
54 Text of the Russian statement from Ljubljana. Online. Available HTTP: <http://www.osce.org/documents/mcs/2005/12/18653_en.pdf> (accessed 1 June 2007).
55 M. Menkiszak, 'Russia's position on the OSCE and its reform', *East Week. Analytical Newsletter* 22, 2005, 2–5, Warsaw: Centre for Eastern Studies.
56 A few months later Russia announced that it could consider introduction of a moratorium on the CFE Treaty and in July 2007 Putin made a final decision on that issue – for more details see: V. Socor, 'Moscow confronts the West over CFE Treaty at OSCE' *Eurasia Daily Monitor*, 25 May 2007. Online. Available HTTP: <www.jamestown.org/article.php?article_id=2372188> (accessed 1 June 2007).
57 Available HTTP: <http://www.osce.org/documents/mcs/2006/12/24411_en.pdf> (accessed 1 June 2007).
58 Buzan and Wæver, *Regions and powers.*
59 On how Russian elites tend to read international relations, see M. A. Lebedeva, 'International relations studies in the USSR/Russia: Is there a Russian national school of IR studies?' *Global Society*, vol. 18, 2004, 263–78.
60 A. Wendt 'Anarchy is what states make of it', *International Organization*, vol. 46, 1992, 394–419.
61 A. Wendt, *Social Theory of International Politics,* Cambridge: Cambridge University Press, 1999, p. 258
62 For a good analysis of the evolution of Russian foreign policy in that period see A. Rahr and J. Krause, *Russia's New Foreign Policy*, Arbeitspapierer zur Internationale Politik, no. 91, 1995.

63 For more on that process see A. Tsygankov, 'Vladimir Putin's vision of Russia as a normal great power', *Post-Soviet Affairs*, vol. 21, 2005, 132–58.
64 D.Trenin, 'Russia leaves the West', *Foreign Policy*, July/August 2006. Online. Available HTTP: <http://www.carnegieendowment.org/publications/index.cfm?fa=print& id=18467> (accessed 1 June 2007).
65 For a comprehensive presentation see his article published by RIA Novosti on 14 August 2006, 'I do not want to court disaster, but I have to say', reproduced in Johnson Russia List on 14 August 2006. Online. Available HTTP: <http://www.cdi.org/russia/ johnson/2006-183-4.cfm> (accessed 1 June 2007).
66 R. Penttila, 'The concert is back, and it seems to be working', *International Herald Tribune*, 28 December 2001. He further elaborated on that idea in a lengthy article in *Russia in Global Affairs*. Online. Available HTTP: <http://eng.globalaffairs.ru/ printver/494.html> (accessed 1 June 2007).

9 Russian regional multilateralism: The case of the Arctic Council

1 For more on the growth of Arctic co-operation, as well as the establishment of the Arctic Council, see E. Keskitalo, *Negotiating the Arctic: The Construction of an International Region*, London: Routledge, 2004; O. Stokke and G. Hønneland (eds) *International Cooperation and Arctic Governance: Regime Effectiveness and Northern Region Building*, London: Routledge, 2007; M. Tennberg, *Arctic Environmental Cooperation: A Study in Governmentality*, Burlington, VT: Ashgate, 2000; O. Young, *Arctic Politics: Conflict and Cooperation in the Circumpolar North*, Hanover, NH: University of New England Press, 1992; and O. Young, *Creating Regimes: Arctic Accords and International Governance*, Ithaca, NY: Cornell University Press, 1998.
2 These documents were formerly available on the official Arctic Council website (www.arctic-council.org). However, following a redesign of the website in the autumn of 2007, several of these documents are no longer available online.
3 See E. Wilson and I. Øverland, 'Indigenous issues', in Stokke and Hønneland (eds), *International Cooperation and Arctic Governance*, pp. 27–49, for a review of how indigenous representatives use the scientific knowledge produced at the Arctic Council level in a variety of multilateral settings.
4 O. Stokke, G. Hønneland and P.J. Schei, 'Pollution and conservation', in Stokke and Hønneland (eds), *International Cooperation and Arctic Governance*, p. 86.
5 O. Stokke, G. Hønneland and P.J. Schei, 'Pollution and conservation', p. 90.
6 For a brief review, see L. Heininen, 'Circumpolar international relations and geopolitics', in N. Einarsson, J. Nymand Larsen, A. Nilsson and O. Young (eds) *Arctic Human Development Report*, Akureyri: Stefansson Arctic Institute, 2004, pp. 207–26.
7 See *Norwegian Chairmanship Programme*. Online. Available HTTP: <http://arctic-council.org/article/2007/11/norwegian_programme> (accessed 10 December 2007).
8 *Address by Minister of Foreign Affairs of the Russian Federation Sergey Lavrov at the Fifth Ministerial Session of the Arctic Council, Salekhard*, 26 October 2006. Previously available HTTP: < www.arctic-council.org> (accessed 1 September 2007).
9 See Gazeta.ru (Gazeta.ru, Sever vsegda krainniy, 12 August 2005. Online. Available HTTP: <www.gazeta.ru/comments/2005/08/12_e_353572.shtml?print> (accessed 1 October 2006) for an editorial characterizing the process of supplying northern cities and settlements as a cyclical one of mismanagement and emergency.
10 See H. Blakkisrud, 'What's to be done with the North?' in H. Blakkisrud and G. Hønneland (eds) *Tackling Space: Federal Politics and the Russian North*, Lanham, MD: University Press of America, 2006, pp. 25–52.
11 Regions that can be clearly considered part of the 'profitable North' are those with existing, developing or potential oil and gas output. Yamal-Nenets and Khanty-Mansi Autonomous Okrug stand out as key producers, while Nenets Autonomous Okrug,

Tomsk Oblast, the Komi Republic, the Sakha Republic, Irkutsk Oblast and Evenk Autonomous Okrug are emerging as important players as well. See V. Kryukov and A. Moe, 'Hydrocarbon resources and northern development', in Blakkisrud and Hønneland (eds) *Tackling Space*, pp. 125–42.

12 See H. Balzer, 'The Putin thesis and Russian energy policy', *Post-Soviet Affairs*, 2005, vol. 21, 210–25 for an overview of some of the key principles driving this policy. See J. Perovic and R. Orrtung, 'Russia's energy policy: Should Europe worry?' *Russia Analytical Digest*, 2007, vol. 18: 2–7 for an updated overview of progress in extending state control.

13 For a Norwegian take on this event, see L. Rowe, 'Den russiske pendulum svinger', *Dagbladet,* 14 May 2007. See also *Norwegian AMEC Co-Chair Expelled from Russia.* Online. Available HTTP: <http://www.bellona.org/articles/kroken> (accessed 10 December 2007).

14 This assertion about 1999 as a turning point is based upon a statement by the USA, expressing 'appreciation for the expanded, vigorous Russian participation in the work of the Council'. *Senior Arctic Officials Meeting Minutes (Draft)*, Washington DC, 18–19 November 1999. Previously available HTTP: <www.arctic-council.org> (accessed 1 September 2007).

15 Stokke *et al.*, 'Pollution and conservation', 98.

16 *Senior Arctic Officials Meeting Minutes (Revised)*, Fairbanks, Alaska, 27–28 April 2000. Previously available HTTP: <www.arctic-council.org> (accessed 1 September 2007).

17 *Report of the Senior Arctic Officials to Ministers at the Fifth Arctic Council Ministerial Meeting*, Salekhard, Russia, 26 October 2006. Previously available HTTP: <www.arctic-council.org> (accessed 1 September 2007).

18 In 2004, a new Senior Arctic Official, Vitaly Churkin, began representing Russia. The involvement of this experienced diplomat, who later became Russia's UN envoy, perhaps indicated that greater importance was being attached to the Council's activities, at least during the Russian chairmanship (Churkin has since been replaced).

19 *Senior Arctic Officials Meeting Minutes (Draft)*, Washington, DC 18–19 November 1999. Previously available HTTP: <www.arctic-council.org> (accessed 1 September 2007).

20 Russia's slow delivery of data for the PAME Arctic Marine Shipping Assessment delayed release of this assessment, although the data was ultimately provided via Finnish involvement and financing. However, an interviewee commented that many countries (including the US) had difficulties bringing the needed data together from multiple sources.

21 *Address by Minister of Foreign Affairs of the Russian Federation Sergey Lavrov at the Fifth Ministerial Session of the Arctic Council, Salekhard*, 26 October 2006. Previously available HTTP: <www.arctic-council.org> (accessed 1 September 2007).

22 For more on the development of the Arctic Council's environmental focus see Keskitalo (2004). For further details on Arctic demography, see J. Round, 'Rescaling Russia's Geography: The Challenges of Depopulating the Northern Periphery', *Europe-Asia Studies*, 2005, vol. 57: 705–27 and D. Bogoyavlenskiy and A. Siggner, 'Arctic Demography', in N. Einarsson, J. Nymand Larsen, A. Nilsson and O. Young (eds) *Arctic Human Development Report,* Akureyri: Stefansson Arctic Institute, 2004, 27–42.

23 *Senior Arctic Officials Meeting Minutes (Draft)*, Washington, DC 18–19 November 1999. Previously available HTTP: <www.arctic-council.org> (accessed 1 September 2007).

24 Report of Senior Arctic Officials to the Arctic Council Minister, Inari, Finland, 7–8 October 2002. Previously available HTTP: <www.arctic-council.org> (accessed 1 September 2007).

25 *Report of the Senior Arctic Officials to Ministers at the Fifth Arctic Council Ministerial Meeting*, Salekhard, Russia, 26 October 2006. Previously available HTTP: <www.arctic-council.org> (accessed 1 September 2007).

26 *Senior Arctic Officials' Meeting Minutes*, Rovaniemi, Finland, 12–13 June 2001. Previously available HTTP: <www.arctic-council.org> (accessed 1 September 2007).

27 *Report of the Senior Arctic Officials to Ministers at the Fifth Arctic Council Ministerial Meeting*, Salekhard, Russia, 26 October 2006. Previously available HTTP: <www.arctic-council.org> (accessed 1 September 2007).

28 D. Trenin and B. Lo, *The Landscape of Russian Foreign Policy Decision-Making*, Carnegie Moscow Center, 2005. Another way of understanding this dichotomy, rather than taking the listing approach used by Trenin and Lo, is Joseph Nye's definition of 'high politics' as of a more symbolic, intense and emotive tenor, whereas 'low politics' are more closely linked to a kind of rational, cost-benefit analysis approach. J. S. Nye, 'Patterns and catalysts in regional integration', *International Organization*, vol. 19, no. 4, 1965, p. 871.

29 *Senior Arctic Officials Meeting Minutes*, Khanty-Mansiysk, Russia, 12–14 October 2005. Previously available HTTP: <www.arctic-council.org> (accessed 1 September 2007).

30 *Concluding Statement by Mr. Artur N. Chilingarov, Deputy Chairman of the State Duma of the Russian Federation*, Salekhard, Russia, 26 October 2006. Previously available HTTP: <www.arctic-council.org> (accessed 1 September 2007).

31 See, for example, *Senior Arctic Officials Meeting Minutes (Draft)*, Washington, DC 18–19 November 1999. Previously available HTTP: <www.arctic-council.org> (accessed 1 September 2007).

32 *Meeting of Senior Arctic Officials, Draft Minutes*, Reykjavik, Iceland, 22–23 November 2004. See also *Senior Arctic Officials Meeting Minutes*, Espoo, Finland, 6–7 November 2001, where the idea was first proposed. Both documents were previously available HTTP: <www.arctic-council.org> (accessed 1 September 2007).

33 *Report of the Senior Arctic Officials to Ministers at the Fifth Arctic Council Ministerial Meeting*, Salekhard, Russia, 26 October 2006. Previously available HTTP: <www.arctic-council.org> (accessed 1 September 2007).

34 See for an up-to-date overview P. Baev, 'Russia's race for the Arctic and the new geopolitics of the North Pole', *Occasional Paper, The Jamestown Foundation*, October 2007. Online. Available HTTP: <http://www.jamestown.org/docs/Jamestown-BaevRussiaArctic.pdf> (accessed 10 December 2007).

10 Russia, the CIS and the EEC: Finally getting it right?

1 M. B. Olcott, A. Aslund and S. W. Garnett, *Getting it Wrong: Regional Cooperation and the Commonwealth of Independent States*, Washington DC: Carnegie Endowment for International Peace, 1999.

2 While the top priorities of the CIS are not difficult to document, whether Russia was actually adhering to these in the manner envisaged is a more complex question. Bobo Lo has argued that the policy doctrines referred to here were devised mainly to provide the illusion of vision and policy coherence in Moscow's foreign policy – a surrogate for policy action (B. Lo, *Russian Foreign Policy in the Post-Soviet Era: Reality, Illusion and Mythmaking*, Basingstoke: Palgrave, 2002, pp. 6–7, 66–98) The declared primacy of the CIS was a 'foundation myth' perpetuated by the Yeltsin administration; according to Lo, it testified to the 'potemkinization' of Russian foreign policy in the 1990s.

3 A. Sergounin, 'Russia and the world: changing paradigms of Russian foreign and security policy under Yeltsin and Putin', in J. M. Godzimirski (ed) *The Russian Federation – Ten Years of Statehood: What Now?* Oslo: Norwegian Institute of International Affairs, 2003. Russian Federation, *Kontseptsiia vneshnei politiki Rossiskoi Federatsii*, Moscow: Ministry of Foreign Affairs, 1993.

4 W. Kononczuk, *The Failure of Integration. The CIS and Other International Organizations in the Post-Soviet Area, 1991–2006*, Warsaw Centre for Eastern Studies, p. 31

5 The CIS had, as Webber and Sakwa outlined in 1999, the following structure: '...The Council of Heads of State [CHS]...is defined in the 1993 Charter as the 'leading organ' of the CIS. Its meeting in April 1998 was the twenty-first since 1991. The CHS grants or denies approval to measures worked out at lower levels and co-ordinates its work closely with the Council of Heads of Government (CHG); inter-ministerial committees which exist inter alia for defence, foreign affairs, internal affairs, special services, and state security, and foreign economic relations; 54 departmental councils to co-ordinate sectoral co-operation between corresponding departments and ministries in CIS states; an executive secretariat set up in September 1993 headed by an Executive Secretary; permanent working agencies in the field of defence...organs of economic competence such as MEK, an Inter-State Bank (inaugurated in December 1993), and Economic Court (July 1994) and a CIS Currency Committee (February 1996); the Inter-Parliamentary Assembly.' R. Sakwa and M. Webber, 'The Commonwealth of Independent States, 1991–1998: stagnation and survival', *Europe-Asia studies*, vol. 51, no. 3, 1999, pp. 394–95

6 W. Kononczuk, *The failure of integration*, p. 36

7 Quoted in Kononczuk, *The failure of integration*, p. 36

8 These include I. Kobrinskaya, 'The CIS in Russian foreign policy: Causes and effects', in Hanna Smith (ed) *Russia and Its Foreign Policy Influences, Interests and Issues*, Helsinki: Aleksanteri Institute Helsinki, 2005; Olcott *et al.*, *Getting it Wrong;* M. Webber, *CIS Integration Trends: Russia and the Former Soviet South*, London: Royal Institute of International Affairs, 1997; Webber and Sakwa, 'The Commonwealth of Independent States, 1991–1998'.

9 Olcott *et al.*, in *Getting it wrong*, attribute CIS failure to incoherent and poor institutional design; suspicion of Russia and coercive and intimidating actions by Russia towards the new states; and reluctance on the part of state leaders to yield newly-won sovereignty and decision-making power to supranational institutions. Mark Webber argues that the reason for the malfunctioning of the CIS lies in the inherent limitations and contradictions in the design of the organization, as well as in the scepticism of its member states towards proposals that might recall the USSR. There have also been profound differences between states in their conception of the CIS and its purpose: while some (among them Kazakhstan and Kyrgyzstan) have been supportive, others have been coerced into joining (Moldova, Georgia) or have viewed membership in purely instrumental terms (Armenia, seeking to secure support in its conflict with Azerbaijan and vis-à-vis Turkey). M. Webber, *The International Politics of Russia and the Successor States*, Manchester: Manchester University Press, 1996.

10 G. G. Rakhmatulina, *Dinamika razvitia integratsionnykh protsessov v gosudarstvakh SNG i perspektivy formirovaniia edinogo ekonomicheskogo prostranstva*, Almaty: Kazakhstanskii Institut Strategicheskikh Issledovanii pri Prezidente Respubliki Kazakhstan 2004.

11 Interview, High-level representative, Ministry of Industry, Tajikistan, Dushanbe, 12 April 2005.

12 Rakhmatulina, *Dinamika razvitia integratsionnykh protsessov.*

13 S. Primbetov, 'EEC i Vsemirnaia torgovaia organizatsia', *Kazakhstan Spekter*, no. 3, 2004, pp. 3–6.

14 Rakhmatulina, *Dinamika razvitia integratsionnykh protsessov*, p. 143.

15 Each member also provided a list of sensitive commodities to be exempted from common external tariff rates. During the transition period before the customs union is completed, each member is allowed to exempt 15 per cent of its trade in sensitive commodities from the commonly agreed tariffs. Tajikistan is allowed to exempt up to 25 per cent

in value terms, but only in aluminium. The shares and values are reassessed each year. IMF, *Country Report Tajikistan*, Washington: IMF, 2005.

16 'Russia TV sums up CIS security and economic blocs' summit results', *BBC Worldwide Monitoring*, 23 June 2006.

17 Rep. of Kazakhstan, *Kazakhstansko-Rossiiskie Otnosheniia*, Briefing to Parliament, Moscow: Embassy of Kazakhstan to the Russian Federation, 2000, p. 2.

18 Rep. of Kazakhstan, *Kazakhstansko-Rossiiskie Otnosheniia: Osnovnye Aspekty Sotrudnichestva*, Briefing to parliament, Astana: Ministry of Foreign Affairs Kazakhstan, 2000, p. 4.

19 'Kyrgyz goods get simplified transit regime in Kazakhstan', *Times of Central Asia*, 30 March 2005.

20 'Glavnoe nachistotu', *Vechernii Bishkek*, 22 March 2001.

21 'Kazakhstan vvedet litsensirovanie importa tsementa is kirgistana', *Vechernii Bishkek*, 14 July 1999.

22 'Iz punkta A v punkt B po miroviim standartam', *Vechernii Bishkek*, 20 February 1997.

23 'Tamozhni sakruchivaiut gaiki', *Vechernii Bishkek*, 9 June 1997.

24 Kazakhstan and Kyrgyzstan Agreement Between the Government of the Republic of Kazakhstan and the Government of the Kyrgyz Republic on Transit of Goods by Road Transport Through the Territory of the Republic of Kazakhstan, 26 March 2004.

25 Ibid.

26 Interview, representative, Ministry of Finance, Kyrgyzstan, Bishkek, 25 February 2005; interview, representative, Ministry of External Trade and Industry, Kyrgyzstan, Bishkek, 21 February 2005.

27 Interview, representative, Department of Foreign Economic Relations, Ministry of Industry, Tajikistan, Dushanbe, 12 April 2005.

28 Kazakhstan and Tajikistan entered into bilateral negotiations under the auspices of the Working Party group. Kazakhstan had completed seven working-party meetings by December 2005. Both countries undertook these negotiations individually and directly with WTO members. The two candidates shared information with Russia, but without involving it in the negotiation process. Interview, representative, Ministry of External Trade and Industry, Kyrgyzstan, Bishkek, 21 February 2005; WTO 'Accessions'. Online. Available HTTP: <www.wto.org> (accessed 12 February 2007).

29 B. Hoekman and M. Kostecki, *The Political Economy of the World Trading System: The WTO and Beyond*, 2nd edn, Oxford: Oxford University Press, 2001, p. 352 This rule forbidding tariff increase after accession proved contentious, and in 1994 a further 'Understanding of the Interpretation of Article XXIV' was issued. Here the WTO reaffirmed that regional agreements should 'to the greatest possible extent avoid creating adverse effects on the trade of other [WTO] members' (Ibid) A transition period for adjustments to ensure correspondence with this rule was set to ten years.

30 IMF, *Country report Tajikistan*, p. 44.

31 'Customs union to be set up after Russia, Kazakhstan join WTO – Russian minister', *BBC Worldwide Monitoring*, 5 April 2006.

32 I. Rakhimov, 'Mezhgosudarstvennoe sotrudnichestvo kak neobkhdimoe uslovie tsivilizovannogo resheniia problem migratsii', *Migratsiia v Tsentral'noi Azii: Problemy i Perspektivy (materialy mezhdunarodnoi konferentsii)*, Almaty: Institut mirovoi ekonomiki i politiki pri fonde pervogo Presidenta RK, 2005.

33 Kazakhstan and Russia established in 2006 a Eurasian development bank with starting capital of US$ 614 million. The bank was tasked with funding large-scale development projects in the EEC area, with the emphasis on projects that would enhance economic integration between member countries.

34 Interview, representative of the US embassy in Tajikistan, Dushanbe, 22 April 2005; M. Mayer *Security or human rights: US foreign policy dilemma in Uzbekistan*, Forsvarsstudier 2, Oslo: Norwegian Institute for Defence Studies, 2006.

35 A. Cooley, 'Base politics', *Foreign Affairs*, vol. 84, no. 6, 2005.

36 P. Guang, 'The Chinese perspective on the recent Astana summit', *Jamestown Foundation China Brief*, 16 August 2005

37 'Uzbekistan becomes full-fledged member of Russia-led security organization', *BBC Worldwide Monitoring*, 17 August 2006.

38 'Russia to pay more for Uzbek gas in 2006', *RFE/RL*, 23 January 2006.

39 Russia formally entered in May 2005; the actual decision was taken at the TAS meeting in Dushanbe 18 October 2004. See 'Russia joins CACO', *RFE/RL*, 19 October 2004.

40 'Putin hails merger of post-Soviet groupings', *BBC Worldwide Monitoring*, 7 October 2005.

41 As late as January 2005, President Karimov commented: 'The CIS could have influenced various events, but it never has. In general there are too many associations of various types in the post-Soviet zone. I am referring to organizations such as the [EEC], the CSTO Collective Security Treaty Organization, and the SES Single Economic Space, which loudly make their presence known, but I personally feel they serve little purpose'. See 'Uzbek president gives wide-ranging interview to Russian paper', *BBC Worldwide Monitoring*, 20 January 2005. In August 2006, however, President Karimov stated that the country's rejoining the CSTO was 'a big event in Uzbekistan's life' and stressed that 'this is a needed body, and, maybe the time will come when we unite the CSTO with [EEC].' ('Uzbek leader moots merger of CIS security body, Eurasian economic bloc', *BBC Worldwide Monitoring*, 16 August 2006.)

42 'SCO not an eastern version of NATO', *BBC Worldwide Monitoring*, 7 June 2006.

11 Russia's trade relations within the Commonwealth of Independent States

1 See Ollus and Simola (S. E. Ollus and H. Simola, 'Russia's true imports?' Bank of Finland, *BOFIT Online*, no. 1, 2007. Online. Available HTTP: <http://www.bof.fi/ bofit/fin/7online/index.stm> (accessed 1 October 2007)) for an analysis that indicates a significant underestimation of the volume of imports from China and an overestimation of imports from Belarus and Ukraine in the statistics of the Federal Customs Service.

2 The correlation is statistically significant: excluding Belarus (and Turkmenistan because of the lack of per capita GNI data), we obtain a Pearson coefficient of 0.814 at a 1 per cent confidence level.

3 According to official national statistics, in 2006 Russia accounted for 20.7 per cent of Kazakhstan's total trade turnover (http://www.customs.kz) and 26.9 per cent of Ukraine's (http://www.ukrstat.gov.ua).

4 Interfaks interview with Maksim Medvedkov. Online. Available HTTP: <http://www. wto.ru/News> (accessed 9 January 2007). German Gref, the economics minister, was more cautious: in early February he said that the schedule was tough but that there was a 'chance' of accession before the end of the year (Online. Available HTTP: <http://www.wto.ru> (accessed 5 February 2007)). By October 2007, Medvedkov was acknowledging that accession would not be possible until 2008 (*Rossiiskaya gazeta*, 13 October 2007, p.1).

5 For the view of President Yushchenko that membership of the WTO was a matter of 'a few weeks' see HTTP: <http://www.wto.ru> (accessed 28 September 2007).

6 On CIS trading relations, see H. Broadman (ed.) *From Disintegration to Reintegration*: *Eastern Europe and the Former Soviet Union in International Trade*, Washington, DC: World Trade Organization, 2006; L. Freinkman, E. Polyakov and C. Revenco, 'Trade performance and regional integration of the CIS countries', *World Bank Working Paper*, no. 38, Washington, DC: The World Bank, June 2004; and J. de Kort, Joop and R. Dragneva, 'Russia's role in fostering the CIS trade regime', Leiden University, Faculty of Law, *Department of Economics Research Memorandum*, no. 3, 2006.

7 de Kort and Dragneva, 'Russia's role', p. 1 (It is claimed that there have been more than 1000 such documents).
8 Database of international organizations. Online. Available HTTP: <http://www.eurasianhome.org> (accessed 12 January 2007).
9 Online. Available HTTP: <http://www.guam.org.ua/211.0.0.1.0.0.phtml> (accessed 10 January 2007).
10 Database of international organizations. Online. Available HTTP: <http://www.eurasianhome.org> (accessed 12 January 2007).
11 *Rossiya*, 2 November 2006, p. 3 (accessed via EastView universal database).
12 Russia 40 per cent; Belarus, Kazakhstan and Uzbekistan 15 per cent each; Kyrgyzstan and Tajikistan 7.5 per cent each.
13 Interview with G. Rapota. Online. Available HTTP: <http://www.eepnews.ru/news/m6284> (accessed 1 November 2007).
14 See S. Glinkina and L. Kosikova, 'Development of Common Economic Space of Russia, Ukraine, Belarus and Kazakhstan in the context of EU enlargement', *INDEUNIS Papers* ('Industrial Restructuring in the NIS. Experiences of and lessons from the new EU Member States'), Vienna Institute for International Economic Studies, August 2006.
15 See HTTP: <http://www.wto.ru> 16 September and 2 October 2003. Gref reiterated this stance in April 2006, stating that an EEC customs union would be possible only when Russia and Kazakhstan had joined the WTO. Belarus was not specifically mentioned, but if it was also included then Gref was in effect postponing a customs union for several years (Online. Available HTTP: <http://www.wto.ru/ru/news>, 6 April 2006 (accessed 1 February 2007)).
16 See HTTP: <http://www.wto.ru>, 27 August and 9 September 2003; *Kommersant daily*, 29 October 2003, p. 15.
17 Online. Available HTTP: <http://en.for-ua.com/news/2006/04/07/110045.html> (accessed 7 April 2006).
18 Online. Available HTTP: <http://www.vedomosti.ru> (accessed 29 August 2005); Online. Available HTTP: <http://www.wto.ru> (accessed 29 August 2005).
19 http://www.eepnews.ru/events/m6386, 21 November 2006.
20 Indicative is the fact that since early autumn 2005 the website devoted to UES matters, (http://www.eepnews.ru), formerly very active, has been almost dormant, the only new items being occasional press reviews and news bulletins, including the one in the previous footnote.
21 G. Rapota, 'Perspektivy integratsii v ramkakh EvrAzES', *Ekonomicheskoe obozrenie EvrAzES+*, 4th quarter, 2006, p. 6. Rapota acknowledges that the aims and tasks of the EEC and the UES are practically identical.
22 Original plans were overoptimistic: in early October 2007, Russia, Belarus and Kazakhstan agreed to create a Commission for the customs union and adopted a three-year plan for the union's formation (*Rossiiskaya gazeta,* 8 October 2007, p. 3).
23 Ministry of Economic Development and Trade data. Online. Available HTTP: <http://www.economy.gov.ru> (accessed 22 August 2006).
24 C. Michalopoulos and D. Tarr, 'Are customs unions economically sensible in the Commonwealth of Independent States', World Bank, December 2004, pp. 18–20. Online. Available HTTP: <http://siteresources.worldbank.org/INTRANETTRADE/Resources/Topics/Accession/438734-1109706732431/CustomsUnionsCIS_Eng.DOC>(accessed 1 February 2007).
25 P. Tumbarello, 'Regional trade integration and WTO accession: which is the right sequencing? An application to the CIS', *IMF Working Paper*, WP/05/94, May 2005.
26 Rossiiskaya akademiya nauk, 'Natsional'nyi investitsionnyi sovet' *Narodnokhozyaist-vennye posledstviya prisoedineniya rossii k VTO*, Moscow, 2002, p. 7.
27 Online, 18 January 2003. Available HTTP: <http://www.rg.ru> (accessed 1 February 2007).
28 'Truby razdora', *Kommersant daily*, 27 December 2006, p. 8.

29 A. Petrachkova, V. Kashin and B. Grozovskii, 'Voiny s sosedyami', *Vedomosti*, 29 December 2006.
30 Putin and other Russian leaders make frequent reference to charging 'market' prices for gas, but this is rather misleading as Russia sells gas only to long-term contacts at negotiated prices. These can be said to be 'market' prices only insofar as they are closer to the contract prices prevailing in Europe.
31 For a vivid expression of this view, see A. Prokhanov, '"Belorusskii konflikt" – strategicheskaya oshibka', *Zavtra*, no. 6, 7 February 2007.
32 See, e.g., D. Mindich and M. Agarkov, 'Taktika bez strategii', *Profil'*, no.1, January 2007.
33 *Moskovskii Komsomolets*, 25 December 2006, p. 2.
34 See HTTP: <http://www.sng-baltia.ru> (accessed 8 December 2006).
35 Y. Zaitsev , 'Tsena vstupleniya Ukrainy v NATO: gibel' VPK i sotni milliomnov ubytka'. Online. Available HTTP: <http://www.mashportal.ru/machinery_world-4410.aspx> (accessed 9 June 2006).
36 Ibid. and I. Plugatarev, 'Khochesh' v NATO – ostavaisya so svoimi dvigatelyami'. Online. Available HTTP: <http://nvo.ng.ru/6555> (accessed 26 May 2006).
37 See M. Kruglov, 'Real'naya integratsiya', *Rossiiskaya gazeta*, 1 December 2006.

12 Russia as a military great power: The uses of the CSTO and the SCO in Central Asia

1 The 1993 Foreign Policy Concept of the Russian Federation stressed as a central goal the establishment of a belt of security and good neighbourliness around the country's borders. Russian Federation, *Kontseptsiia vneshnei politiki Rossiskoi Federatsii*, Moscow: Ministry of Foreign Affairs, 1993. See also: A. Sergounin, 'Russia and the world: Changing paradigms of Russian foreign and security policy under Yeltsin and Putin', in Godzimirski (ed) *The Russian Federation – Ten Years of Statehood: What Now?* Oslo: Norwegian Institute of International Affairs, 2003.
2 V Putin 'SCO – A New Model of Successful International Cooperation', 14 June 2006. Online. Available HTTP: <http://www.indonesia.mid.ru/ros_asia_e_4.html> (accessed 1 June 2007). See also A. Bailes, P. Dunay, P. Guang and M. Troitskiy, 'The Shanghai Cooperation Organization' *SIPRI Policy Paper No. 17*, Stockholm: SIPRI, 2007, p. 32
3 This is exemplified by the incursions into the Batken region of Kyrgyzstan and Uzbekistan by the Islamic Movement of Uzbekistan (IMU) in the summers of 1999 and 2000, the attacks in Tashkent in 2004, and the growing activities of Hizb-ut Tahrir in the Ferghana Valley.
4 Azerbaijan, Georgia and Belarus joined in 1993. The treaty was renewed in 1999, but Azerbaijan, Georgia and Uzbekistan decided to withdraw. In October 2002, the six member states of the CST signed a charter creating the Collective Security Treaty Organization. In June 2006, Uzbekistan joined the organization.
5 A limited unified air defence system was indeed maintained. However, this development proved to be more of an exception than a rule, in terms of preserving a united military structure within the CIS/CST framework.
6 Domitilla Sagramoso, *Russia's geopolitical orientation towards the former Soviet states*, PhD thesis School of Slavonic and East European Studies, UCL, January 2000.
7 R. Allison, 'Regionalism, regional structures and security management in Central Asia', *International Affairs*, vol. 80, no. 3, 2004, p. 470.
8 The mining of border areas by Uzbekistan aggravated relations with Kyrgyzstan and Tajikistan even further.
9 In August 2004, the CSTO conducted an extensive military anti-terrorism exercise, *Rubezh 2004*, in Kazakhstan and Kyrgyzstan to test the CSTO's rapid deployment force

in action for the first time. A similar exercise was held a year later – *Rubezh 2005* – in Tajikistan. The aim was ensure the rapid deployment of joint troops to counter a terrorist threat. Various Combat Commonwealth exercises were also held by CSTO states in 2004 and 2005 to ensure co-ordination and inter-operability in anti-aircraft and anti-terror operations.

10 R. Allison, 'Regionalism, regional structures and security management in Central Asia', p. 471.
11 R. Maksutov, 'The Shanghai Cooperation Organisation: A Central Asian perspective', Stockholm: SIPRI, 2006, p. 3.
12 The secretariat has a staff of 30 persons and was initially allocated a budget of US$ 2.6 million, Bailes *et al.*, 'The Shanghai Cooperation Organization', p. 1.
13 It has been endowed with a separate budget of US$ 3.1 million.
14 The first stage of the exercise was held in Kazakhstan and involved Russian, Kazakh and Kyrgyz troops; the second stage was held in Xinjiang province in China and involved Kyrgyz and Chinese troops.
15 The Peace Mission 2005 exercises were the first bilateral military manoeuvres held between Russia and China, and by far the largest drill undertaken either by the SCO or the CSTO at the time. China provided 7000 personnel while Russia supplied 1800. The drill involved assault ships, submarines and strategic aviation.
16 'SCO: Pragmatism gains the upper hand', *Moscow News,* 29 September 2006.
17 Ibid.
18 P. Guang, 'The Chinese perspective on the recent Astana summit', *Jamestown Foundation China Brief,* 16 August 2005
19 Bailes *et al.*, 'The Shanghai Cooperation Organization', p. 6.
20 RFE/RL, 'Eurasia: US security expert talks about SCO exercises, summit', 8 August 2007.
21 See note 19 above.
22 Maksutov, 'The Shanghai Cooperation Organisation', p. 13.
23 V Putin 'SCO – A New Model of Successful International Cooperation'.

Index